⊃8/2⊂
F

ALUES IN SOCIAL WORK

Also by Derek Clifford
Social Assessment Theory and Practice: A Multi-Disciplinary Framework

Also by Beverley Burke
Anti-Oppressive Practice Social Care and the Law
(*with J. Dalrymple*)

Anti-Oppressive Ethics and Values in Social Work

Derek Clifford
and
Beverley Burke

First published 2009 by
PALGRAVE MACMILLAN

Palgrave Macmillan in the UK is an imprint of Macmillan Publishers Limited,
registered in England, company number 785998, of Houndmills, Basingstoke,
Hampshire RG21 6XS.

Palgrave Macmillan in the US is a division of St Martin's Press LLC,
175 Fifth Avenue, New York, NY 10010.

Palgrave Macmillan is the global academic imprint of the above companies
and has companies and representatives throughout the world.

Palgrave® and Macmillan® are registered trademarks in the United States,
the United Kingdom, Europe and other countries.

ISBN-13: 978–1–4039–0556–7
ISBN-10: 1–4039–0556–8

This book is printed on paper suitable for recycling and made from fully
managed and sustained forest sources. Logging, pulping and manufacturing
processes are expected to conform to the environmental regulations of the
country of origin.

A catalogue record for this book is available from the British Library.

A catalog record for this book is available from the Library of Congress.

Printed and bound in Great Britain by
CPI Antony Rowe , Chippenham and Eastbourne

Contents

Acknowledgements

We would like to thank a number of people who have influenced and/or supported us in the writing of this book. We would thank Catherine Gray in particular from our publishers, Palgrave Macmillan, for suggesting it in the first place whilst on a visit to our University, and for her subsequent valuable comments, help and patience. We would also like to thank the anonymous reviewers for their comments on the first draft, and colleagues for helpful contributions at various stages. We would like to thank Professor Michael Preston-Shoot, Dr Elizabeth Lynn, Dr John Powell and others, including staff, students and service users associated with the social work courses at Liverpool John Moores University, Clive Kendall for the original cover design, and also Sarah Lodge of Palgrave Macmillan. Despite all the helpful comments we of course take full responsibility for the final content of this book.

DEREK CLIFFORD
BEVERLEY BURKE

Introduction

> *Social workers need to be genuine, committed, and caring — not coming into the profession for the wrong reasons. They should be genuinely interested in the job — it's not just a job — it's about people's lives.*
>
> (Comments by service users on the training of social workers in values and ethics: Voices in Partnership, 2003)

In preparing for the book we met with a service-user group to discuss with them what and how we should teach the subject of ethics in social work (Clifford and Burke, 2003). Our perceptions of their interests are incorporated into what follows. References to service users and their views are scattered throughout the book, and in our teaching we involve service users who engage with the case studies and put their point-of-view in discussion with students. Service users told us amongst other things that they thought it was important for us to ensure that students had a good understanding of the differences between each other, as well as between themselves and service users. Our approach in this book is consistent with that. Teaching and learning methods can only benefit from discussions about ethical issues in which differing perspectives, including those of service users and carers, can be represented.

WHY 'ANTI-OPPRESSIVE ETHICS'?

We have some qualifying remarks to make to begin with about the phrase 'anti-oppressive ethics'. We are well aware that both within the profession and outside it, the use of 'anti-oppressive' as an adjectival phrase is certainly not universally accepted or approved. Indeed, even those who have used it with approval can also condemn its use: 'as a gloss to help it [social work]

1

feel better about what it is required to do' (Humphries, 2004, p105). We take it as read that any word with positive connotations for some will not have them for long without the term being reinvented, abused, misunderstood, neglected or rejected completely: language is a changing and disputed territory. The powerful will seek to incorporate critical terms into their dominant discourses if at all possible. We would contend that the phrase currently indicates a position that we – and others – take up about the seriousness of social diversity and inequality in relation to ethical professional practice. We think our approach is consistent with the widely accepted *Definition of Social Work* from the International Federation of Social Workers (IFSW) and International Association of Schools of Social Work (IASSW):

> The social work profession promotes social change, problem solving in human relationships and the empowerment and liberation of people to enhance well-being. Utilising theories of human behaviour and social systems, social work intervenes at the points where people interact with their environments. Principles of human rights and social justice are fundamental to social work.
>
> (IFSW/IASSW, 2004, Section 2)

Evidently, to be 'anti-oppressive' is to be in favour of the objectives listed in this definition, and whilst all its terms are open to debate, it does at least make clear that ethical and political concepts such as rights, social justice, empowerment and liberation are fundamental to social work. This book looks more closely at what some of these concepts might mean.

It may be objected that 'anti-oppressive' is an unnecessary way to qualify 'ethics' since almost any ethics should be anti-oppressive. However, it has been pointed out some time ago that the adjective 'anti-oppressive' seems useful to mark out the range of structural oppressions (as we do) rather than just individual or local prejudice, for which 'anti-discriminatory' seems adequate (cf. Phillipson, 1992, p15). We use 'anti-oppressive' as an inclusive term to cover both. However, this is not the only way to use these terms. For example, Thompson (1998) prefers to use 'anti-discriminatory practice' to refer to both radical and liberal aspects of equal opportunities. A currently popular adjective which seems to have partially replaced both 'anti-oppressive' and 'anti-discriminatory' is 'critical' (cf. Adams *et al.*, 2002), or 'critical best practice' (Ferguson, 2003). However, from our perspective 'critical' is a very broad term, and like 'empowerment' does not necessarily indicate the importance and interconnectedness of structural social difference, inequality and ethics. 'Anti-oppressive' is still very general, but at least a little more connotative of the idea that injustice and unethical practices are a pervasive feature of societies and endemic within social structures rather than simply a matter of individual prejudice or vice, and with our further explanation of it in Chapter 1, it provides a basis for the agenda that follows.

Ethics is always open to debate, so no one should be surprised to see criticisms of the use of 'anti-oppressive' in relation to ethics both by those in favour of the ideas behind it, and by those against. They need to be assessed on the merit of their arguments, as we hope our own interpretation will be. Whilst we think our account of anti-oppressive social work ethics is firmly based on contemporary discussions of ethics, and upon theory and evidence in the social sciences, we acknowledge that we have only sketched some complex ideas, and that there are lots of ways of conceiving of ethical ideas in social work differently from ours. We therefore present an 'approach' to anti-oppressive ethics rather than claim to have a fully worked out ethical theory (an approach that is sketched out in Chapter 1).

We would contend that in this context there is no logically or ethically acceptable way of avoiding *tentative* commitments to ways of explaining and evaluating social situations. The only option is to do so in an open way on the basis of reasoned argument and evidence, including the evidence of human experience and feeling. Contemporary work in both philosophy and the social sciences cautions professionals in any area to make modest claims. However, social workers are very aware of their participation in decisions about people's lives that have great potential for both good and ill. Our contention is that this involvement both is and should be critically influenced by the evidence of the nature of the social oppressions which constitute and structure the situations in which professionals find themselves, including their own social location, organisational role, and personal qualities.

Idealism and reality

An anti-oppressive approach to ethics is not helpful if it does not attempt to engage with the 'realities' (however defined) of complex social situations (Beckett, 2008). It is always too easy, on the other hand, to undermine any ethical position, including ours, by contrasting its supposed idealism with the alleged 'realities' of the social world. What assumptions are being made about the 'real' and who exactly is defining it – and to whose benefit? However, it is also always a serious possibility that an ethical stance will be used to hide vested interests – in this case including those of the social work profession itself (cf. Baistow, 1994/5). With an anti-oppressive ethic it is clearly possible to envisage as ideals different ways of organising society as well as different ways of acting within it, and this might be justifiably if unsympathetically viewed as idealistic and/or self-serving. However, a sympathetic reading of anti-oppressive ethics may *also* underscore the sense of distance between values and 'realities'. In this case the irony would be occasioned by a sense of alienation from enduring and unacceptable social practices, rather than ridicule at unattainable ethical standards (cf. Ferguson and Lavalette, 2004). What might well be seen as disingenuous is the espousal of ethical terminology and ideas, yet with no apparent commitment or perceptible change in behaviour of either individuals or organisations. The point of an ethic of anti-oppressive practice is that the individual social work professional is invited to take responsibility for themselves in the light of a realistic analysis of the dynamics of micro- *and* macro-social situations, and to intervene with at least some degree of confidence and sensitivity in an uncertain world. Attempting to be ethical in an unethical world is an invitation to continual perplexity and reflection – but not one that we think can seriously be refused by social workers, and, in many cases, nor has it.

We also do not make assumptions about whether this approach will necessarily overcome any particular form of oppression. It may not be possible in some situations to 'liberate', 'empower', or even help individuals when the social worker is herself implicated in controlling care, manipulating power and authority, and rationing resources. There is no need to assume some ideal end-state must be in sight (cf. Tew, 2006). Moreover, it will always be possible to make things even worse than they are (intentionally or not) and to limit the damage that is likely to occur may be the highest aspiration that is possible. However, sometimes it may be feasible to make decisions that are positive and constructive, challenging oppressive situations, and releasing the potential of individuals and groups. We hope that social work can contribute at both individual and collective levels to freeing people to live the lives they choose, and realise their human potential, but there is no guarantee that this will happen, since social work is usually a small part of the numerous factors impinging on people's lives. However, social workers have always been aware of the interweaving of care and control, and the aim of this exercise is to assist recognition of what is ethically desirable and/or possible and how best to act in the circumstances, even if that means having to choose the lesser of two evils. It has been fairly pointed out that ethical choices are not necessarily about 'emancipation' – the reality of the social work task includes controlling dangerous behaviours (Beckett, 2008). We are advocating a position that releases ethics from a narrow concern with individual moral behaviour, towards a more social understanding of human relationships and how to nurture and change them for the better – or in some circumstances prevent them from getting even worse. Whether it succeeds depends on both individual and collective action and upon historical, social and economic forces that can either assist or undermine the most determined efforts. The challenge is both to understand and endeavour to change for the better human social situations.

ANTI-OPPRESSIVE PRACTICE

Offering guidance to ethical practice from an anti-oppressive perspective implies support for anti-oppressive practice. However, some recent authors have been critical of what they have seen as anti-oppressive practice as a popular trend in social work. Their criticisms concern the limitations of an anti-oppressive approach to the explanation of and guidance for practice. Such a range of criticism obviously has negative connotations for a book on an anti-oppressive approach to ethics. In addition, there has been a revival of interest in religion and 'spirituality' which also has implications critical of social work's anti-oppressive values in so far as the secular teaching of social work has laid little emphasis upon the religious values of service users, or (in their view) shown much concern for the spiritual needs of service users and carers generally. There are a number of preliminary points we thus need to make to clarify our position on these issues, and justify what we see as a valuable – indeed essential – contribution that an anti-oppressive approach to ethics makes.

Criticisms of anti-oppressive approaches to practice

The criticism of anti-oppressive practice sometimes draws on conservative post-modern themes concerning the role of anti-oppressive values as an 'ideology' that can be subjected to a liberal critique of its apparent moral idealism. This is discussed further in Chapter 1, where the positive value of some post-modern themes is acknowledged but the anti-oppressive basis of this book is defended. It is important to add here that recent criticisms continue to be produced, but do not always grasp the relevant issues. On the contrary there is sometimes more than a hint of stereotyping and pigeon-holing of anti-oppressive ideas. The implicit criticism, often not clearly articulated, is that as a form of moral idealism it is more suited as an object of academic analysis, rather than as a tool of analysis. It is part of a continuing strong academic tradition to assume a neutral attitude towards anything that smacks of ethical commitment, regardless of the objection that such a position requires its own ethical and analytical premises (and its own utopias). Millar (2008) adopts a conservative functionalist sociological theory to characterise anti-oppressive values as a system of ideas that serves a particular function in relation to the way social workers perceive themselves. There is indeed no question that any set of ideas will influence social reality in contradictory ways, and that moral ideas in particular are notorious for being used in diametrically opposite ways to that in which they appear to be intended. Marx, 150 years ago, also used a functionalist argument against liberal 'bourgeois' moral ideals, regarding them as instrumental for the protection of systemic capitalist interests. More recent analyses of the related concept of 'empowerment' make it abundantly clear that it is plainly usable as a means of questionable ethical ends (Humphries, 1996). 'Empowerment' as a social work value can be seen as a morally important (or naïve) concept, but it can also have a role in justifying the way that the profession sees itself, and presents itself to the world.

Any set of values, including anti-oppressive values, can be subverted in practice (and in theory) and may serve roles and functions for which they are not intended. This includes especially the advocates of those values, some of whom may adopt an intolerant attitude towards any who differ from them. Neither academic neutrality nor intolerant commitment will serve the purpose of anti-oppressive practice. It is necessary to use reason and evidence to question situations where social difference and inequality give rise to ethical issues: the tentative nature of these values is evident in these assumptions from the beginning because of the integration of the relativising concept of *history* into the framework (see further discussion below in Chapter 1). In particular we would argue that (*pace* Millar and other critics such as Wilson and Beresford, 2000) the *reflexive* dimension of anti-oppressive values (see further discussion below in Chapter 1) necessarily means that an anti-oppressive analysis always has to be turned against its own practice, and be reflective about its own powers to abuse, be co-opted for other purposes, or to have unintended or latent functions. Social circumstances change, interacting with varying degrees of personal and collective awareness of change. What used to be an effective and ethical approach may turn out to have a different meaning in a new environment for different people. The meaning of the concept is (or should be) always problematised, and especially when a worker is directly involved with others – a service user, client, carer, or other professionals – and simultaneously working for an organisational agenda.

If a professional's practice is not reflexive, and the worker or writer unable to assess the impact of power and specific social location for themselves and others, then it is not an anti-oppressive approach as we understand it, and the suspicion may be that it is being cited unethically and/or without sufficient understanding. Thus critics are often setting up a straw target. Sakamoto and Pitner (2005) seem to think that an anti-oppressive approach is limited to structural concerns, but any such approach would inevitably fail to grasp the qualitative complexities of difference and inequality in specific lived experiences – and this is not a new concern. Black feminists especially have been emphasising this for at least a quarter of a century, from bell hooks, writing in the 1980s (hooks, 1982) and up to the present (Graham, 2007). Similarly, Millar's reference to Healy (2000, p4) expressing puzzlement about the apparent lack of self-doubt amongst people who advocated anti-oppressive values, suggests either that those people did not have a very good grasp of the values they espouse, or else that the observer concerned may have misunderstood the context of that discourse – or indeed that the people concerned may have had limited commitment to those values, and used the language for their own purposes. Amongst those who attempt to realise them in practice, self-doubt and questioning are continually on the agenda: they are a basic part of this perspective. It is more culturally dominant concepts which are usually presented as 'natural' or as 'authoritative', supported by 'evidence' which those of low social status (service users or social workers) are not expected to question. We are not as convinced as Millar that anti-oppressive concepts have as much influence as he thinks, and when they do have some impact they are often undermined by over-simplification and co-option. An example is given in a paper purporting to be critical of anti-oppressive concepts yet illustrating this by means of the case of 'senior managers' who, having co-opted the concept of ageism, were unable to understand it (Lloyd, 2006, p1177) – hardly a good example of anti-oppressive ideas being put into action, and one that is obviously easy to criticise. However, in so far as 'anti-oppressive' values do become influential within social work, then it is certainly appropriate for this to become a matter for continual reflexive criticism.

Service users, carers and anti-oppressive ethics

A good example of the complexity and self-doubt involved in a reflexive anti-oppressive approach to ethics in practice must be the way in which social work values have evolved in relation to service users and carers. Dalrymple and Burke (1995 and 2006) have discussed the positive aspects of the various service-user movements, and many writers with anti-oppressive values in mind (including the present authors) have explicitly drawn upon the experiences of those in dominated social groups as a guide for attempting to work out what might be considered anti-oppressive (cf. Clifford, 1998). From the start anti-oppressive practice has developed as a matter for professional workers concerned about the impact of their actions and decisions on vulnerable others, and aware of the need to learn from marginalised social groups, and to be self-aware of their own membership of both dominating and marginal groups. It has also reflected an understanding of how social justice issues cut across the private and political spheres of action (Dalrymple and Burke, 2006, pp7–23). At the same time professionals have been aware (some more than others) of the unavoidable clash between the interests and perceptions of the professionals as against those on the receiving end of their work, whether 'clients', service users or carers. An anti-oppressive approach to practice necessarily has to address this issue, and it has done so, often in an uncertain world where so-called self-determination of service users can sometimes mean leaving vulnerable individuals to fend for themselves. But there are always questions about whose perception is being assumed, and who is controlling what decisions, and for whose benefit? This is the reason why anti-oppressive perspectives take seriously the position of subordinate groups who continually question accepted norms and expectations.

The earliest studies of service-user perceptions (Meyer and Timms, 1970) demonstrated a large gap between the worker and the 'client', and the service-user movement has grown apace since then, along with the growth of the various social movements of the late twentieth century. The impact made by Dalrymple and Burke's (1995) dedicated approach to anti-oppressive practice in the 1990s included a clear commitment to service-user participation in decision-making, and also indicated the complexity and self-questioning that was required of the practitioner in recognising and acknowledging the power differences (Dalrymple and Burke, 1995, p144). Wilson and Beresford's claim (Wilson and Beresford, 2000) that anti-oppressive authors have taken over the ideas of service users seems to ignore evidence that (at least) some to which he refers have explicitly acknowl-edged the lead provided by service users and carers, the debt owed to them, and positively advocated alliances with them. Additionally, professionals (and academics) are often also service users themselves, and the relationship between professionals in social services and service user has often been dialectical. Social workers' experiences of being a service user, carer or member of a dominated social group underpin, consciously or not, their values and perceptions of others. Ultimately they have responsibility for making judgements about risk-taking and need, and their assessment of a particular service user has to include taking account of the possibility of service users having acted in ways which are ethically unacceptable, most obviously in abuse cases. This does not excuse a social worker from seri-ously considering how to work in partnership with perpetrators of abuse. Nor does it ignore the possibility that the social worker may be the one who is criminally using their power to abuse others. The relationship between them for anti-oppressive ethics is necessarily complex and open to self-doubt and criticism, and the growth of service-user movements has high-lighted that fact. Part of the current challenge is how to critically assess the way service-user involvement is co-opted by management (Cowden and Singh, 2007), and of the over-simplification of relationships between service-user organisations, their leaders, their members, and related social groups and organisations.

RELIGION, SPIRITUALITY AND ANTI-OPPRESSIVE ETHICS

A second example of the complexity and self-doubt necessary in anti-oppressive ethics is in relation to the new wave of 'spirituality' that has gained popularity in social work in recent years. This is itself a reflection of the awareness of cultural diversity that has been forcing itself onto Western societies in the shape of the challenge of Islamic ideas, amongst other factors. One of the implications has been an acceptance that differ-ences in religious cultures need to be respected whatever the religion, and that differences between secular and religious values have also to be recog-nised and accommodated. A view that has been expressed recently is that social work values have paid little attention to 'spirituality', and this is inconsistent with anti-oppressive social work ethical ideals of respect for the values of service users, whose religions differ, and whose commitment to them may be an important aspect of their lives (Holloway, 2007). Indeed, the commitment of any individual to a meaningful understanding of their own identity, existence and place in the world, whether religious or secular, can be defined as the 'spiritual' meaning of their life, involving needs that social workers ought to understand and be prepared to meet as they arise in working with service users and carers (Canda and Furman, 1999; Moss, 2005).

The previous history of social work has been variable in different countries in relation to its engagement with religion (Holloway, 2007). In the UK a growing secular trend in the twentieth century may recently have been halted or at least slowed by the challenge of Islamic ideas, the influx of people with various religious convictions (such as Polish Catholics), and the reaction of Christians to the challenges to their faith. Anti-oppressive values have grown mainly out of a secular radicalism, but sometimes also with the support of religious ideals, and have always been based upon the notion of tolerance of differing religious values. Although the USA rather than the UK is known for its separation of church and state, in practice the statutory social services ethos in the UK is one of equal services to all citizens separate from and regardless of their religion. However, there is also a long history of the provision of social services by religious organisations, continuing to this day, and possibly increasing with the global emphasis on voluntary and private rather than state provision of services. Yet there is also a chequered record of commitment to providing *universal* services when religious groups tend to their own constituencies rather than offering an equal service to others (as for example in fostering, adoption and education, where religious organisations have often favoured their own memberships). Currently, there are extreme examples of this in the Middle East, where differing religious groups in one state offer services to their own, thus marginalising those who are judged not to 'fit', and resulting in a divided patchwork of provision (Jawad, 2007). It may be that services in 'Western' countries may go part-way down the same road, but an anti-oppressive approach to values places a high regard on acceptance of both religious and cultural toleration, but also on providing equality of services to all groups, and especially vulnerable or 'deviant' groups, however defined. Therefore a religious ethic is inevitably limited *to the extent that* it is incompatible with this value. Some religions and denominations within religious groups are able to manage this, but others have notably drawn the line in the provision of services to (for example) gays and lesbians, a current stumbling block for a number of religious groups across the world. It is also arguable whether various religions even now offer equality of opportunities to women.

Anti-oppressive ethics and the meaning of people's lives

The key anti-oppressive component of personal and social history discussed in Chapter 1 includes understanding and valuing the cultural and spiritual heritage of the families and communities within which individuals are situated, but recognising the continually changing dynamics of that experience. What individuals understand as the meaning of their life is mediated by their particular experiences of local cultures. The anti-oppressive ethical practitioner therefore needs an ability to understand, appreciate and tolerate the variety of local values to be found in communities and families, but also a commitment to critical questioning of local values (including their own) in the light of wider norms. It thus requires a commitment to a professional approach to ethics that overlaps but may be in some tension with personal ethics. The commitment to be (and to stay as) a postholder in a profession that is governed by codes of practice and laws relating to universal human welfare is itself a demand for competency in ethics made upon oneself. In so far as either a religious or secular ethics is so rooted in its own traditions that it cannot provide an equal service to all citizens, then it is open to criticism. Similarly, if 'anti-oppressive values' are ever used oppressively against people with religious values, then such a usage clearly transgresses against its own premises, unless that religious tradition can be shown to be failing to offer equality to service users and carers, or otherwise advocating intolerant or oppressive practices. In this sense, anti-oppressive approaches cannot and should not avoid commitment to the overriding values inherent in the position, as described in Chapter 1. They are perfectly compatible with respect for and recognition of the spiritual dimension to people's lives, in the sense outlined above, but they cannot afford a commitment to a narrow religious interpretation of the 'spiritual', nor any particular religious conviction that would deny equal citizenship and rights to human beings of all sorts of persuasions. Nor are they compatible with a view, whether religious or secular, which is based on certainty and the absence of questioning and self-doubt – we further discuss some of these issues in Chapter 5.

It follows from this that an anti-oppressive approach to ethics must necessarily be reflexive about the ('spiritual') values held by the worker. Whether the worker belongs to a religious tradition *or* has secular values, then the question is the same: how far those values should be allowed to influence their practice, especially where those vulnerable to them (clearly service users and carers) are of a different persuasion. How will non-religious workers be able to support and counsel someone of a religious background, and how will religious professionals be able to offer an equal service (if at all) to users they regard as deviant – except possibly in a paternalistic way, which devalues the meaning the service user or carer themselves give to their life? These are significant ethical issues which an anti-oppressive approach to ethics draws attention.

GENERAL STRUCTURE OF THE BOOK AND OUTLINE OF THE CHAPTERS

The purpose of this book is to enable readers to think critically about their values and ethics, and explore the links and discontinuities between practice, ethical theory and anti-oppressive ethics. We have developed an anti-oppressive approach to ethics which critically evaluates the various traditional ethical theories from the basis of feminist and anti-oppressive values so as to provide a framework that is sensitive to power differentials. It acknowledges the complexity of decision-making within professional situations, and supports practitioners' efforts to think and act ethically.

After the first two introductory chapters, laying the foundations of our approach, the following chapters (3–8) have a particular format, each focusing on a particular ethical theory. Each chapter will also be focused on a key anti-oppressive concept – one that is announced in the title of each chapter. This does not mean that other concepts are not relevant, but to avoid repetition we have only briefly referred to the other concepts at the end of each chapter, and have concentrated on discussion of the concept indicated in the chapter heading. Chapter 8 is an exception to this in the sense that it does not focus on one anti-oppressive concept but is more broadly inclusive of anti-oppressive concepts, because, in our view, feminist relational ethics has a lot to offer an anti-oppressive approach to ethics. At the beginning of most chapters, readers will find a 'Key Ideas' box. This box highlights some of the main ethical concepts that will be addressed in the body of the chapter. This box is followed by an introductory paragraph to the chapter. What follows next is a detailed case scenario that poses a particular moral and ethical issue, which is explored from a particular ethical perspective. This exploration is then in turn analysed from an anti-oppressive ethical position. In keeping with our aim of wanting to write a book that actively engaged the reader and reflected our commitment to the principle of reflexivity, we have included our own perspectives, reflecting on how we might have responded if we had been the social worker involved, focusing on the key anti-oppressive concept highlighted in that chapter. The chapters conclude with a brief summary of the chapter and further reading.

A key feature of Chapters 3–8 is the prominence of a practice scenario. The decision to begin each chapter with a practice dilemma was based on our experiences of teaching in the area of values and ethics and our attempts at helping students to make the links between theory and practice. We felt that it was important to begin with the realities of practice and then move on to explore the ethical and moral implications of the situations presented with reference to theory.

The aim of Chapter 1 is to discuss the key words in the title of the book, and defend our anti-oppressive approach to ethics in the light of possible criticism, and to show precisely how anti-oppressive ethics requires critical and reflexive thinking.

Chapter 2 attempts to critique from an anti-oppressive perspective the legal and policy context, the values and codes of ethics which guide the actions of practitioners and in which practice is located.

Chapters 3–8 take as their starting points particular ethical practice dilemmas. The ethical perspectives of Kantianism, utilitarianism, Virtue ethics, Marxian, Rawlsian, post-modernist, existentialist and feminist ethics are all used to explore practice. In the final, ninth chapter we attempt to set out guidelines appropriate to any professional intervention, focusing on reflective practice and decision-making.

The concluding chapter summarises the key arguments in the book and does so by addressing our concern that individual ethical action needs to be seen in the context of organisational and structural change, by reviewing how an anti-oppressive approach to ethics might be applied to problems arising in the organisations within which social workers are employed.

BACKGROUND

We are both university teachers of social work who have behind us varied experiences of generic and childcare social work, and of being ourselves service users and carers.

We have been working together in our present positions for a number of years, and have cooperated in teaching modules on Social Work Theory and Practice, Ethics and Anti-Oppressive Practice, and Social Divisions and Auto/Biography, and other social work modules. We have researched and published together and independently in related areas. However, we have different backgrounds and experiences, and our social location makes a difference as to how we react to situations. Part of our approach to anti-oppressive ethics is to insist on the importance of a 'reflexive' awareness of how individuals and groups act. An important aspect of that is to be clear about your own social location and its impact on yourself and your relation to others, as we will explain later. We will thus be commenting on the case scenarios throughout the book, and we begin here by commenting on our own background in writing it.

Beverley's perspective

My values are very firmly rooted in my experiences of being black, female and someone whose formative years took place within a working-class, multiracial and multicultural community. The experience of leaving home to study for a degree in the social sciences allowed me to reflect on my values in the light of coming into contact with a diverse range of people who had very different life experiences to my own. My experiences as a youth and community worker and then as a social worker challenged as well as confirmed my understanding of issues of inequality and oppression, testing my capacity to understand the nature of human relationships, and providing the impetus to question my values and the values of other people. I have learnt that it is important to actively listen to the stories of others, because it is through the continual exploration of the differences between us in honest and respectful communication that we begin to make sense of who we are, our relationship with others and the values that we hold.

Derek's perspective

My interest in ethics and values dates back a long time. As a student in the turbulent 1960s I could hardly be unaware of the impact of changes in values on society in general, or on myself. I went to Manchester University from a white 'working-class' background. I studied and taught about differences in values in Departments of Politics, then Philosophy, in universities in the UK, the West Indies and Australia. Following these varied locations, I went into social work for a decade, mainly in childcare work, experiencing some of the realities of values in practice. Returning to higher education to teach social work has given me the chance to think through again some of the issues about differences and changes in values and ethics. Being part of the white ethnic majority, being male, able-bodied, and (now) older and 'middle-class', I've had to learn about people very different from myself, and their values. I'm still learning – and reflecting on the ethical implications.

Chapter 1

Anti-Oppressive Ethics and Ethical Thinking

The aim of this book is to introduce the reader to anti-oppressive ethics in social work. In this chapter we will define and explain the terms being used, and describe key anti-oppressive concepts which we will argue provide a guiding framework in social work ethics. We will make connections with some long-standing issues frequently discussed in ethics, and show how our approach relates to them. In addition we want to show how anti-oppressive ethics requires reflexive thinking that includes but goes further than some conventional assumptions about logical thinking in ethics, but also requires a more socially critical approach than some recent discussions of social work ethics. We begin by stating what we mean by the key words in the title of this book, explaining them as clearly as we can, and defending our position against possible misunderstanding.

Stereotypical assumptions are sometimes made about 'anti-oppressive' practice which pigeon-hole the concept as an outdated structuralist position unsuitable for contemporary practice, and inconsistent with contemporary post-modern thinking. We argue that this is a straw target. Our conception of anti-oppressive ethics takes account of recent developments, and demonstrates an open-endedness and a capacity to challenge preconceptions and practices where other approaches are more limited. This book therefore draws on other ethical theories, but critically assesses their boundaries. We also argue that without an anti-oppressive approach to ethics a critical dimension of ethics is missing – one that is vitally important for social work, and a basic part of what is best in the social work heritage.

KEY IDEAS

Oppression includes both the exploitative exercise of power by individuals and groups over others, and the structuring of marginalisation and inequality into everyday routines and rules, through the continuing acquisition and maintenance of economic, political and cultural capital by dominant social groups over long periods of time, reflecting the existence of major social divisions. Oppression therefore arises from inequalities of power that can be *both* stable *and* fluid, affected by situational changes in individual and group circumstances, and by people's responses to them.

Social divisions are widely perceived differences between large groups of people, characterised by inequalities in power and access to material and cultural resources, both individually and collectively. These differences vary through time and place. They are often long-standing, but can sometimes alter quickly during periods of general social change.

Anti-oppressive ethics are approaches to guiding action in the light of the recognition of inequalities and powerlessness damaging to individual and collective freedom and welfare, especially in relation to groups and individuals marginalised through membership of dominated and diverse social divisions.

AN ANTI-OPPRESSIVE APPROACH TO ETHICS

Some basic ideas

Anti-oppressive social work ethics is an approach to applied ethics which is especially relevant to social care and social work, and especially (but not only) drawing on some key ideas in feminist ethical theory. We do not assume that there is agreement between feminist theorists (some of the differences are discussed in Chapter 8), but we will be drawing on some of the commonly held views of feminist social and moral theorists which are particularly useful in this context. We also do not assume that there is a fully worked out ethical position called 'anti-oppressive ethics'. We believe that more work would need to be done to justify such a claim. However, there is enough space to argue for what we claim to be a useful *approach* to ethics – using anti-oppressive concepts which provide some guidance for the application of ethical concepts in a way that is consistent with social work values.

The aim of anti-oppressive ethics is to provide guidance to oppose, minimise and/or overcome those aspects of human relationships that express and consolidate oppression. The point of adding the descriptive term 'anti-oppressive' to qualify 'ethics' is to emphasise individual behaviour as inseparable from the unequal political and social contexts in which it occurs. Whilst some ethical theories have made such connections (particularly feminist ethics, for example), we think that most do not do so adequately, and that ethics is often regarded as a purely individual and personal matter. Although we accept that ethics is *peculiarly* related to individual personal responsibility for behaviour (as in the commonly used meaning of the term), situations involving social difference and inequality between people are the areas where issues of personal ethics become critical. As one feminist theorist so aptly puts it: 'all significant differentials in power are critical hot spots in social-moral order' (Walker, 1998, p218). They are aspects of social life that cut across the different levels and areas of social existence, connecting individuals and groups, from family and friends, to businesses, organisations and social and economic systems, across space and time, and it is at these points of human interaction that ethical behaviour is brought most clearly into focus. It does *not* mean that we exclusively emphasise the structural aspect of oppression, as some writers still assume (Sakamoto and Pitner, 2005, p436). It is an important part of our approach that it recognises the pervasiveness of oppression in the micro-situations of everyday life, and the *dynamic interdependency* between such personal interaction at intimate and local levels, and wider organisational and structural influences.

Our view of the nature of ethics admits the possibility of giving reasons, drawing on both knowledge about the social world, and on the feelings that are common (and uncommon) to human experience, but without assuming that rationality, empirical evidence or human feelings can either by themselves or even together provide an absolute basis for ethics. Too much is known about the variability of human values and the limitations of human rationality to make such an assumption complacently.

There are many inequalities of wealth, status and power, both reflecting and leading to cultural and structural social divisions. The social context of the professional working with vulnerable individuals and groups demands recognition of the need to act in a way that minimises or overcomes some of the complex effects of discrimination and oppression, rather than adding to them through collusion, neglect or lack of self-awareness. Even worse, obviously, would be intentionally adding to existing oppression and exploitation. What matters is the possibility of dialogue between individuals and groups – the attempt to act in an anti-oppressive way is itself an endless search for ethical values in which we continually negotiate with and learn from each other – and especially from the 'other', in the sense of one who is socially and culturally different.

It is important to emphasise that 'oppression' is not intended simply to refer to situations where a powerful person or group exerts a tyrannical influence over others – though it does include this. More importantly, it also refers to the structural injustices which arise from (often) unintentionally oppressive assumptions and interactions which occur as the result of institutional and social customs, economic practices and rules. Oppression thus operates at both structural and personal levels at the same time. It also does not necessarily mean that the same people are 'oppressed' by the same 'oppressors'. The situation is always complicated by differential membership of social divisions, specific situations, and people's responses to them. An individual may be vulnerable in terms of their membership of one social division, but powerful in another. A classic example in social work is the male service user and the female social worker. Female workers have the benefit of professional employment and agency support, but they may still be vulnerable to an aggressive male service user, and subject to male hierarchies in employment and other agencies, not to mention wider male cultural and political power. Individuals may be able to temporarily increase their power in particular situations, and people can join together collectively to increase their power, but it is often not easy to do for subordinate social groups.

Throughout this chapter we will be drawing on the contribution of various feminists to the development of an anti-oppressive approach to ethics, because feminists are consciously attempting to reflect the experiences of one of the most important globally subordinated social groups, and one which is particularly significant in social work, as service users and as professionals. An important aspect of feminist work is their recognition of their own and others' need to avoid being misled by ethical concepts which may reflect dominant norms. One example amongst many is the influential social and political theorist Iris Marion Young who has written about the 'Five Faces of Oppression' (Young, 1990, ch. 2). The personal interactions which are the subject of ethics are an integral part of social situations, in which 'oppressions are systematically reproduced in major economic, political and cultural institutions (Young, 1990, p41). She analyses the different kinds of oppression as five different categories: exploitation, marginalisation, powerlessness, cultural imperialism, and violence. These processes function at the level of regional, national and international social systems, where politics and economics play a significant role, influencing the course of individual lives. However, they can *also* operate at the level of individual and group interactions, within organisations and networks: 'the conscious actions of many individuals daily contribute to maintaining and reproducing oppression' (Young, 1990, pp41–2). For example, when men use their power to abuse women, it includes the whole range of oppressions from cultural stereotypes, to physical violence, exclusion from various jobs (especially ones with decision-making roles), low status and poor rewards. These ends are routinely accomplished by many ordinary men in the course of their lives without any particular planning, and often without the intention to 'oppress' (but also sometimes with that intention). This example clearly raises all sorts of ethical issues that relate simultaneously to the behaviour of individuals, and also to the social and moral context in which such situations arise. Similar things could be said, albeit in somewhat different ways, for the range of other social divisions.

What we mean by the social divisions is *not* simply a shortlist of the major social groups, such as gender, class and 'race'. Other social divisions are also important such as disability, sexuality, age, religion, health, region, mental health and HIV status, and yet others too may be of great consequence, especially for the individual. The crucial issue here is one of 'empirical' examination of what social divisions are *generally* significant in a particular society at a particular time. For a specific individual it is a matter of assessing which social inequalities matter most (and to whom?) at any one particular place and point in time.

Young has suggested that after much debate about social divisions at the end of the twentieth century, 'a consensus is emerging that many different groups must be said to be oppressed in our society, and that no single form of oppression can be assigned causal or moral primacy' (Young, 1990, p42). This approach to understanding society, based on the central importance of the social divisions, is supported by sociologists (e.g. Payne, 2006; Bradley, 1996), but does not preclude debate about which social divisions are more important in any given place and time, or about the nature of social divisions. Payne, for example, lists nine 'core characteristics' of social divisions, focused on clear-cut material and cultural differences persisting through time (Payne, 2006, p348). It has also become clear that membership of social divisions will cut across the lives of individuals and groups in a complex way: 'group differences cut across individual lives in a multiplicity of ways that can entail privilege and oppression for the same person in different respects' (Young, 1990, p42). For example, an individual can be disabled and lack access and opportunities to which others can aspire. Yet that same disabled person may be a white male whose opportunities, social class and self-esteem may be high in comparison with an unemployed black male or a white woman subject to 'domestic violence'. The complexity of social division in the lives of individuals is magnified by the continually unsettled meaning of the terms used and the debated concepts involved: what do 'black' and 'white', 'male' and 'female' mean in any particular place and time?

Post-modernists and post-structuralists vary markedly in their views, but are usually critical of what they see as the questionable assumptions of an 'anti-oppressive' position (see the useful social work summary in Healey, 2005, pp188–91). In particular they emphasise the importance of language as a key area for analysis rather than social or economic 'realities', and query the changing meaning of the terms used and the 'binary' opposition of powerful and dominated groups in anti-oppressive theory. They question the alleged fixed identity of members of oppressed social groups, and continual reference to macro-social structures that 'determine' people's life chances, often by means of powers possessed by some groups and individuals who exercise it over the powerless. However, post-modernist arguments are sometimes anticipated by anti-oppressive and feminist writers, whilst at other times post-modernism creates straw targets, omitting consideration of key issues.

Clearly what matters to individuals and how they see themselves varies enormously depending on their changing lives and circumstances. Nevertheless, it remains the case that individuals have commonalities as well as differences. These are certainly subject to perception and interpretation. The commonalities may be well or poorly understood by any particular individual member of a social group, and continually debated by social scientists. However, the conditioning of life chances by 'external' structures such as lack of employment; segregated job markets; institutional discrimination; unequal distribution of wealth and income; stereotyping in the media, and many other factors, will still affect them and shape their lives. They will also have varying degrees of 'agency': that is ability and awareness as participants to actively engage with powerful social systems, rather than passively accept or collude with them. There is absolutely no need at all for an anti-oppressive perspective to accept the view that individuals and groups are simply determined by macro-social or macro-economic structures. It is obvious that mezzo-level social structures, such as organisations, and micro-level groups, such as families, impact on individual lives, and that individuals respond to social circumstances in active ways which can sometimes change or deflect (or reinforce) their impact. An anti-oppressive perspective regards all these changing social factors, including language itself as potentially leading to the maintenance of oppression: there is no guarantee that things get better. The response of individuals in terms of their own behaviour is likely to further that oppression or undermine it –

depending on their circumstances, their grasp of the issues involved, and their ethical and political attitudes.

What may be misleading is the construction of a straw target against which 'post-modernism' is favourably contrasted – a technique that post-modernisms sometimes fall into (Outhwaite, 1999). For example, it is a common criticism of an anti-oppressive approach that: 'the prioritization of structural analysis of clients' experiences, can lead social workers to neglect individual psychological and personal factors' (Healey, 2005, p189). However, our framework specifically highlights the tensions between individual action and personal history and the various levels of social relationships with which individuals interact. The aim of an anti-oppressive ethical framework is to examine rigorously the interaction between individual action and the micro-, mezzo-, and macro-structures of personal and social life. Oppression operates at all these levels where inequalities and diversities multiply, and cannot seriously be envisioned as a simple unidirectional, top-down exercise of power. This was always the case – except in naïve, simplistic or stereotypical accounts of anti-oppressive practice. It follows therefore that we have no difficulties in appreciating the variety of forms of power, and their positive as well as negative potential, and for that potential to be unevenly wielded for good and ill by all social actors, as well as being implicated in the whole range of social structures.

Another common reproach of anti-oppressive theories is that: 'A contradiction exists between anti-oppressive theorists' claim to promote dialogue in practice and their assumptions that they hold a true and correct analysis of the world' (Healey, 2000, p190). However, it is obviously questionable whether the various forms of post-modern and post-structural thought do not themselves involve assumptions about what is true about the world. Indeed it is hard to imagine how anyone writing about the social world could logically avoid some general assumptions about the 'reality' being considered. We therefore specifically include ourselves as participants within the anti-oppressive theoretical framework, which is itself radically historical and reflexive. It follows therefore that this framework cannot but be a construction of the concrete social world it attempts to evaluate. It is a corollary of our position that there can never be a 'correct' account of reality. So far from inhibiting dialogue, that is precisely what makes it so important: we have to share accounts from our very different perspectives. However, in addition it also means that there is an unavoidable recognition that there is a perspective which is consciously being taken. There is no pretence of an objective, academic position which avoids 'taking sides', and we openly acknowledge that there are ethical and political implications. Academics sometimes appear uncomfortable with ethical or political commitment, but we see it as undesirable to present the appearance of neutrality, or pretended universality, or to appear to avoid ethical commitment (Humphries, 2004, p281). Despite this, it is certainly not one of the implications of our position that ethical commitment entails a rush to judgement, omitting careful consideration of both 'facts' and possible alternative values, and the inevitably limited, social location of our own position. In the end there is always some tension between dialogue and commitment: we would suggest that is a common experience not unique to an anti-oppressive argument. Indeed any claim about ethics is always torn between asserting a position with conviction, yet recognising that it is disputed and disputable.

Equally, there is also some tension between the various perspectives and values through which realities are filtered, and the brute nature of externalities which impinge on our consciousness and language. A 'wishlist' approach to ethics is not what we are advocating here: intending or hoping that a situation might be free of oppression does not make it so (cf. Beckett, 2007). Whilst agreeing that a 'true and correct analysis of the world' may be a naïve form of realism, precisely because of the variety and plurality of intervening perspectives, it is not the case that empirical evidence about the world should be ignored. Social work cannot afford to abandon the realities of oppression (at micro- and macro-levels of society) that physically and psychologically constrain the lives of service users and carers. This means that an anti-oppressive approach to ethics needs to take seriously case and research evidence about the realities of social life (whilst rigorously questioning the adequacy and provenance of the research programmes involved). Associating fashionably acceptable ethical concepts with proposed actions or policies does not make them ethical. Rather we see a rigorous approach to evidence informed by anti-oppressive concepts as a demanding process, which involves both dialogue with others *and* attention to logic and evidence, especially evidence that is apparently conflicting, which may be revealed through dialogue with the different perspectives of colleagues or service users and carers from different social backgrounds, as well as through examining relevant research evidence. This process requires skills in reflexive and critical thinking which are described later in this chapter.

ETHICS: SOME SPECIFIC DISTINCTIONS

KEY IDEAS

Applied ethics is a discussion of the ethical aspects of particular situations, and the ethical decisions that might be reached. It could begin with a practical decision and ask what ethical theories are being applied or assumed. Alternatively, it can begin with moral concepts and theories, and consider how they might be applied to specific situations.

Normative ethics is a discussion of those norms or standards by which people make moral choices. It involves questions about duty; questions about moral values, and about what constitutes a 'good' life.

Meta-ethics is the theoretical discussion of the nature and meaning of moral language.

Ethics is the study of human conduct, and is often sub-divided as in the box above, though the different aspects are also interrelated. Moral philosophers may discuss any of these aspects, but will certainly pay particular attention to meta-ethics. Practitioners will obviously be most interested in applied ethics, but need to be aware how these different aspects of ethics interconnect. The discussion of normative ethics will be one of the themes built into the case studies in this book, with each case study linked to a particular approach. We would argue that anti-oppressive ethics has something to learn from many of these ethical principles, but that it also adds to them.

THE POSSIBILITY OF ANTI-OPPRESSIVE ETHICS: COMMON ARGUMENTS

Moral philosophers have discussed for centuries the meta-ethical questions, and, whilst it is not the intention of this book to focus on these issues, we need to acknowledge that they cannot be wished away and they unavoidably impinge on the issues of applied and normative ethics. In particular the reader needs to be aware that the approach we are recommending for professionals is one which can always be subject to fundamental criticism, especially in the light of three meta-ethical positions which not only have been defended (and attacked) by moral philosophers, but also will be either argued by ordinary people and professionals themselves or assumed in their daily lives. These positions are views about the nature of ethical language. If you accept one of them, it would appear that you immediately cut the ground from under whole areas of discussion of applied ethics, and therefore we need to indicate the implications of arguing for anti-oppressive ethics.

We limit our selves to considering here three general meta-ethical positions which people often use in ordinary discussion, and may well arise in the course of student seminars as objections to anti-oppressive ethics. We have made this limited selection partly because these particular views are commonly held by students (and probably by many others). A paper discussing 'student relativism' has identified these kinds of arguments (Erion, 2005), and we have contrasted them with an absolutist position (which may be religious or secular), to bring out the implications all the more clearly. It is therefore useful to consider how they relate to our anti-oppressive approach to ethics.

I   'It's just about an individual's emotions and preferences'

This view is known as non-cognitive ethics in which it is asserted that the meaning of the language of ethics is essentially about individual feelings, preferences and emotions. It is, by contrast, explicitly *not* about matters of 'cognition', that is: knowledge about any aspect of the world or how it works. Admittedly, the feelings involved are typically not casual preferences such as a taste for a particular kind of ice-cream. They are usually strongly held feelings about how people should behave. Nevertheless, a really important implication of this view is that you cannot easily have a rational discussion about ethical practice because there may be little room for either logical argument or empirical evidence. People may never agree: they may just have different feelings.

For example, the act of female genital mutilation produces strong but very different feelings in people across the globe. For many, such a practice induces strong feelings of revulsion and moral disgust. However, it is also obvious that for many others it is a traditional, and sometimes a religious practice, which can be associated with very strong feelings of approval. It makes no difference to point out to those who practise what they describe as 'female circumcision' that there are facts about human development – and empirical evidence – which might suggest that the consequences might be physically or psychologically unhealthy. This is something they value despite any possible pain or suffering: it arouses strong feelings of obligation and loyalty. It would also make no difference to point out the apparent logical inconsistency between their feelings of respect for women in regard to other matters and non-respect in this. All that matters (on this account of moral language) is that for them it is a strongly held view which expresses their feelings and preferences, and that is what makes it moral for them. If other individuals have strong feelings against the practice that makes it immoral for them, there is little more that can be said about it.

Some moral philosophers have based their own arguments on this view, often called 'emotivism', sketching out the nature of ethics from this perspective (e.g. Ayer, 2002; Stevenson, 2002). Its function is to 'emote' or express someone's strong feelings. It was very popular in the West before and after the Second World War, but is less so now. However, there are at least two matters which anti-oppressive ethics need to take into account from non-cognitivist ethics.

First, an awareness of the strong feelings that underlies people's actions is not uncommonly associated with ethical values that may be very different from other people's views. In particular, it may be the case that a service user has an ethical and strongly emotional commitment to a practice that the worker finds ethically unacceptable. Taking account of their feelings is, at the least, a prudential thing to do (because of your responsibilities as an employee with a specific role to play) and most would agree it may also be ethical, even though we may have very different but equally strong feelings ourselves. But exactly how far can or should we empathise with the feelings of someone who practises something we find abhorrent? This is a significant moral dilemma to which we will return.

Secondly, the realisation that ethical language is significantly and commonly associated with feelings and emotions is one that feminists have re-emphasised in more recent times in ways that are also relevant to anti-oppressive ethics. Although not wishing to ignore the relevance of evidence and logic, they have pointed out that ethics is also fundamentally about the expression of emotions related to human caring, sympathy and understanding, and the feelings that people have towards each other in various social contexts should be an essential part of any ethical analysis. They also point significantly to the *interconnection* between the cognitive and emotional aspects of ethical concepts such as compassion, which requires cognitive judgements to be made about whether the circumstances are serious and justifiable (Nussbaum, 2005, p133).

The point here is to admit that the anti-oppressive approach that we are recommending is one in which logic, empirical evidence and also feelings are *all* recognised as important components of ethics. This approach is therefore not consistent with a rigorous non-cognitivist position.

One reason why this seems appropriate is precisely because the focus on feelings *alone* does not assist the practitioner to discuss and resolve difficult issues. It especially does not help in the opposition to oppressive practices, which needs to be supported by good reasons drawing on empirical evidence and using logical arguments, *as well as* appealing to ordinary 'human' feelings in a sensitive way that respects differences between people.

For example, whilst we know that there are many different views about exactly what constitutes child abuse in different times and places, it does not seem acceptable to *simply* accept the variability of human feelings on this very serious topic, so that anyone can claim to have an 'ethical' position, no matter how damaging. The relevance of evidence about human welfare and suffering, and logic and consistency in the use of evidence cannot and should not be ruled out of consideration.

2   'It's all about the variety of different cultures and religions'

On this view of ethical language it makes no sense to generalise or try to say that ethics has a rational or universal basis. From the factual evidence of cultural difference this argument concludes that there is no universal basis for ethics: a position known as Relativist Ethics. It *may* involve the giving of reasons, and *may* use logic and evidence as well as emotion, but the essential nature of ethics is that it is always *relative* to a particular society and a particular historical time. Societies are very different in time and space, and they espouse very different ethical perspectives which cannot be reduced to a single set of universal ideas. They are simply different. Ethical language therefore is primarily about the discourse engaged in by particular moral traditions, rather than being about individuals and their preferences – emotional or rational. The evidence for a relativist position on ethics is regarded as almost self-evident to anyone who cares to consider societies other than their own. There are just so many examples of people and groups having very different values in societies across time and space. The example given above of female genital mutilation is not simply about *individuals* having different feelings. It is one of many where very different cultural traditions of different social groups come into conflict.

A well-known objection to relativism is that its conclusion that there is no way of judging what is ethical outside a particular tradition is not always a very helpful position in a multicultural, shrinking world. It may or may not lead to tolerance, depending on which value system is dominant. The reality of our world is also argued to be one where there are significant overlaps and engagements between differing moral traditions, and in this situation we are able and need to search for ways of using ethical language that will be meaningful *between* traditions, whilst recognising how difficult this is.

There is also a familiar logical conundrum about relativism. This is that in asserting the truth of relativism there is the presumption that the statement made is itself *not* relative. But if the statement is true then it also can only be relative to a particular discourse – and this leaves it open to someone to disagree with relativism itself as a particular cultural tradition. It thus has a well-known, inherent self-contradictory element.

From an anti-oppressive perspective two points need to be drawn from relativist ethics: first it is important to recognise that anti-oppressive ethics depends on the recognition of the seriousness of the social divisions that occur within and between cultures and traditions on ethical issues, involving religious and secular commitments that are sometimes worlds apart. To people socialised into different ethical traditions their values are often mutually incomprehensible. However, these traditions also change over time and historical difference adds to the real sense of the relativity of ethical language, and the difficulties that arise from this.

Secondly, it is important to reject the view that everything is equally culturally relative and that there is no way of discussing ethics which will be able to cross the social divisions that exist between differing social groups and traditions. Precisely because differing (and sometimes overlapping) traditions also use logic and evidence as well as appealing to common human feelings, experiences and capabilities (Nussbaum, 2000) there is the possibility of – and the responsibility for – dialogue that will assist practitioners in minimising or avoiding oppression and discrimination between people. Feminist discussions of this intractable issue also contend that 'respect for cultural difference may be combined with claims to postconventional moral objectivity' (Jagger, 2004).

3   'What matters is what is true, and what we all have a duty to do'

Absolutist Ethics regards the language of ethics as consisting of universally valid concepts, applicable to everyone. These approaches therefore claim that there are ethical propositions which are absolutely true, and are not relative to particular societies, and certainly not mere expressions of individual feeling. They have the advantage of apparently providing a firm foundation for ethical decisions. However, they can be based on very different justifications of the claim to absolute status. For example, they can be based on religious traditions of various kinds that insist on their proclamation of *the* truth as a result of divine revelation, an authority that cannot and should not be questioned. Other versions of this approach are not religious, and are based on the view that ethics has a fundamental basis in reason; therefore the essential tenets of morality are applicable to every rational human being.

Similar to the other two meta-ethical issues, an anti-oppressive approach to ethics both draws on and rejects aspects of this approach:

■ It cannot base itself on one religious view of absolutist ethics because to do so would link it to a particular religious tradition and alienate it from others. The aim of minimising and overcoming oppression requires anti-oppressive ethics to avoid a partial commitment which would bias it in favour of specific social groups, and implicate it when other groups might be oppressed or discriminated against.

■ Although anti-oppressive ethics must make good use of reasoning to oppose instances of discrimination and oppression, there are problems with a theory of universal reason, which ignores the significant empirical variations and differences of perspective between individuals and groups in relation to ethics and values, and the limitations of human reason. The evidence of attempts to build rational theories about what is universally applicable tends to show that they often end up looking rather parochial. There are also problems about reliance on a concept of reason which sidelines or ignores altogether the role of feelings and experience in human relationships.

However, anti-oppressive ethics has to search for ways of reaching towards *a degree* of rationality, and consistency with human feeling and experience, as well as knowledge of how societies work. This is because the aim of reducing oppression depends on being able to identify whenever it occurs, and being able to produce rational arguments for action in order to reduce it. It need not assume some form of absolute rationality against which there is no appeal. Nor does it have to be committed to a grand theory of how the world works. However, it does need to examine the rationality of arguments carefully, and it certainly needs to question assumptions about society, and research thoroughly the relevant evidence, with the expectation that any conclusions may only be temporary and open to revision in the light of further evidence. It also needs to consider being partial, or committed, at least on a strategic basis, in favour of oppressed social groups.

ANTI-OPPRESSIVE ETHICAL GUIDELINES

This framework draws on the range of ethical theory, but especially on feminist ethical theories (see Chapters 8 and 9 for further discussion), which will be referred to throughout. There is a consistency in the position we have argued in that we are advocating a strategic alliance with a theoretical position (feminism) which is clearly focused on experiences of oppression, rather than drawing solely on the classic moral philosophies. Our approach to anti-oppressive ethics is to view all the traditional ethical injunctions through the lens of some key concepts drawn from feminist ethics, *and* from the writings of members of other subordinate groups, many of whom have experiences of being service users and/or carers. We regard it as essential that the following concepts are always taken together in order to provide an adequate framework for anti-oppressive ethics. They provide a guiding framework for thinking through specific situations, a particular approach requiring positive application to specific circumstances. They will not provide 'the answer' to ethical dilemmas, but they will certainly bring forward key issues that should be considered seriously. We believe they make a major contribution to good practice generally because they combine a concern for good outcomes and understanding of the social world, with an awareness of differential perspectives, unequal powers and the importance of reflexivity.

I   Taking thorough account of social difference

Whilst ethical concepts like 'treating people with respect', or looking at outcomes, or character will all have a place within the repertoire of social workers, the key issue in understanding them is whether membership of the social divisions is adequately understood. For example, having respect for individuals – in the abstract – is a fine ethical principle, but respecting concrete individuals who are very different from ourselves is the real test of an ethical commitment. A 'thorough account' of social difference implies:

- Thinking through *all* the major social divisions in relation to the person and the situation being considered, even when it is not immediately clear how or whether they are relevant.
- Considering whether it is justifiable to find out about the membership of social divisions which are not apparent, and/or finding out more detail about those that are apparent.

▣ Thinking through the detailed specifics of the major social divisions rather than just the broad categorisations, including minor social divisions that may be important in the given circumstances.

▣ Thinking through the qualitative differences that are engendered by the intersection of social differences in individual lives, including simultaneous membership of dominant and subordinate groups.

▣ Considering what the significance of this information is for understanding the values, rights, wishes and perspectives of service users, carers and professional colleagues, and in relation to other members of society and other social groups.

The 1970s were dominated by feminist concerns about commonalities between women, and this is reflected in the women's standpoint of the 'ethics of care', as promoted by earlier women's writing on ethics (Noddings, 1984; see also Chapter 8). However, differences of 'race' and ethnicity, social class, sexuality, age, disability, and others, combined with post-modern interests in difference and fragmentation soon led to a questioning of the category of 'woman' in the 'ethics of care' as an adequate basis for ethics. More recent writings of feminist ethicists have clearly integrated into their theories an awareness of the differences between women, and the importance of the intersection between the differing social divisions (e.g. Held, 2006). This is well expressed in the assertion that: 'gender, race, class hegemony and subjectivity are not optional aspects of moral theory but necessary elements of any account of morality' (Hekman, 1995, p48). Contemporary feminists wish to include within their consideration of ethics the whole range of social divisions: whereas 'traditional ethics heard a single truth of disembodied moral principles, feminist ethics listens and hears multiple voices' (Porter, 1999, p20). On the other hand there is also the re-appropriation of the concept of 'women' as a significant social category, in spite of the complex and contradictory experiences of and between women, and the theoretical objections of post-modernism to the categorisation of social groups (Ahmed, 1998).

An anti-oppressive ethics needs to take a thorough account of *all* social differences and inequalities, not only whether the social worker or service user is male or female. Part of the thinking through of social difference will be the way in which social difference either distances the social worker from, or associates them with, other individuals and groups in any specific situation. The gender of the social worker will be one important aspect of social division to be factored into any ethical assessment of a situation. We regard it as essential to think through the ethical implications of the membership of social divisions of all those involved in a situation, directly and indirectly, in as thorough and as intelligent a way as it is possible to do, even (and especially) when it is difficult to investigate. These social differences are fluid and changing, but they are often also enduring and highly significant. This concept is discussed further in Chapter 7.

2   Evaluating the range and impact of social systems and relationships

Taking care of the needs of individuals is a complex business, involving both immediate close relationships, and more distant and/or indirect relationships with other individuals placed in different social systems and organisations. The constraints and possibilities afforded or denied by other individuals and other social systems are part of the landscape within which ethical decisions have to be made. Therefore ethical decisions and discussions need to take account of the varied contexts of actual and potential relationships that exist in a specific situation. The 'private' area of family life should be seen in continuous interaction with the 'public' areas of friends and peers, communities, organisations and national and international institutions. Therefore the anti-oppressive ethic requires attention to be given to the whole network of relationships in which the specific service users, carers and professional colleagues are involved.

Feminist ethics is centred on the possibilities of dialogue between people, a dialogue that takes place in many different ways, and on different levels, both 'private' and 'public'. The 'ethics of care' began by paying close attention to the relationships within families, starting with gendered parent–child relationship, and other dependent relationships, but broadening this out to wider social relationships (Held, 2006). In addition to family nurturing there is also the nurturing of friendships – an activity where women have also traditionally excelled: 'Research seems unequivocal in showing that at every life stage, women have more friendships than men and the differences in quality are marked' (Porter, 1999, p34). Recent feminist ethical theorists have also wanted to broaden out their attention to include not only family social systems, but the whole range of social systems in which individuals relate to each other directly and indirectly: 'not just between those providing care and those requiring it, but also between different groups with care needs' (Orme, 2002, p805). Women have always emphasised the connections between the public and the private, and the differing levels of social interaction where maintenance and care of relationships needs to take place. This will include intermediate levels of social systems such as peer groups, organisations and communities, as well as large-scale social groups and systems such as the social divisions themselves, and national and international organisations. Feminist and other writers about subordinate social groups are also well aware of the cultural aspect of these different social systems, and how internalisation of dominant social values can impact on the lives of individuals and groups.

Black women writers also stress the significance of community relationships, not only among women but also between men and women (e.g. Collins, 1990; Graham, 2007). It is a feature of black and white feminist ethics to be aware of the relationships of power and inequality as well as relationships of care within social networks. It is important to be aware of the distribution of power and legitimacy in hierarchical systems requiring an 'understanding of the political nature of oppression' (McLeod and Sherwin, 2000, p276), and to make strategic decisions about how to advocate, negotiate, and intervene in large organisational structures, and in community and political contexts, as well as within families, and between individuals and organisations. An anti-oppressive ethic will thoroughly assess the multiple social relationships that exist between individuals and groups, both intimate and informal, distant and official, and caring and controlling, realising that these pairs of opposites can co-exist within the same social networks. This concept is discussed further in Chapter 6.

3   Understanding the specific social histories of individuals and groups involved

An anti-oppressive ethic requires the social worker to respect the concrete particularity of individuals and groups through a shared appreciation of their personal and family histories by discussion with them, and through study of what is justifiably known about them, *and* about the wider social history which contextualises their lives. It is simultaneously a matter for ethical judgement about the extent to which knowledge of the personal histories, and extended discussion with those concerned *is* justifiable – from their point-of-view, *and* from the perspective of the social worker's role and task on this occasion. Is it intrusive and controlling, or is it welcomed and therapeutic (or both)? Is such a discussion and investigation of personal and family history genuinely required to help understand and resolve a complex case, or is it meeting the immediate wants (appropriate or not?) of service users or carers – or the social worker? It is important that life stories and social histories should not be limited to assessment of psychological development – though that is certainly included. It is also important that a holistic appreciation of changing personal and family histories can be open to disconfirmation, and based on evidence that can be shared (as much as possible) and critically discussed. It is essentially about understanding the development of social identities across time; the experiences that people have had, their deepest values and the ('spiritual') meaning they give them, and the events and trends in their lives that have led to where they are, and who they are today. The histories of other individuals such as the social worker and her colleagues, and the history of organisations, especially those with which users have been involved, are also relevant to understanding the specifics of the current situation.

A feminist position on ethics insists that collaborative ethical discussion has to draw critically on existing (past and present) understandings, resisting 'any attempt to abstract away from the relevance of a person's life experiences' (Koehn, 1998, p161). It needs to supportively explore personal and family history to understand the pattern of an individual's life, the experience of oppression, and the evidence of previous capacity (and opportunities) for making decisions. Being able to make decisions and express your opinions and feelings 'has a lot to do with trusting your own judgement about their accuracy and relevance *in discussion with others*' (McLeod and Sherwin, 2000, p273, our emphasis). If an individual is capable of making a decision, she will be able to share some understanding of herself and her past experiences: 'The capacity to have a past and to reflect on it is crucial to selfhood' (Lloyd, 2000, p122). Conversely, 'A narrative selfhood focuses on the concreteness of individuals with specific histories, identities, emotions and attachments' (Porter, 1999, p11). The attempt to understand other people has to utilise the evidence of shared discussion, including knowledge of 'hidden' experiences from personal, family and social history, as well as the coherence of arguments and empirical evidence that colleagues or relevant friends or relatives may present. This attempt to grasp the real person behind the label therefore requires genuine effort to find out the details of their past. However, the attempt is inevitably limited by the mutual perceptions of the participants in the discussion, including the social worker's personal social history, as well as by the practical and ethical considerations relating to the immediate circumstances. It may not be possible and/or ethical to investigate details of personal and family history, but it therefore remains correspondingly important to be aware of the possible information that may remain unknown to you at a given point in time. This concept is discussed further in Chapter 4.

4 Analysing different kinds of power

Anti-oppressive ethics alert the worker to the variety and complexity as well as the inequality of powers in social situations and their significant connotations for ethical action. The worker needs to examine both the cross-cutting impact of powers arising from simultaneous membership of different social divisions, and the intervening effects of intermediate sources of power such as organisations or families. It also recognises that power can be wielded by the most unlikely sources – even if only for short periods of time or with limited impact. It is produced in social interactions between people and groups whose powers will not be static but will vary with the changing situational specifics, producing differing vulnerabilities and strengths. Taking account of these potential differences is essential for an anti-oppressive ethic. Clearly the power of the social worker as representative of an authorised agency is another relevant factor, although again, it is a relative one, given the limited powers of individual social workers to influence their own agency, or to access resources. Similarly, the powers of users and carers may also vary and have a very significant impact in a range of different ways, for good and ill.

A central concern of feminist ethics is about the existence of power in social relationships: the social divisions and all other social relationships are both enabled and disfigured by unequal and complex powers. Koehn argues for an approach to ethics 'capable of cultivating thoughtful attentiveness not only to the unjust power dynamics affecting women', but 'to the world as a whole' (Koehn, 1998, p163). The point is well expressed by Walker: that '*all* significant differentials in power are critical hot spots in social-moral order' (Walker, 1998, p218, our emphasis). These differences exist not only between major social divisions but also between care-givers and receivers, and understanding the power relationships involved is fundamental to this development in feminist ethics. The point is made that differing social positions reflect differences of perspective in which power and knowledge are intertwined so that: 'morality is not *simply* about guiding actions' – 'actual moral orders . . . may . . . be a core of dominant understandings' (Walker, 1998, p218). Feminists are well aware that: 'powers of several types . . . can allow some people to rig both the arrangements and the perception of them' (Walker, 1998, p219), and this means that a feminist ethics requires both 'reflective analysis' of forms of life, and 'critical reflection' (Walker, 1998, p9) on the specific features of dominant values and the differing powers expressed in all relationships, thus facilitating any possibility of improvement. The complex relationships are part of a social world in which 'social segmentation and hierarchical power-relations are the rule', and 'the commonplace reality is different moral identities in differentiated moral and social worlds' (Walker, 1998, p17). Clearly, the characteristics of the social world that underpin moral concepts on this account are precisely the relationships of caring and social inequality which women experience in diverse ways, and that conventional ethics tends to ignore (Held, 2006). Anti-oppressive ethics draws on women's understanding of the variety and complexity of powers produced by and affecting individuals and groups across all the social divisions.

This approach also takes account of, yet is critical of, post-modern concepts of power which conceive of power as ubiquitous and multidirectional. The nature of power is indeed complex, but Lukes (2005) has argued that post-modern concepts have their limitations – Foucauldian notions of power in particular (see Chapter 3). The existence of varieties of forms of power and their multidirectionality is accepted, but there also needs to be an emphasis on unequal powers, and the consequent inequalities between individuals and groups of people holding power. It is important to take account of the existence of domains of power characterised by the *absence* of decision-making by those powerful enough to control agendas, as well as the possibilities for those in 'weak' positions to utilise power on limited occasions in specific situations. This view of power is important for both feminist and anti-oppressive concerns with inequality and difference (cf. Thompson, 2007). This concept is discussed further in Chapter 3.

5   Examine reflexively your own social location and the possibility of dialogue

The anti-oppressive view of 'reflexivity' requires more than either a 'reflective' approach or a post-modern understanding of reflexivity. Examining the language and assumptions that the social worker uses in dialogue with others is certainly part of the requirement (Taylor and White, 2000). More importantly the professional has to assess how the language and assumptions they use are related to the specific social locations they themselves occupy, taking a critical look at their own values, without assuming that they can easily 'reverse positions' with others, in order to grasp their meaning. We mean here the interrogation of the worker's social position, language, behaviour, experience and motives in relation to the service users' and carers' perspectives and the dialogue that takes place between them. It needs to be done with an awareness of both the distant and the local variables which condition the discourse and understanding of both parties.

In particular a thorough analysis of the membership of the social divisions of the social worker in relation to specific others is a key issue. In addition their status, role and position as professionals and as agents of a powerful organisation in relation to service users, carers and colleagues is also an important factor that needs to be taken account of by the social worker. The nature and the possibility of dialogue between the parties will be constrained and/or facilitated by consideration of these issues. How well will the social worker be able to 'hear' the various muted voices of service users and others, especially those affected by disability (e.g. hearing or speaking impairments), or culture (language, values and accent), and more subtly but equally significantly by differences of social location, experience, perspective, and unequal powers. Awareness of your involvement, your strengths and limitations, and your responsibilities in a complex dialogue with others is therefore essential (Stanley, 1992).

Feminists have been critical of the Kantian assumption that moral action requires us to be able to 'take the position' of the other, in order to have a universally applicable rule. In recent times this has been associated with Jurgen Habermas, who argues that moral discourse requires people to be able to come together on the basis of freedom and equality to discuss problems and issues (Habermas, 1990). Recent social work academic interest has also linked Habermas with virtue theory, arguing that the emphasis of virtue ethics on personal character and commitment complements the Habermasian argument on open discourse in a way that provides a good foundation for social work (Gray and Lovat, 2007). The feminist concern with a form of moral discourse that helps to resolve differences respectfully has also drawn on the discourse ethics of Habermas, but not without qualification. Benhabib, for example, is a feminist who values Habermasian ideas about the fundamental political and ethical importance of free and equal public discussion (Benhabib, 1992). The Habermasian argument assumes that in principle all people can communicate with each other in a rational way. However, the assumption of reversibility of perspectives between dominant and subordinate is sometimes regarded as incoherent and undesirable: 'asking the oppressed to reverse perspectives with the privileged ... may itself be an injustice and an insult' (Young, 1997, p48). The Kantian and

Habermasian traditions have not on this view taken the problems of inequality between social groups seriously enough, and the kind of discourse needed has to take account of the 'complex and difficult activity' of 'hearing across the social divisions' (Jaggar, 2000, pp238–9). This requires both the development of practical skills in communication, and understanding the importance of 'moral humility' (Young, 1997, p49) when listening to individuals whose experiences of oppression (and domination) are very different from your own, but particularly when those experiences encompass living with social oppression. In other words, you are not pretending to take up a 'universal' ethical position, nor assuming that you can easily communicate with others. You recognise that you yourself are a participant with a particular social location and particular interests that impinge on your understanding of the situation, and on other participants' perspectives, including their understanding of you. This clearly requires an evaluation of the differences between the social locations of the specific actors involved in a situation. However, since some of the aspects of social positioning are not always visible or easy to classify, and are usually complex, there is therefore a further reason for moral humility. The precise nature of a person's experiences of oppression may not only be hidden, but it may not be possible or appropriate to find out in the given circumstances. This seriously complicates the assumption that Habermasian rules for speaking are sufficient for ensuring ethical dialogue (cf. Houston, 2003). It emphasises the need for an anti-oppressive view of reflexivity as a basic ethical tool.

The term 'spirituality' is sometimes used to describe the search for meaning and purpose, and although usually associated with religious ideas it is related by some to the notion that every person (religious or secular) belongs to a particular family and culture, and thus possesses a meaningful view of the world. The implication is that a social worker needs to be aware both of their own culture and that of others, if they are to work in a multicultural society: 'If we . . . appropriately locate *ourselves* (our emphasis) in matters to do with religion and spirituality, it will help us . . . to do justice to the other person's experience' (Moss, 2005, p43). An anti-oppressive approach to ethics must include this but go beyond it, taking account of dominant cultural and social powers, avoiding the imposition of particular religious or secular concepts, whilst maintaining dialogue with individuals from various cultures and embodying various social differences, as far as that is possible.

An anti-oppressive approach to ethics will thus encompass this notion of reflexive awareness, but locate it more effectively within *all* the major social divisions that structure people's lives, of which religion will sometimes be one, its importance relative to local values. It needs to be seen in terms of the specific histories of individual and group experiences, rather than deduced from nominal allegiances, and be thoroughly inclusive of both religious and secular values – and those with no particular answers to 'meaningful' questions. It certainly needs to be thought of in a reflexive way, affecting the interaction between the service user or carer and the worker, and demanding the worker's thoughtful consideration of the impact of their own social location, their organisational position and membership of *all* the social divisions (including secular or religious cultures), on the nature of their professional relationships. This concept is discussed further in Chapter 5.

REFLEXIVE AND CRITICAL THINKING IN ETHICS: SOME PRACTICAL IMPLICATIONS

In this section of the book we introduce two of the skills necessary for anti-oppressive ethics, basing ourselves on the above discussion of how an anti-oppressive approach relates to continuing ethical issues. We asserted that an anti-oppressive approach needs to be able to use evidence rationally; to argue logically; to draw sensitively on human feelings and emotions, but also to take account of the way all individual ethical understanding, feeling and behaviour is situated in particular historical times and social formations. In particular it relates ethics to particular historical contexts of social difference and inequality of powers and conditions in which the real dilemmas of both personal and professional practice arise.

KEY IDEAS

Practical reasoning in ethics from an anti-oppressive perspective requires *both*:

Reflexive thinking – taking account of your own social location, powers, values and perspectives, and your membership of the social divisions, in relation to specific others, recognising the inequalities and diversities of particular social situations in all your interactions with others.

Critical thinking – rigorously examining the relevance and cogency of evidence, and the logic of ethical arguments to make them as well-supported and intelligent as possible, taking account of different perspectives. We use this term, not in a post-modern sense, but in a more conventional way, but one that is reconfigured by its connection with reflexive thinking.

THINKING REFLEXIVELY

An important skill in ethical thinking is the ability to be aware of one's own position in relation to others. In some forms of ethics, this has been limited to the idea that one should make the attempt to:

1   understand the position of the other person, and
2   be prepared to act in ways that take their humanity and/or needs into account as well as your own.

It tends to be implicit that understanding the other's position is generally not an insoluble problem – with the application of some imaginative intelligence, and that there are sufficiently common notions of 'humanity' to support this strategy. Moral behaviour requires an effort to go beyond mere self-interest, and to act in the light of that knowledge. Self-interested action is regarded as 'prudential' rather than ethical – something which helps us to live our own lives, but is not necessarily related to anything or anyone else.

The notion of reflexive thinking (as we use it here) requires the actor to go beyond both prudential and ethical thinking (in the above sense) in ways that are consistent with an understanding of oppression in social life. The individual is not simply an abstract moral agent making decisions about what ought to be in hypothetical situations. The actor is a real human person in concrete social situations, in which each person has (changing) social locations. By the phrase 'social location' we mean the actor's simultaneous membership of the various social divisions, their particular position in social time and place, together with the specific roles they play within formal and informal social systems. The social location is critical in defining the ethical issues for each person involved, and their differing perceptions. The actor is either male or female, and will have a specific ethnic background. They may or may not be disabled, and their particular age, sexuality and social class will all affect how they will be perceived by others, and how they will see themselves as well as how they see others. They will also be part of various organisations and communities, with varying degrees of power over others – and others over them.

The moral actor is a participant within a complex situation, both as an observer of it, and as one who occupies a specific participant location of relative power. We draw this idea from a number of feminist ethical sources, as indicated above, including feminist research methodology where 'Reflexivity as a principle of good feminist research is widely agreed'

(Ramazanoglou with Holland, 2002, p118). The mutual involvement and dialogue between people both in feminist research practice and in social work practice implies that the perceptions of the observer and the subject interact. The values and perspectives of both are therefore central to the process of understanding. However, this process can only be fully understood in the context of the power differentials between them. This personal interaction is not only a matter of personal ethics, beliefs and psychology, but also of sociology, history, and politics. The differences in location and perception mean that understanding each other is often not at all easy. In the context of social work the dialogue between service users and carers is a key site (but not the only point) at which reflexive issues need to be carefully considered by workers, who themselves need to relate ethically to both the vulnerable (*and* the powerful) as socially located participants, rather than as 'neutral' professionals. The dialogue between differing kinds of professionals in the context of working together is another key area where reflexive issues are unavoidably important. The diagram below gives the reader the opportunity to begin to consider the personal implications of reflexivity. A similar diagram, but without the dimension of social class, can be found in Kallen (2003, p33).

The table opposite inevitably suggests simplistic assumptions about the categories of social division. An individual may not 'fit' easily into some positions, and may move from one to another, and will certainly combine membership of both dominant and subordinate groups in unique ways. The suggested categories will vary in time and across societies, especially between Western and non-Western countries. They are not suggested as an exclusive list – others will also be relevant, and the relative importance of a social division will vary with particular places and times. However, this diagram helps to *begin* thinking through your own social location systematically. It is especially important to consider the interconnection of social divisions – an abstract separate analysis of each category is inadequate. Each category needs to be considered separately *and* together as a qualitative rather than a merely additive exercise. Only this will provide an adequate basis for a reflexive anti-oppressive ethics. The diagram also focuses on the social divisions: *it does not say anything about an individual's social location within relevant social systems – the various social groups, communities and organisations in which they play a specific part.* This aspect of social location *also* needs to be considered – in conjunction with examination of membership of the social divisions – when thinking reflexively about particular situations.

Locating the self across unequal social divisions	Dominant groups	Subordinate groups
Gender (Note changing social and family perceptions of gender roles)	Men	Women
Social class (Note changing historical complexities of class in different societies)	Upper class; middle class; professionals	'Working class' Unemployed
'Race' (Note specific ethnicities and people of mixed ethnic heritage)	In the 'West' often white ethnic groups of 'Anglo' extraction	Minority ethnic groups – in the West often 'Black', Asian, Jewish, Irish
Sexuality (Note different constructions in differing societies)	Heterosexuals	Gay, lesbian, bi-sexuals and transsexuals
Disability (Note range of types and degrees of disability)	Able-bodied	'Disabled' people – however defined, including learning disability
Age (Note variations between societies and through time)	Adults – especially 'young middle-aged'	Children and young people Older people
Others		
1. Religion. Note the need to be specific about religious variations within and between countries.	In the 'West', major Christian groups The secular majority in some countries?	In the 'West', Muslims; Hindus; minority Christian and other religions
2. Mental health	Assumed 'normality' of people not labelled as 'mentally ill'	The mentally distressed and 'mentally ill'
3. Physical health	The 'healthy'	Especially those with chronic conditions and severe illness that diminish life opportunities

In the middle chapters of this book the concept of reflexivity will be put into practice for the reader to see for themselves. The examples of cases which require ethical consideration not only are discussed by the authors in relation to specific ethical theories (and compared with anti-oppressive ethics), but are also considered in relation to the authors' own social location, with comment on what difference the ethics of each case might have been if we the authors had been involved. We suggest that you the reader might consider what difference it would make if you had been in that position.

An important aspect of reflexive thinking is about coming to terms with the feelings that we have about various issues, and the circumstances that face us in particular situations. Having identified and recognised aspects of our own identity and their connections to concrete social factors in our lives, we also need to be aware of the way our experiences and feelings will colour our perspectives. In thinking reflexively, our awareness is not only in relation to deficits in our experience, but also to our strengths, and to our feelings about ourselves and others. We need therefore to think and feel creatively about ethical dilemmas – to be 'open-hearted' in our thinking (Weston, 2002, p75). We see this as an important part of both intellectual and emotional 'literacy' in ethics, and an essential component of anti-oppressive ethics. The issue is about whether our feelings are appropriate, and help us to understand people, or whether they help or hinder our understanding of ourselves and others, and whether our emotions are inappropriately clouding or colouring the issues (Thomson, 1999, pp143–52). In addition it involves the recognition of other voices than our own, and the need to engage in dialogue with them. Their specific social location has to be taken account of in the process of engagement.

THINKING CRITICALLY

The basic skills of critical thinking in ethics are similar to thinking skills in other disciplinary areas where rational procedures are necessary in order to achieve any form of agreement on what is a valid argument. These skills are relatively easy to spell out at a basic level, but they are often not so easy to actually put into practice. We are using the term 'critical' in this section in a conventional way, to refer to processes of logical thinking – but we suggest how these processes are re-figured by an anti-oppressive perspective.

In discussing ethics and values from an anti-oppressive perspective we need to be able to give good reasons: ethics has to relate to the realities that exist, including the realities of oppression in everyday life. When we enter into dialogue with people over ethical issues we use arguments that are not just about presenting information. It is a matter of presenting conclusions that are soundly based on a reasonable argument that may draw on three distinct elements: *evidence, values and the logic of the argument* itself. In other words:

[1] We should know the facts about the situation being considered. We need to know as accurately as possible the facts about what is happening, what has happened, the motives of those concerned and the predicted outcome of what is being done (if any outcome can be

predicted). We should consider if there are any particular circumstances that make this action unique, and what evidence there is that might *disconfirm* our initial view of the facts of the case (see below).

[2] We should consider carefully the norms and values by which that action is to be evaluated, and be as clear as possible about the grounds upon which ethical claims are made, and the values that are implied. This will include legal and professional norms as well as personal values. We also need to be aware of any possible challenge that could be made to that claim, and to our norms and values.

[3] We should think carefully about the logical basis of arguments. A conclusion may be challenged on various basic grounds: either we may not argue logically from the premises to the conclusion, or we may be wrong about the premises, or about the facts, or about the norms.

[1] Thinking critically about the facts is important for any kind of ethical argument, but is especially important in anti-oppressive ethics, because there is no assumption that it will be at all easy to tell what are 'the facts'. In the past ethics examples sometimes required the actor to clearly distinguish facts from values, with the assumption that this is at least in principle always possible, and usually possible to do without too much difficulty. Generally speaking a statement of fact or an 'empirical' statement about the actual social world does *not* involve a 'should' or an 'ought': it simply describes what is the case. Ethical statements can often be identified by the actual or implicit presence of such key words. An ethical argument often (but not always) involves an 'ought' and implies an appeal to a rule or norm. Thus:

Fact: A has had occasion to harm B
Ethical norm: harming people is wrong
Conclusion: A ought not to have harmed B.

However, this example is very simple, and relies on a universal norm. Social workers know that their cases usually involve differences of perspective in which the facts are hotly disputed and are viewed from very different angles. This does not excuse anyone from examining carefully the nature of the evidence on which ethical arguments are based. On the contrary, it means that facts need to be scrutinised, and assessed, and in particular, it means that the research principle of 'disconfirmation' needs to be applied to empirical statements about the social world on which ethical conclusions are based. This means that the actor should not only search for what she believes are the facts of the case, but should also search for what would conflict with what are believed to be the facts, but might support a different explanation. These facts would '*dis*confirm' rather than confirm the actor's initial beliefs about the situation. In the above example the 'fact' of what was said is very possibly disputable. Did A *really* say just that, or was he misheard, or joking, or saying it for some justifiable reason?

[2] Thinking critically about the norms, principles and moral concepts on which ethical arguments are based is also of even greater importance for anti-oppressive ethics than it is for some other types of ethics. This is because there is so little agreement on ethical norms between different ethical and cultural perspectives, and an anti-oppressive ethic is specifically oriented to take account of a range of different views. In addition, an anti-oppressive ethic will take account of legal, organisational and professional norms, yet will need to be particularly sensitive of the need to be critical of established and 'authoritative' statements, even if legitimated by agreed political and bureaucratic processes. Just because an 'authority' lays down norms, principles and concepts does not mean that these have to be accepted as ethical. A social worker cannot ignore the socially legitimated policy and law of the land that is required by the employing agency, but at the same time has to take account of their own personal and professional values and culture, and in addition those of the service users, all of which may differ from each other in significant respects.

Two imperatives follow from this consideration of varying norms for anti-oppressive critical thinking. First, there is the importance of knowledge and understanding of the different perspectives, including law and policy; the service users' cultures, and the worker's own. Secondly, where possible, dialogue between the interested parties is needed to negotiate an area of agreement where people may act ethically with as little compromise of their own or others' values as possible, and with as much sense of their own integrity as possible. This means considering carefully the areas of apparent conflict and areas of agreement, not only between the worker and service user perspectives, but also between those of other professionals, other carers and users, and the policy and law relevant to the agency. This requires considerable mental effort in principle, although in practice much of this is taken as read, or as already 'covered' in training and induction. Nevertheless anti-oppressive critical ethical thinking abhors complacency on these issues, which need to be reviewed and reconsidered when ethical decisions are being made.

[3] Thinking critically about the logic of ethical arguments raises some particular issues for anti-oppressive ethics. There are some common logical considerations which help to distinguish between arguments that are regarded as legitimate, and arguments that are unacceptable. Anti-oppressive ethics requires careful examination of some of these issues. Some 'fallacies in ethical reasoning' (cf. Fox and DeMarco, 2001, on which the following is based) that are of particular concern to anti-oppressive ethics are as follows:

- *The fallacy of authority*. People will often appeal to various authorities, but logically a proposition should be true regardless of any authority to which appeal may be made. This is particularly true of anti-oppressive ethics because of the awareness of differing cultural and religious icons and authorities, which may have meaning for some but not for others.
- *The fallacy of expertise*. The appeal to expertise is fallacious if it is misplaced, i.e. the person concerned is not actually an expert on the issue in hand (but may be on something else). This is also important for anti-oppressive ethics because the justification of anyone's claim to expertise needs to be closely scrutinised when explanations of 'fact' are so closely tied to variable perspectives and values, particularly so when spokespersons for dominant value systems claim expertise without knowledge or experience of subordinate groups.
- *The fallacy of 'ad hominem' arguments*. This means one should be evaluating an argument because of its inherent validity, and *not* on the basis of sympathy for, or prejudice against, the person advocating that argument. An 'ad feminam' argument would mean the same thing but referring to a different gender. For anti-oppressive ethics, it seems important to consider the argument *both* on its own merit, regardless of who made it, and as an expression of the values and experience of a particular socially located person. If an unemployed disabled mother and a male city stockbroker say the same thing when expressing their values, do they *mean* the same thing or are they really saying something different?
- *The fallacy of legitimate power*. Within contemporary democratic societies the government of the day constitutes the legitimate power. However, the government's law and policy relevant to social situations and social services agencies may contribute to, but they cannot be assumed to be the end of an ethical argument. The 'powers that be' may be able to force compliance, and even insist on what is 'right', but that

does not make the action ethical. Clearly this is an important consideration for an anti-oppressive ethic.

- *The fallacy of generalisation.* Generalising statements about what is the case should be based on good evidence about the things being referred to, but ethical arguments may easily involve fallacious generalisations when they are drawn from limited evidence or experience. This is particularly important for anti-oppressive ethics, where the existence of social divisions is clearly recognised, and the consequent danger of someone generalising from their own experience (or from the experience of members of their own group) runs the risk of ignoring completely the evidence and experience of different others.

- *The fallacy of meaning.* Obviously words have different meanings (and/or different words have the same meaning) and in an ethical argument there can easily be misconceived arguments resulting from differences in meaning or changes of meaning. In anti-oppressive ethics the possibility of this is magnified by awareness of the pervasive influence of social difference. Our differing perspectives usually involve different understandings of the meaning of apparently common terms, and this can easily lead to difficulties in ethical argument. Thus attending very carefully to what is meant is extremely important. The fallacy is to assume that the same term means the same thing to everyone – it often does not. Similarly the use of different terms does not necessarily add anything to the argument if the different words mean essentially the same thing, in which case the arguer is simply 'begging the question' by repeating the argument but using different language.

- *The fallacy of the slippery slope.* These are arguments where the logic is assumed to be one of a chain of consequences. If X happens, then Y might be a consequence, and an unacceptable Z might occur as a result of Y. Therefore we should not start on this 'slippery slope' and should ensure that X does not happen as a result of our actions. This is only a fallacy if the connections cannot be shown to be likely to happen. The argument looks logical, but it all depends on empirical evidence about the probability of something happening. Such evidence requires both data and interpretation, and from an anti-oppressive perspective the problem is that differently located people will evaluate the evidence for probability differently. It is therefore a serious issue.

It has been a growing concern that social workers should consciously engage in 'practical reasoning', taking responsibility for their own actions, and demonstrating relevant skills and understanding to enable them to think through the ethics of the situations in which they find themselves (Clark, 2006). We would suggest that the kind of practical reasoning that is necessary for an anti-oppressive approach to ethics in social work needs to combine the reflexive thinking described above with the more traditional 'critical' consideration of evidence and argument just discussed. The two modes of thinking need to work together to form an adequate basis for anti-oppressive ethics.

CHAPTER SUMMARY

In this chapter we have explained the nature of oppression and social division, laying particular emphasis on inequalities and diversities across a range of social groups and dimensions of power – personal, cultural, political and economic. We have suggested some meta-ethical issues can usefully be discussed in order to understand anti-oppressive ethics, with its respect for both reason and feeling, as well as experience and empirical evidence. We have set out a guiding framework of concepts which can be used to explore anti-oppressive ethical issues in any situation, and have argued that anti-oppressive ethics involves both thinking critically, empirically and logically about arguments, but also reflexively, with feeling and sensitivity, in the light of our own social location.

FURTHER READING

Banks, S. (2006) *Ethics and Values in Social Work*, 3rd edn. A comprehensive account of ethics and values in social work.

Clifford, D.J. and Burke, B. (2001) 'What difference does it make? Anti-oppressive ethics and informed consent.' This paper attempts to illustrate the difference that anti-oppressive ethics makes in practice.

Dominelli, L. (2002c) 'Values in Social Work'. An anti-oppressive approach to values in social work.

McLaughlin, J. (2003) Chapter 3, 'The Ethics of Care'. A summary of work in feminist ethics.

Orme, J. (2002) 'Social work: gender, care and justice'. A summary of the contribution of feminist ethics to social work, with special reference to community care.

Young, I.M. (1990) *Justice and the Politics of Difference*. A broad introduction to anti-oppressive values.

Chapter 2

Social Work Values, Codes and the Law

This chapter provides the backdrop against which the practice situations discussed in later chapters should be critically analysed. The scenarios which we present not only explore the complex nature of social work in contemporary society, the multidisciplinary context in which practitioners deliver services, but also the diverse experiences of users within their families, their communities and the society at large. In this chapter we critique, from an anti-oppressive perspective, the values, codes of ethics and practice, and the legal and policy context which guide the actions of practitioners and in which practice is located.

KEY IDEAS

Code of ethics: Usually a written document produced by a professional association, occupational regulatory body or other professional body with the stated aim of guiding the practitioners who are members, protecting service users and safeguarding the reputation of the profession. (Banks, 2004, p108).

Code of practice: Usually a written document which may be produced by government with professional and lay consultation, but which has the force of legitimate authority and may be backed with penalties for non-compliance, similarly aiming to protect service users and guide practitioners.

SOCIAL WORK AND VALUES

Most would agree that 'social work is a diverse and shifting activity' (Jones, 2002, p41) and that consequently it is difficult to capture its essence in a single static definition. Post-modernists would object to the notion of it having an essence and we would agree at least to the extent that differences of definition are related to different values. However, the widely accepted international definition of social work (International Federation of Social Workers, 2004) asserts that at its core social work claims to promote social change, and be informed by a human rights and social justice perspective, thus emphasising the value and moral base of social work as a complex and morally demanding activity (Bisman, 2004; Clifford and Burke, 2004; Dalrymple and Burke, 2006). Practitioners are faced on a daily basis with a range of situations which reflect the detailed complexities of people's lives and their relationship to social structures. Practitioners need to have the ability to work with situations of uncertainty and with the 'ethical complexity which is at the heart of all practice' (Jones *et al.*, 2008). Within a context where the profession is subject to the challenges of limited resources, increasing managerialism, privatisation, fragmentation, de-regulation and routinisation of social work tasks (Healey and Meagher, 2004), it is important for social work to maintain its humanitarian value-based mission.

Historically social work values have been seen as an important component of what social work both 'is' and 'should be'. The well-known principles identified by Biestek (1961) relating to individualisation, acceptance, non-judgementalism, self-determination and confidentiality centrally informed social work's identity as a helping profession for many years, and are still enshrined in codes of ethics and practice, especially in Western countries. However, Biestek's principles were based on a definition of social work as individual 'casework' – with the therapeutic relationship as a key component. Not surprisingly, in more recent times this has been criticised for 'being highly individualised and culturally specific, that is, tied to Western culture' (Dominelli, 2002c, p18). The definition of social work as individual casework is also limited by its relative failure to take into account that social workers work with some of the most socially disadvantaged, marginalised and excluded people. It could be said that one of the important roles of social work is to make visible the connections between individual distress and social structures and confront 'a social order that thrives on the backs of poor people; challenge the legitimacy of unequal social relations and demand the personal and structural changes required to fulfil its mandate' (Dominelli, 2004, p249). However, the continued presence of these values within social work, albeit at times in modified form, is testimony to their continuing relevance to and influence on social work.

The internationally agreed definition of social work issued by the

International Federation of Social Workers and the International Association of Schools of Social Work (2004) explicitly implies that there are other dimensions to social work practice than the 'moral individualism of the liberal tradition' (Jordan, 2004, p6). Social work is defined as promoting social change and the empowerment and liberation of people. At the heart of this definition is a commitment to the principles and values which underpin human rights and social justice: social work is viewed as being able to make a contribution to change on a personal and structural level. This international definition of social work appears to imply, as Jordan says, the 'potentially emancipatory' character of social work (Jordan, 2004, p1). However, the meaning of 'empowerment' and 'emancipatory' cannot be taken for granted. 'Empowerment' especially has been widely used within right-wing discourse as a code for getting individuals to be responsible for themselves without the need for help, in direct opposition to the recognition of the politics of social injustice and exploitation. It is thus possible to 'read' even this definition of social work in various ways, just as it was possible to read earlier statements of social work values in contradictory ways (see Humphries, 1997). Social work has the potential to be emancipatory but this potential will only be realised if the profession clearly identifies 'what is distinctive about its values, knowledge and practice methods, and create strong links between all practitioners committed to these, in a whole range of public, voluntary and commercial agencies' (Jordan, 2004, p17).

However, the basic issue here is the inevitable and variable involvement of contested social work values (however defined) in codes of ethics and practice, policy and the law. Social work codes of ethics, if treated as a 'living document' (Bowles et al., 2006, p84), can assist practitioners to 'respond to the moral imperative of caring for the neediest among us' (Bisman, 2004, p109). If used critically as a tool in which differing social values, both locally and globally, can be taken into account by the practitioner engaging in decision-making processes, the ethical dimension of practice will thus be placed at the 'forefront of professional consciousness' (Bowles et al., 2006, p84).

Values and codes

Professional codes of ethics and codes of practice generally aim to promote ethical awareness and behaviour (see definitions above). Both kinds of codes are used by a range of professions and usually incorporate a range of values which have been found to be 'useful in structuring moral life, and . . . may include seeking justice, equality and liberty for all, and respect for persons and their autonomy' (Pattinson, 2001, p7). By identifying the general values and principles of ethical conduct the codes in essence are describing the practitioner as a person who is expected to have certain 'virtues' such as being compassionate or respectful, and who has an awareness of injustice, especially in the health and social care professions. The codes establish and maintain a particular professional identity. Professional codes vary in length and detail but on the whole they can be seen to embody the theoretical, practical and ethical basis of a range of professional groups. For example, the United Kingdom Central Council for Nursing, Midwifery and Health Visiting (Nursing and Midwifery Council, 2002) *Code of Professional Conduct* and the British Association of Social Workers *Code of Ethics* (BASW, 2002) provide practitioners with the relevant professional framework which guides and regulates the conduct of its members. Codes not only make tangible the nebulous qualities of values but with their blend of values, ethical principles and rules governing behaviour they can be used to assist – and control – the practitioner.

In codifying rules of conduct the contested values of social work have been filtered down to produce a degree of coherence. However, the difficulty even with codified values is that they can still mean anything to anyone as 'values are, inescapably, relative to the actor's view; plural and inherently contradictory; contingent on time, community and situation' (Clark, 2000, p30). However, they are also, and oddly, often viewed as unproblematic, universal and agreed. Yet it is in practice that the evidence of the uncertain quality of values comes to the fore: 'the fluid movement of values through complex interactions in helping relationships suggests that the certainty and stability that surround values are illusionary' (Dominelli, 2002c, p16). If values are socially constructed, culturally and historically specific, and open to individual interpretation, is it possible to construct an agreed code that will guide ethical practice? Or will the codes appear as ephemeral entities in practice – their vagueness, generality and internal inconsistencies limiting their application? Does this mean that professional generalisations drawn from fundamentals of ethics are unhelpful? These questions are relevant and need to be addressed but equally this does not mean that it is not worth trying to gain agreement regarding minimum standards of practice (Hugman, 2007). The International Federation of Social Workers (IFSW) and the International Association of Schools of Social Work (IASSW) *Ethics in Social Work, Statement of Principles* (IFSW/IASSW, 2004) provides, with all its attendant difficulties, a set of values and general ethical principles which are aimed at encouraging ethical debate and reflection amongst practitioners and assisting them to make ethically informed decisions. It is expected that the international statement would be used to inform national codes of ethics. This expectation acknowledges the possibility that a global set of values relevant to social work can exist but equally can and should co-exist with varying degrees of consideration for the particularities of different cultures, communities and countries (Healy, 2007). This is an important corrective if the international ethical code is not to be seen as a universal tool for promoting Westernised ideologies and values associated with individualism, failing to acknowledge, for example, the existence of values that stress collectivity, communality, and reciprocity which are important from an anti-oppressive perspective. Social work has developed in specific national contexts and, as a consequence, values and ethical principles from the international ethical statement will be differentially received and interpreted. It is therefore important that the statement is viewed as a vehicle which can promote international discussion regarding the meaning of social work values and principles as well as consider the extent to which these 'agreed' values and principles can be universally applied. Commentators such as Healy (2007) and Yip (2004), have raised questions regarding the relevance and applicability of international statements to all contexts which, in their attempt to be of universal relevance, promote rather than challenge 'cultural hegemony' (Hugman, 2008). The extent to which ethical rules are fixed or contextual are central to Healy and Yip's critique. Yip proposes 'that in international terms social work ethics ought to be treated as a dynamic exchange between cultures' (Hugman, 2008), where there is mutual respect between the different values which exist within and between countries. 'This means that not only non-Eurocentric countries should respect western ideologies such as rights, equality, empowerment and social change, but also the Eurocentric countries should respect eastern ideologies such as responsibility, collectivity, social norms and relation' (Yip, 2004, p610). Healy also advocates the need for cultural sensitivity in relation to social work values but warns against going down the path of pure relativity as this can lead to practitioners failing to act and actually violating the profession's commitment to the values of human rights and equality. The *Ethics in Social Work: Statement of Principles* (IFSW/IASSW, 2004), if seen as a dynamic and interactive document, has a role to play in facilitating ethical awareness and guiding ethical action in diverse cultural contexts. The document states clearly that it is the responsibility of the national member organisations to develop and regularly update their own codes of ethics so that they are consistent with the statement of ethics. Given this responsibility, a national code of ethics needs to be made specific to the context in which it is to be used. There is then still some value for the profession of having a code of ethics at both global and national levels to which social workers can be called to account, but which always requires critical reassessment and interpretation (Banks, 2004).

Codes of ethics in conjunction with codes of practice act as guidance for practitioners and help to ensure that minimum standards of practice are adhered to (Clark, 2007). Importantly, they are also the means by which service users can judge the standard of the service that is being provided. The code of ethics can be seen as the means by which the ideals of the profession are translated into practice, and, given the lack of status of social work, this could be seen as an important part of the struggle for recognition and respect of a profession that is often criticised and marginalised. However, evidence (Holland and Kilpatrick, 1991, cited in Congress and McAuliffe, 2006; Hekmans *et al.*, 2007) suggests that social workers, though aware of a code of ethics, are not always familiar with its content or use it in any systematic way to assist in their ethical decision-making. Given its important function there is therefore a need to ensure that staff have access to copies of codes and that they have the space in which to critically debate their content and their relevance to practice situations. In fact the British Association of Social Work's code of ethics does suggest that social workers should ensure that their employers are made aware of the code and that as practitioners they should 'uphold the ethical principles and responsibilities of the code and use the values and principles of the code to resolve conflicts between ethical principles and organisational policies and practices' (BASW, 2002, p11, para 4.3). However, codes of practice, where supported by the authorities, make social workers accountable to central government regulatory bodies, and they may also be used by employers as part of a contract of employment. They are part of a 'regulatory discourse consistent with the wider disciplinary activity of the state' (Humphries, 1997, p644). The existence of the codes and how they are implemented can influence practice to reinforce government policies, but they can *also* be used to critically evaluate 'the impact and ethical worth of policies and procedures' (Bowles *et al.*, 2006, p81).

There are clearly arguments in favour of codes as well as against, and an anti-oppressive ethical perspective cannot be complacent about either. Our conclusion is that, in practice, an anti-oppressive ethic needs to take the rules of conduct and seek to interpret and apply them within an anti-oppressive framework of concepts which are developed and used throughout this book, and elaborated further in Chapter 9.

Codes, ethics and practice

Despite the cultural variations between nations, social work values are often also common across different societies and reflected in the content of many professional codes of ethics (Banks, 2004; Healy, 2007). For example, many of the agreed universal values expressed in the *Ethics in Social Work, Statement of Principles* (IFSW/IASSW, 2004) can be found in the BASW *Code of Ethics for Social Work* (2002) as well as in other national codes. This convergence between various codes of ethics and practice of different countries could well be a 'response to the forces of globalisation and post-modernism' (Bowles *et al.*, 2006, p85), as well as being a direct response to the demand that the international statement of ethics should inform national and local codes of ethics. The UK BASW *Code of Ethics* provides practitioners with guidance as to how they should engage in ethical, theoretically informed practice, underpinned by the needs and rights of service users and carers. It reflects *both* liberal individualistic values and values which emphasise 'mutuality and democratic solidarity' (Jordan, 2004, p17). The BASW code takes as its starting point the international definition of social work, indicating a belief that social work is a politically and ethically informed activity. Given their similarity and the links between codes of ethics and codes of practice, we will review their content by focusing on one we know well in the UK, the General Social Care Council *Codes of Practice* (GSCC, 2002), but referring also to other codes and countries in passing.

The GSCC *Codes of Practice* contain a list of statements that describe the standards of professional conduct and practice required of social care workers. The GSCC codes are intended to reflect existing good practice and it is hoped that workers will recognise in the codes the shared standards to which they already aspire. Social workers are expected to meet the following six standards:

1 Protect the rights and promote the interests of services users and carers;
2 Strive to establish and maintain the trust and confidence of service users and carers;
3 Promote the independence of service users while protecting them as far as possible from danger or harm;
4 Respect the rights of service users while seeking to ensure that their behaviour does not harm themselves or other people;
5 Uphold public trust and confidence in social care services; and
6 Be accountable for the quality of their work and take responsibility for maintaining and improving their knowledge and skills (GSCC, 2002).

Although the GSCC codes are not called a code of ethics, they can be seen to fulfil the function of a code of ethics as well as a code of practice. However, unlike the BASW *Code of Ethics* they are enforceable. Using criteria developed by Banks (2004, p108) from her review of a range of different professional codes of ethics, we find that the GSCC codes contain similar elements to codes of ethics:

- Statements about the core purpose or service ideal of the profession. For example, the purpose of social work can be seen to include a commitment to protecting the rights of service users, promote social justice and contribute to social change. The Australian Association of Social Workers (AASW), North American National Association of Social Workers (NASW) and the British Association of Social Workers (BASW) all incorporate social justice as a core value in their codes.

- Statements about the character/attributes or virtues of the professional. For example: 'Professional practitioners should be honest and trustworthy, reliable and dependable' (GSCC, 2002, paras 2.1 and 2.4). In suggesting that practitioners have to be a certain type of person the code clearly emphasises the 'importance of "virtues" in social work ethics and reminds us how the personal and professional are intertwined' (Bowles *et al.*, 2006).

- Ethical principles. Banks points out that codes are often 'loosely related to universal ethical theories such as Kantianism and utilitarianism' (Banks, 2004, p107), and are embodied in the following statements which can all be found in the GSCC code of practice: treating each person as an individual (para 1.1), respect for the autonomy of service users (para 1.3), respecting and maintaining the dignity and privacy of service users (para 1.4), respecting diversity and different cultures and values (para 1.6). Similar statements can be found in other professions such as the UK Nursing and Midwifery Council *Code of Professional Conduct* (Nursing and Midwifery Council, 2002), and in the codes adopted in other countries.

- Rules of professional practice provide very specific guidance relating to professional practice, for example practitioners may be reminded that policies and procedures exist in relation to accepting gifts and money from service users and carers (GSCC, 2002, para 2.7).

- Principles of professional practice. The GSCC codes are intended to reflect existing good practice as well as identify what workers should aspire to in relation to their own practices – so they contain statements such as helping service users and carers to make complaints, taking complaints seriously and responding to them or passing them to the appropriate person; and 'recognising and using responsibly the power that comes from working with service users and carers' (GSCC, 2002, paras 3.7 and 3.8), the practice principle of working in collaboration with colleagues is encapsulated in the following statement: 'recognising and respecting the roles and expertise of workers from other agencies and working in partnership with them' (GSCC, 2002, para 6.7). The Australian and American codes of ethics also view consultation with other professionals as an ethical responsibility of practitioners (Congress and McAuliffe, 2006). The Australian code of ethics states clearly that 'in making ethical decisions consultations with colleagues, supervisors and/or competent professionals [are] advisable' (AASW, 1999, p22).

The value of codes of ethics then is that of creating and maintaining a professional identity, helping to establish and reaffirm the qualities required of a professional practitioner. They are aspirational, educational and political documents (Banks, 2004), but they cannot and should not be a substitute for practitioners engaging in ethical reflection. Codes are a useful starting point and a helpful guide that can shape and inform organisational cultures as well as the actions of individuals. They should not be seen as a rigidly prescriptive framework for ethical practice, as uncritical use of the codes may well contribute to and reinforce technicist and managerialist approaches to practice issues and dilemmas.

In addition to the commonalities between codes identified by Banks (2004) there are of course some differences of emphasis, and occasional departures from the norm that relate to the particular experiences of specific countries. For example, it is interesting to note that the Canadian code of ethics includes a commitment to environmental sustainability. Social workers, it states, 'shall advocate for a clean and healthy environment and shall advocate for the development of environmental strategies consistent with social work principles' (Bowles *et al.*, 2006, p90). Cultural differences and understanding of our relationship with the physical world are also reflected in some codes, for example in the Indian code people are seen as 'part of nature, needing to live in harmony with other non-human existence' (Bowles *et al.*, 2006, p90).

Codes of ethics can be considered to be the tangible outcomes of the profession's attempts to 'codify professional morality' (Beauchamp and

Childress, 2001, p5) and by specifying the professional's moral responsibilities, they 'perform a controlling function by seeking to prevent deliberately 'unethical' behaviour on the part of social workers' (Ife, 2001, p103). But what are morally acceptable terms for professions that are working with vulnerable people, and who decides and on what basis? How far can codes successfully guide practitioners who are engaged in very complex moral situations? Should codes of ethics be seen as tools to promote ethical practice or do they merely act as a conduit through which the power that professionals have over relatively powerless service users' is legitimated?

Codes of ethics have been criticised on a philosophical and sociological basis by a number of commentators. Beauchamp and Childress claim that some professional codes over simplify moral requirements (Beauchamp and Childress, 2001, p6). By presenting moral principles as unproblematic there is a failure to recognise that they are in fact underpinned by complex philosophical ideas. For example, little guidance if any is provided for managing decisions in relation to competing moral principles. Another example is that the right to self-determination at times conflicts with the authority of professionals to intrude into private life, particularly if a person's decision to act in a particular way is seen to endanger their life.

Ife (2001) argues that codes of ethics are 'essentially modernist' in their formulation and function' (Ife, 2001, p106) and are a tool of the powerful rather than an instrument that attempts to reflect the diverse perspectives of those who are often subject to those who have power and control. They fail to reflect the competing viewpoints of all the players in practice situations. Ife also points out that the code of ethics may suggest that there is only one way of practising. This attempt to 'encompass the varied and complex roles of social workers into a single ideal way of practising' (Ife, 2001, p106) could also be subjected to criticism by some feminist (Gilligan, 1982; Noddings, 1984) and post-modernist (Baumann, 1992) approaches which emphasise the partial nature of any general ethical principles, and suggest that the search for a single authoritative account of practice is not only unachievable but is unhelpful and impractical. For one would have to develop a comprehensive code of ethics to cover every eventuality. It could also lull professionals into a false sense of moral security, believing that by assiduously following the rules of the codes this will guarantee they are working in a morally acceptable way. However, an unreflective following of prescribed rules leads to practice that is defensive, conservative and disempowering.

Despite some of the more social values expressed in some codes, they tend to promote an individualistic perspective (Ife, 2001). The practice details and the inevitable challenges of working openly, cooperatively and respectively with colleagues, working in partnership with service users or working within a multidisciplinary team are not explored within the codes. Different professional groups will have their own particular understanding of value-laden terms such as 'partnership' and 'collaboration'. From an anti-oppressive perspective the ethical implications of working in a multi-professional team within culturally diverse communities needs to be acknowledged. The stress on personal morality is always open to query, as an overemphasis on personal morality can be a way of evading the complexities of social relationships and wider issues of social justice.

Codes of ethics and codes of practice are not neutral tools. De Maria, (1997, cited in Bowles *et al.*, 2006), suggests that codes of ethics can be used to protect employer organisations rather than those practitioners attempting to challenge the organisation's practices. A similar point is also made by Thompson who states that 'contemporary codes are designed to gain the practitioner's compliance rather than commitment' (Thompson, 2002). They reflect particular interests and commitments as socially constructed documents, which 'inevitably articulate the occupational/professional ideological and moral aspirations of their creators' (Butler, 2002, p240). It always needs to be remembered that despite the apparent 'universality' of the listed rules, 'They need to be contextualised and situated. They are not for always and for everywhere' (Butler, 2002, p240). Workers need to be 'ethically articulate' (Bowles *et al.*, 2006) so as to be able to negotiate between moral principles, social and legal policies, practice standards and agency policy and procedures, and thus act as best they can in morally contentious and ambiguous situations.

THE LEGAL AND POLICY CONTEXT

In an attempt to clarify terms, 'social work law' has been usefully defined by Preston-Shoot *et al.* (1998) to refer to those powers and duties which provide social work practitioners with their specific mandate to practise. 'Social work law' should be distinguished from 'social welfare law', which refers to statutory provisions of which social work practitioners should be aware, in order to advise and advocate effectively with, and on behalf of, people so that they can provide a service which meets service users' needs. This dual legal framework forms part of the context in which social workers practice. The law defines the roles and responsibilities of practitioners and directs practice in the areas of prevention, protection and rehabilitation. This does not mean, however, that practitioners 'merely implement the law' (Adams, 2002). Social workers in fact draw on a range of academic disciplines, such as psychology, sociology, politics, philosophy, social policy, and evidence from practitioner-informed research and service-user experiences, to explore and understand the context in which the problems people face are located. Consequently the relationship between social work and the law is not straightforward. There is inevitably in reality a dynamic relationship between the law and social work practice. Therefore deciding when and how to use the law is not a neutral act: it is one that has an ethical dimension to it. The law is not always informed by anti-oppressive values and is just as likely to compound inequality as well as protect vulnerable individuals (Preston-Shoot, 2003; Dalrymple and Burke, 2006; Brown and Kershaw, 2008).

The law, at a general level and in relation to social work, *can* contribute to the development of practice which is beneficial, supportive, and promotes anti-oppressive values (Dalrymple and Burke, 2006; Braye and Preston-Shoot, 1997; Roche, 2002; Williams, 2004). However, its anti-oppressive potential can be realised only if it is used critically, and interrogated from an ethical perspective (Preston-Shoot *et al.*, 2001). There are parallels between law and some ethical theories as both attempt to resolve difficulties by prescribing action that needs to be taken. However, the comparison is limited as answers to complex human questions and social problems require more than legal rule following (even though sometimes ethics is reduced to a set of rules). The fundamental difference between the law and ethics is that:

> ethics is basically an open-ended, reflective and critical intellectual activity . . . These principles are not the kind of thing that can be settled by fiat, by agreement or by authority. To assume that they can be is to confuse ethics with law-making, rule-making, policy-making and other kinds of decision-making.
>
> (Ladd, 1998, p211, cited in Banks, 2004, pp113–14)

It has relatedly been remarked that a total 'reliance on the law, fails to address the problems people face and may in fact exacerbate them' (Braye and Preston-Shoot, 1997, p3). However, it is perhaps better to view the law as more open-ended like ethics – as something which: 'provides authority and a structure for decision-making rather than solutions: it provides a framework in which individual social workers have to act' (Cull and Roche, 2001, pxiii). However, the law can also be an insensitive, imprecise and blunt instrument with which to understand and resolve the delicate and complex nature of peoples' lives. A legalistic approach to human problems often fails to address directly questions of inequality 'and the damage done by inequitable and discriminatory social structures' (Braye and Preston Shoot, 1997, p3). The law does not always facilitate the resolution of sensitive personal problems to the satisfaction of all participants. We only have to look at the process and outcomes of rape trials (Kennedy, 2004) and child abuse cases. Within these situations it is clear that the interests of all parties are not always acknowledged, particularly in adversarial court arenas where rules of evidence and the evident unequal power relationships that exist can militate against justice being achieved.

Nevertheless, practice that is effective and ethical relies upon the worker having a clear understanding of the law and using it to guide practice that respects service users and is sensitive to their concerns. However, practitioners have to be aware of the contradictions inherent in the law and the fact that some pieces of legislation conflict with each other to such a degree that use of the law is not an impartial activity, and can be constraining and oppressive rather than facilitative of emancipatory practice. Practitioners have to be aware of the intimate relationship which exists between the legislative and policy frameworks and the provision of services. For example, Humphries (2004) suggests that the failure of the profession to critically analyse the ideological basis of legislation and social policy has led to the failure to identify the inherent racism within immigration legislation. Resulting in situations where practitioners actively cooperate 'with the removal and deportation of people' (Humphries, 2004, p104), an aspect of practice that is antithetical to its stated values.

The discriminatory potential of the law has to be recognised (Brayne and Martin, 1990; King and Trowell, 1992; Braye and Preston-Shoot, 1992; Humphries, 2004; Kennedy, 2004; Dalrymple and Burke, 2006), and therefore its utility to promote practice that can be said to be ethical and empowering should be questioned. Helena Kennedy powerfully exposes the gendered value base of the law. Kennedy argues that the 'law mirrors society with all its imperfections and it therefore reflects the subordination of women' (Kennedy, 1993, p30). However, it is not only women whom the legal system fails but also people who are labelled as 'Black', who have a disability, who are gay or lesbian, who are viewed as

working-class (Kennedy, 1993). The potential of the law to make a difference can be realised 'if those involved in the administration of justice have
a special obligation to reject society's irrational prejudices' (Kennedy,
1993, p30). Justice, Kennedy points out, is obtained by 'giving a fair and
unbiased appraisal of each person and situation without relying on
preconceived notions' (Kennedy, 1993, p31). The law has the potential to
radically affect the way in which we relate to each other and live our lives.
It can be used to challenge decisions that deny people's rights, liberty and
equality.

In order for the law, social policies, and practice guidance documents to
be of assistance in relation to the development of good practice their underpinning values need to be examined, and questions need to be asked about
how far they address the issues of equality, justice and rights. Social work
educators have a key responsibility in enabling students to critically understand and apply the law with 'sophistication and sensitivity' (Brown and
Kershaw, 2008) to ensure that the rights of the individual and communities
are protected. The discourse of human rights provides a framework in which
debates regarding tolerance, diversity, inequality, individual and collective
rights and responsibilities can take place. The Human Rights Act 1998 (with
all its imperfections) is underpinned by values such as 'tolerance; respect for
the dignity and lifestyle choices of others; allowing others to speak their
mind or to protest without obstruction; and treating others fairly without
discrimination or degradation' (Klug, 2002, p197). These are values and
principles consistent with our view of ethical practice, and an example of
how the law can be used positively.

The anti-oppressive framework discussed in Chapter 1 provides some key
concepts which should assist the practitioner on questioning various codes
and laws. For example, the way that social divisions are accounted for – or
ignored – is an obvious matter that needs to be thought through rigorously.
We have already discussed above some of the general ways that the law fails
to deal fairly with issues of gender, ethnicity and other matters relating to
social divisions. This can hardly be surprising when the law and codes reflect
the dominant values of the societies that produce them. It needs to be reconsidered for each specific case. Equally, the nature and multiple directions of
power are issues that need to be carefully assessed when using the law or
applying codes of ethics: who is in a position to wield power, and who is
vulnerable to them? This includes social workers, and the officers of the law
itself – a notoriously hierarchical system in which middle-aged white males
often predominate and use their power in questionable ways (Kennedy,

2004). The interacting social systems that constitute legal and regulatory processes also need to be assessed in relation to the impact that differing organisations can have on individual lives. In addition the anti-oppressive requirement of paying attention in a reflexive way to the histories of people involved in interactions remains important when considering who is involved in legal and regulatory processes. This applies equally to officials, social workers and service users: an understanding of the unique histories of those involved provides important clues as to how they will react, and how needs may be more effectively met. Social workers need to think carefully about interpreting and using codes of ethics and practice and the law, in relation to specific individuals and groups. The law needs to be used critically and creatively, with awareness of its limitations and oppressive potential, as well as any positive opportunities it may afford.

CHAPTER SUMMARY

In this chapter we have discussed the context of social practice that is provided by professional codes of ethics, codes of practice and the law, with the aim of emphasising that an anti-oppressive approach to these contextual factors is neither uncritically for or against. There has to be a recognition of the responsibility of the practitioner to interpret and apply the law and work with the relevant codes, but this needs to be done with reference to an anti-oppressive conceptual framework that can both make positive use of and, if necessary, resist various aspects of codes, regulations and laws.

FURTHER READING

Although as UK academics we suggest looking at the UK codes, it would be useful to critically examine your own country's code of ethics and/or codes of practice and compare this with the international code, and with codes developed in other countries, and other codes of ethics produced by other professional groups.

British Association of Social Workers (2002) *Code of Ethics for Social Work.*
General Social Care Council (2002) *Codes of Practice for Social Care Workers and Employers.*
International Federation of Social Workers (IFSW) and International Association of Schools of Social Work (IASSW) (2004) *Ethics in Social Work, Statement of Principles.*

OR: the codes of ethics and practice of your own country.

Banks, S. (2004) *Ethics, Accountability and the Social Professions.* This looks at professional ethics and values, including codes in social work and related professions.

Bowles *et al.* (2006) *Ethical Practice in Social Work: An Applied Approach*, includes a chapter on codes of ethics.

Dalrymple, J. and Burke, B. (2006) *Anti-Oppressive Practice Social Care and the Law*, includes a chapter on how the law can be used to promote anti-oppressive practice.

Hugman, R. (2008) 'Ethics in a world of difference', a paper on the international code of ethics.

Chapter 3

'Rational' Ethical Principles and Unequal Powers

KEY IDEAS

Autonomy: the power of a person to act (1) freely and intentionally; (2) with substantial understanding; and (3) without controlling powers forcing them to choose to act in one way rather than another. The term 'self-determination' has a similar meaning.

Parentalism: the making of a decision on behalf of someone else on the grounds that they are unable to make the decision for themselves (thus treating that person as if they were a child). The term 'paternalism' has a similar meaning, and is more commonly used, but its roots refer only to the father's role.

In this chapter we discuss a common situation where someone is on the margins of being able to understand their own situation, but needs to make a difficult decision. When is it right to make decisions on behalf of someone else, when they are only questionably able to fully understand the decision that is required? Who should decide, what else should be taken into account, and how should the person be dealt with? This issue can arise in a variety of circumstances, but it often arises in the context of the care of older persons, and our case study examines a realistic and complex situation, loosely based on actual circumstances known to one of the authors. We will then assess Kantian ideas in relation to the case study, followed by analysis from the perspective of an anti-oppressive approach, with a particular focus on the concept of power.

Across the globe many countries have policies on informed consent since it is such a basic concept, involving human rights which are widely respected – at least in theory. The International Federation of Social Workers (IFSW), and the International Association of Schools of Social Work (IASSW) both make it clear that: 'Social workers should respect and promote people's right to make their own choices and decisions', and therefore service users need to be able to consent to decisions about their own lives (IFSW/IASSW, 2004, para 4.1). Similarly, there is guidance in the UK's National Health Service on informed consent (DOH, 2001) and also the UK's General Social Care Council's *Code of Practice* (GSCC, 2002) clearly lists the importance of 'supporting service users' rights to control their lives and make informed choices about the services they receive' (GSCC, 2002, para 1.3). This aim is based on classic ethical ideas going back to the philosopher Kant – and beyond. We want to consider what this ideal might mean, and examine the question of what difference an anti-oppressive ethic makes when there are dilemmas about how best to interpret and achieve this end, and what the idea of autonomy means.

CASE STUDY: ELSIE'S STORY

Elsie is an older woman who is suffering from a disease leading to gradual deterioration, for which there is no cure. The social worker Fliss has been provided with medical advice that Elsie is not functioning at a level sufficient to enable her to participate in decisions about her own care. Prior to hospital admission she lived alone, and wandered out at night, but had help from a care assistant from social services, and from her daughter Jean, who has mild learning difficulties, and who visited almost every day. She also has another daughter Carole, who lives a long way from her mother but who is in touch with the hospital. Carole and the nursing staff are agreed that Elsie now needs full-time residential care, and Carole has also expressed some confidential concerns that Jean's care has been partly motivated by easy access to her mother's income.

The ethical question concerns the autonomy of the service user and the respect that is owed to her as a human being so that she can be informed about, and significantly participate in, decisions that intimately concern herself. In addition there is the complication of working with two carers who advocate opposing courses of action. Carole and the nursing staff feel that to actively discuss the issue at all with Elsie would only lead to considerable distress, and that in the light of the medical opinion she is not able to participate in such a discussion. However, Jean takes offence at the implication that her support for her mother was or is no longer adequate. She also thinks her mother of sound mind, except just prior to, and immediately after, admission. She believes that her mother has the right to decide for herself.

The case story ends in a compromise, with the service user being fully informed about the plans by Fliss the social worker, but with the nurses and Carole achieving their aims (that Elsie will be discharged to a residential home), and Fliss feeling that she has at least tried to treat the service user with respect. Jean, who has been the main carer, is angry that her mother is not coming back home.

THE PROBLEM

Fliss, the hospital social worker, is faced with a double problem in that the situation is complicated by the involvement of powerful professional groups as well as carers whose conception of Elsie's best interests and capacity to choose are radically different. The nursing staff have told her that Elsie does not have the mental capacity to make a decision, and that this has been supported by the consultant's doubts about her. She knows that the medical profession is normally obliged to get a patient's consent to proposed courses of action, especially where medical treatment is concerned. She also knows that the consultant has a waiting list of patients all of whom need to take up the bed that Elsie would vacate. The organisational pressure on both Fliss and the consultant was to ensure that hospital waiting lists were kept as low as possible, and that meant getting Elsie discharged quickly – as long as the process could be justified as reasonable and ethical in the circumstances. What made this difficult was that Jean was making it hard to simply go along with what seemed a perfectly acceptable and rational plan. Jean tried to impress upon Fliss that Elsie was capable of making a decision. She admitted that Elsie was temporarily disoriented by the illness and the admission to hospital, and when interviewed by the doctors was unable to untangle her thoughts. Nevertheless, Jean claimed that she knew how to interpret her mother's ideas, and that Elsie was getting better at expressing herself. However, it was not obvious how much Jean's understanding of her mother's needs could be trusted.

A KANTIAN SOLUTION?

Fliss thought that it was not at all difficult to justify a position which went against Jean's wishes, because, though she sympathised with Jean, the fact of the matter was that the consultant had expressed doubt about Elsie's mental capacity. Carole agreed that the nursing staff and the consultant's view had to be accepted, and that the removal of Elsie to a local residential home was necessary and justifiable without upsetting Elsie about her consent to something she couldn't understand.

However, Fliss considered the objections of the main carer, Jean, and thought seriously about the possibility that Elsie ought to be respected as a person despite the doubts about her mental capacity, and offered a choice about when and where she should be discharged. This approach was more consistent with the ethical position she had been taught, and if Jean were right, then Elsie was being treated unethically as a means to a different end (of making her bed available for someone else), and her autonomy as a human being was being by-passed. However, Carole had planted a seed of doubt in her mind about Jean's motives and capacity in wanting her mother to be free to choose to go home. Her confidential information had to be respected and considered. In the absence of other evidence, it was not easy to assess, but it suggested that Jean had a motive for exaggerating her mother's mental capacity, as well as limited ability to understand her mother's limitations.

The nursing professionals agreed with Carole that Elsie would be disturbed and upset by any attempt to discuss discharge issues: it was not in either her short- or her long-term interests. She decided that there was therefore only room for a residual recognition of the principle of respect for persons in this case, because Elsie was not able to understand the nature of the decisions that needed to be made, and Jean's understanding was also uncertain. With the consultant's agreement she arranged for Elsie to be admitted to a Local Authority Home for Older People that was capable of supporting her. She informed Elsie about this placement a couple of days before she was due to go there. She tried to soothe Elsie into thinking it was an extension of hospital care which was being provided for her benefit. Fliss thus accepted that Elsie was not capable of autonomy – but she attempted to show respect for Elsie as a person by sharing the information with her as soon as she thought it was desirable, and encouraged her to look forward to her new home. She later felt badly about Jean's telephoned complaints about how her mother had been treated, but defended her decision as reasonable in the light of the medical advice and the circumstances as she knew them.

KEY IDEAS
Respect for persons: valuing people as ends in themselves, not as objects or as means to other ends.
Confidentiality: respecting private and personal information, unless there are overriding ethical reasons for not doing.
Consent: obtaining the agreement of individuals whose interests will be affected by proposed actions, decisions, policies or laws.

COMMENT: THE ETHICS AND LIMITS OF SELF-DETERMINATION

Most social workers, including educators and administrators, pay at least lip service to a broadly Kantian interpretation of appropriate professional values, and most would accept that it remains a serious *practical* consideration in relation to a holistic view of service users' rights and expectations, even though (and also perhaps because) there is considerable tension between the ethics of respect for persons and the demands of bureaucracies. Superficially at least, the principle of informed consent is also designed to ensure that research participants are made fully aware of the nature of the research in which they are taking part, and the consequences of their participation. Our view is that whilst these often-used Kantian values have provided an important basis for encouraging workers and researchers to reflect on the ethics of their interventions, there has been a lack of understanding of the significance of an anti-oppressive critique of these values. This is not to deny that potentially critical concepts of autonomy and self-determination have been and should remain a part of social work ethical discussion, but it is to assert that the moral concepts upon which social workers draw need to be re-framed in the context of socially informed anti-oppressive ethics.

The approach that Fliss the social worker took would have been well appreciated in the hospital not only because of the pressure to avoid 'bed-blocking' and remove Elsie to a more suitable place as quickly as possible (thus freeing valuable resources for meeting the needs of others – an ethical consideration in itself), but also because the nursing and health professions are themselves also concerned about treating people with respect, and therefore with having an ethical justification when the right to self-determination is denied – as in this kind of situation. Although medical ethics has historically tended towards the principle of beneficence (or aiming to do good – see next chapter) as its ethical touchstone, it has in recent times become more concerned with the principle of respect for persons and their autonomy (Beauchamp and Childress, 2001, p12). Nursing ethics has usually had respect for persons at the centre of its concerns: 'what we want to stress . . . is the importance of the principle of autonomy' (Chadwick and Todd, 1992, pviii).

The basis of social and health care professionals' interest in autonomy has been the ethical views of Kant, a European moral philosopher of the late eighteenth century (see further reading, at the end of this chapter). The recent popularity of his views emerged especially after the Second World War as a way of affirming the equal worth of human beings whatever their ethnic background. Some German doctors had been complicit in some of the experiments of the Nazi period. In other Western countries people with learning disabilities, and black Americans were also sometimes 'treated' (very badly) without their full consent, on the grounds that medical experts knew best (e.g. Black *et al.*, 2002, p140). Never again did health or care professionals wish to treat with such contempt the personhood of their patients, despite believing they know what is best for their patients' health because of their expertise.

The attraction of Kant's ethics was that it was based on reason and freedom – two key values of the post-war democratic societies that dominated the West. In addition the Kantian formula was consistent with traditional Christian and Jewish ethics, but did not depend on belief in or obedience to God as the basis of morality. The key Christian ethic is often summed up in the 'Golden Rule': 'Do unto others what you would have them do to you', although some would argue that this is not sufficient to meet the demands of an ethic of love consistent with Jesus' teaching (Preston, 1993, p95). In Kant's version this rule is expressed in various (subtly different) ways, but its essence is regarded as the fundamental or 'categorical' basis of all morality. However, instead of relying on divine revelation as his justification, he argued that all persons (with some key exceptions – see later) had the capacity for free choice, and for the exercise of their reason. He then argued that rationality demanded that anyone seriously thinking about what they should freely choose to do could not rationally choose something that could not be made into a universal law of behaviour. If we were proposing to act in a certain way, then to be ethical it must be possible to make a rule that *everyone* could follow. In other words, it would be unreasonable for you to expect others to behave differently from the way you thought it was good to behave yourself – and vice versa.

This 'categorical' rule was based on the perceived fundamental equality between all persons who have the capacity for free choice and rationality. The adherence to this principle of behaviour is therefore recognition that others are 'persons' capable of the same feelings and reasoned behaviour as you yourself. They should therefore be treated not as objects for you to manipulate, or as means to your own ends, but as persons in their own right, as 'ends' in themselves. Professionals should thus try to treat people with respect, as free autonomous persons, capable of determining their own lives.

As we have mentioned, there are some limits to this universal rule. It should be fairly obvious that Kant's argument depends on accepting others as capable of rational thought, and some people are just not able to meet this criterion. The mentally ill and children are obvious groups who may be thought to have difficulties with this today – and in Kant's day there was little doubt about that, although representatives of both groups in our present age would challenge this assumption. It has also been pointed out that many of the classic philosophers were part of the elite male establishments of their time, and it did not occur to them that women were equal to men in their capacity to reason, and therefore women were also not regarded as equally persons in their own right. Kant was not the only male thinker subject to this criticism: 'Almost every canonised philosopher up to the 20th century has explicitly held that women are lesser . . . moral agents' (Walker, 1998, p20). In addition Kant (and many others before and since) also regarded various ethnic groups, especially non-white groups, as being unable to meet this demand for rational thought (Graham, 2002).

In today's world there should be no question that women and the various oppressed ethnic groups in nations around the globe are to be regarded as equal to white males in their capacity for thought. Nevertheless, there are still places in the world where that is questioned, and everywhere women and members of oppressed ethnic groups are often understandably suspicious that their views are not regarded equally. The classic Kantian respect for autonomy seeks to avoid coercion, compulsion and ignorance, but it does so on the basis of the neutral provision of information to a service user who either does or does not have the freedom and cognitive capacity to make a decision. However, as McLeod and Sherwin point out, *social oppression* 'tends to interfere with an agent's ability to develop or exercise autonomy' (Mcleod and Sherwin, 2000, p261). Historically there was no allowance for social oppression – women, ethnic groups and various others who did not meet the male white standards of rationality and autonomy were automatically excluded. In many contemporary societies, despite the rhetoric of equality, there remains the continuing reality that the white male standard of rationality is still the norm by which others are judged, with little allowance for different understandings of human interaction.

There are important issues relating to how far children, or the mentally ill or, as in this case, people with learning difficulties (Jean) or people with seriously deteriorating health (Elsie) can equally be regarded as persons in their own right if their capacity for thought has to reach the given standard. The advocates for children's rights, and for mental health and learning disability service users, would claim that they also cannot be automatically assumed as incapable of rational thought, quite the contrary. In Elsie's case her daughter's intellectual ability may place her at a disadvantage, and Elsie's capacity for thought has clearly been damaged. How far does this affect her ability to be an autonomous person, able to decide her own future, and be treated with respect? The short answer is that the capacity for thought does not have to be exactly the same for everyone. In addition the stereotypical notion of decision-making oversimplifies the process of reaching decisions. What needs to be considered are what *'levels of involvement in decision-making* are feasible and desirable for her (O'Sullivan, 1999, pp45–50). Variations are inevitable, and what matters is that the views and wishes of service users and carers should both be taken as seriously as possible. But exactly how far is that possible or desirable?

ANTI-OPPRESSIVE ETHICS AND POWER

Using an anti-oppressive framework, there are a number of questions which need to be considered in this case study. We will focus in this chapter especially on the issue of power, but all the issues are interconnected, and therefore some indication of the relevant issues relating to each basic anti-oppressive concept will be briefly sketched after dealing in more detail with the issue of power.

I   Power dynamics

Taking decisions for someone is an exercise in power – traditionally seen as 'paternalism' or 'parentalism' – treating people as children, and by implication without the respect due to a self-determining adult person (we bracket out here the issue of children as persons). However, as in Elsie's case, the person concerned has to be in a position to be able to take their own decisions – they need to be as free as possible from the power of others. The difficulty is that 'paternalism is especially problematic when applied to patients whose auton-omy is reduced by virtue of their oppression' (McLeod and Sherwin, 2000, p267). Elsie's powers of decision-making for herself are significantly impaired not only by her physical and mental illness, but also by the subordinate and relatively powerless social position she occupies because of her membership of oppressed social groups – especially (at least) gender, disability and age in her case. Her relative powerlessness is also exacerbated by being near the bottom of the organisational 'hospital hierarchy', in addition to her subordinate rela-tionship to the social services department and the social worker. In addition to all that, she is not an atomised individual to whom can be allocated a specific power index; she is part of a web of social relationships in which various powers are inscribed, generated and/or exercised and which can change with time. An anti-oppressive ethics, properly understood, draws attention to all those features of social situations in which both overt and hidden mechanisms of power operate to condition, influence and constitute ethical issues.

Kantian ethical perspectives have tended to focus on the ethical decisions of individual persons, and on the universal principle of respect for individ-ual persons – whatever their specific personal social biography and position. Issues of power have often been seen as 'political' matters not necessarily relevant to a person's duty. However, it is important to take account of the way that an individual's autonomy – their ability to make their own deci-sions – is significantly connected to their social location within changing relationships of power. Indeed a feminist view of this emphasises the critical importance of power as the basis for generating ethical issues (Walker, 1998, p218). The model of the abstract rational individual doing his (*sic*) duty in the light of universalisable rules is a simplification of the realities of the 'political' and ethical complexities faced by individuals as a result of cross-cutting effects of power. Despite the continuing importance of Kantian ideas as a baseline of respect for persons, it is lacking in its capacity as a frame-work for ethics in contemporary societies, and especially in relation to social work. It is a basis for ethical thinking that needs continuing incorporation into a framework that can complement its insights with an appreciation of the significance of the inequalities and the varied and dynamic nature of power. A position more consistent with an anti-oppressive ethic is explored in recent feminist studies of 'relational autonomy' (Mackenzie and Stoljar, 2000). This concept is based on a view of the individual as embedded in social and historical contexts with *unequal distributions of power* rather than conceived of as a rational individual abstracted from such contexts (Code, 2000; Fricker, 2000).

The nature of power has in any case long been contested. In Lukes' recent critical review of the topic (Lukes, 2005) he judiciously exposes the main dimensions, and provides a useful overview for an anti-oppressive concept of power – one that takes seriously the structures of power that oppress whole social groups and individuals, but also one that can account for the complex and productive nature of the variety of kinds of interleaving powers. For example, the fact that power is a disputable concept upon which there is no agreement demonstrates the importance of values and differing perspectives on power and their implications for ethical action (Lukes, 2005, pp61–2). That 'ought' implies 'can' means that power is always a critical element in ethics, since responsibility and blame are determined by the extent to which individuals or groups can be said to have known about and been able (have the power) to act upon information relevant to ethical behaviour (Lukes, 2005, pp66–7). He distinguishes between two commonly used concepts of power – 'power over' and 'power to' (Lukes, 2005, p73), but also discusses the distinction between dominant and non-dominant 'power over' people, where the former is described as: 'the ability to constrain the choices of others . . . impeding them from living as their own nature and judgement dictate' (Lukes, 2005, p85). It is possible to be in a position of authority, and *facilitate* rather than impede the ability of individuals to pursue their own aims (for example, being a parent, nurse, social worker). It is also obvious that it is possible to both facilitate and impede, or abuse in the same role.

Lukes takes to task some of the more exaggerated claims made for the Foucauldian concept of power, and defends his concept of the neglected 'third dimension' of power. It is commonly asserted that Foucault's view of power has provided a post-modern (and thus better) account of power than 'modernist' accounts, including traditional sociological accounts as in Weber or Parsons, as well as feminist and Marxist versions. Key aspects of the post-modern understanding of power usually include:

1   the way power is 'no longer' seen as a 'thing' to be possessed, but a potential that exists in all social relationships;
2   the multidirectional, fluid nature of power, rather than its flowing in a steady 'top-down' direction
3   the 'productive' nature of power, as a positive generative force, rather than just an oppressive feature of social relationships.

This conceptualisation is sometimes used to belabour anti-oppressive accounts of power, on the assumption that they are more consistent with modernist concepts (Healey, 2000, pp111 and 126; Tew, 2006, p37). However, whilst it is inevitably the case that oppressed social groups will be concerned with the oppressive restrictions placed on their actions and choices by those who have power over them, this is not necessarily because an anti-oppressive understanding of the concept of power has to be naively modernist or structuralist – except in stereotyped straw versions, or overly partisan accounts.

Foucault's arguments about productive power are widely supposed to have undermined the Kantian model of the rational autonomous agent as the origin of action and power (Lukes, 2005, p92; Tew, 2006, p35). However, when examined closely Foucault's views amount to 're-stating some socio-logical commonplaces: individuals are socialised: they are oriented to roles and practices that are culturally and socially given: they internalise these and experience them as freely chosen' (Lukes, 2005, p97). As Lukes asserts, despite Foucault's claims about the ubiquity of powers, there still remains a distinction between dominating and non-dominating uses of power, and the possibility of questioning the ways in which compliance is secured through willing consent. This 'third dimension' of power, as Lukes puts it, logically requires the imputation of interests to individuals which are to some degree unrecognised by those individuals (Lukes, 2005, pp144–51). It is this step that the Foucauldian arguments seek to avoid, and by so doing dismiss a major aspect of oppression. It does *not* imply that the enlightened academic or practitioner can 'expertly' ascertain what are an individual's or service user's 'real interests'. This is a common charge against an anti-oppressive orientation (e.g. Wilson and Beresford, 2000; Tew, 2006, p34). What it does mean is that there is no value-free way of assessing the impact of the mechanisms through which dominating powers secure willing consent. The academic or practitioner therefore necessarily engages in participative moral enterprise in attempting to understand (and intervene in the case of practitioners) the ways in which individuals and groups might be conceived to have interests other than those of which they are fully aware. This is not hard to imagine, given the prevalence of misinformation, censoring, concentrated ownership of the media on the one hand, and cultural, economic and political institutionalisation of 'natural' differences (e.g. institutional racism), and other institutional practices which prioritise the interests of some over others. The academic or practitioner herself is not outside these influences, but also subject to them, and possibly colludes with them. It has long been obvious that 'empowering others' is not necessarily altruistic, but is in itself a vested interest of the helping professions and personally for the worker, and is itself an exercise of power that may or may not be acceptable to the service user or carer (Baistow, 1994/5).

This understanding of the ethical importance of the variety and complexity of powers does not assume the passivity of individuals and groups. On the contrary it assumes their active involvement, sometimes colluding with, sometimes resisting powers in their everyday lives. It also does not mean that the pattern of local powers can be deduced readily from macro-level social divisions: the variety and fluidity of powers ensures that interpretation is always open to question – and therefore has evaluative moral and ethical implications. However, *neither* does it mean that individuals and groups inhabit a free-floating world where major social divisions, or the state and large public and private organisations have no powerful impact 'over' their lives. Such an assumption is not plausible: almost whatever sociology is used will reveal (for instance) stubbornly persistent educational differences between social classes, or income levels between genders (Bradley, 1996; Payne, 2006). These interrelated and more slowly changing macro-structural powers have to be assessed in relation to the range of other powers at micro- and mezzo-levels, *both* productive and oppressive (Clifford, 1998, chap 5).

From an anti-oppressive ethical perspective, then, power is a crucial but contradictory element. This is not a new observation (cf. Humphries, 1996), but seems to need repeating in view of the characterisations (already cited) of anti-oppressive perspectives as inevitably modernist and structuralist. The implication of a broader view of power relevant to anti-oppressive ethics is that practice may aspire to be 'emancipatory' but given the contradictions of power this may not be possible, and other less noble outcomes have to be accepted. The worst scenario must include the possibility that unexpectedly poor outcomes may occur as a result of good practice. This certainly includes practice informed by service user or carer involvement, since neither they nor the worker can give an absolute guarantee of positive outcomes. The claim that any practice is 'emancipatory' (Tew, 2006) has to be made with caution. Anti-oppressive ethical practice is *not* necessarily emancipatory. It is bound to have contradictory effects. It may only be able to maintain a poor situation and prevent it getting worse. Clearly, it aims to improve the conditions of life of those most vulnerable to oppressive powers of all kinds, but there is no guarantee of success, even for competent practitioners working in partnership. In the case example the worker would be supporting a poor outcome for someone whichever course of action is chosen. The two carers are in disagreement, and the worker Fliss may use her power positively and productively to assess and nurture the powers of the service user to recall her past and her preferences, as suggested by Jean, dismissing the concerns of Carole the second carer. Or she may accede to the wishes of the second carer and the advice of nursing staff in the light of what she assesses as expert medical knowledge of cognitive ability, thus disappointing Jean. She needs to consider how she will positively use her powers, which powers to oppose and which to reinforce.

Anti-oppressive ethics always challenges both the worker's understanding and integrity in taking into account the complex balance of powers in any situation, with the demand to make an ethical and political decision consistent with anti-oppressive values. It does not depend on some ideal end-point at which all powers are equal – it can afford to be agnostic about that possibility (it is always a long way off and may never be achieved). Nevertheless it is informed by the sociological, psychological and historical evidence that unequal powers are endemic in modern societies, and that they lie at the root of ethical issues in everday life. Ethical issues are thus also 'political' in the feminist sense, and failure to link ethics with the *whole* range of powers is a failure in ethical imagination. Individual autonomy in the Kantian sense may be an inappropriate focus for ethics if it ignores this critical dimension of moral life. An overemphasis on ethics as personal morality is a way of evading the politics of social justice implicit in the inequalities of powers assigned to different social divisions, and ignores the internalisation of dominant values, and the limited rationality of all human beings. Conversely, an overemphasis on a deterministic sociology ignores the responsibility of people individually and collectively to meet the ethical challenge to try to understand and act locally with integrity and with an understanding of the multiple impact of powers, as informed by an anti-oppressive framework.

2 Social divisions

The prominence of the social divisions of age and gender are obvious in this case, with age being a particularly complex issue, involving differences between the service user, the carers, and the social worker and colleagues in health and social services. There are also some obvious issues about both intellectual and physical disabilities in relation to Elsie. These are critically important issues which should be appreciated in the context of the concept of social division, *not* simply as an issue of individual characteristics. That is to say that Elsie's gender and disabilities should signal a specific ethical caution about how she is treated, involving reflection on how far social constructions are implicated in her position and in her treatment.

Although 'race' and ethnicity are not mentioned in this case study, the ethnic background and culture of the service user and her carers cannot be assumed by the social worker. It may also have a bearing on the decisions to be made and how Elsie is to be treated. In the absence of information about her ethnicity the usual assumption is that the 'default' ethnicity is that of the dominant ethnicity in local society, but this 'normal' assumption not only may be mistaken, but, even if true, it may also still hide her particular culture, which may involve attachments to specific communities or religions. These differences may inform the clash between the carers, and how they perceive Elsie would want to be treated especially in her declining years, and as she approaches death.

Other social divisions are not so prominent, but may also be important to Elsie and her carers. Sexuality and social class are often ignored in case studies, and are not always understood as relevant. Yet they should also be considered as potentially important contributors to the dynamics of interaction between the people and situations involved. The sexuality of the family members involved may be relevant to their relationships, and the social class of all the individuals will certainly be an important underlying theme in personal relationships, and may also surface as a key element in financial considerations that will inevitably arise in considering the cost of whatever care package is decided (not to mention as a common factor, amongst others, in sibling rivalry). Anti-oppressive ethics explicitly raise issues about the social context and structuring of people's lives that are not the centre of consideration by Kantian ethics.

3   Social systems

The Kantian emphasis on the duties of individuals acting according to principles which stand up to rational examination is attractive to an individualist society where entrepreneurs are seen as role models. However, it does not take account of the way in which our understanding of ethical action and our actual decision-taking depends on first learning, and then negotiating our ideas of what it is right to do in the context of changing social relationships and social systems. This includes micro-level groups such as family, friends and peers, but also macro-level groups such as cultures, media and religions. The Kantian concern with the autonomous individual needs to be modified by an anti-oppressive ethic towards a more socially informed view of autonomy, as for example in the model of 'relational autonomy' which has recently been developed by feminist moral philosophers (see further discussion in the closing chapters of this book, as well as the previously cited Mackenzie and Stoljar, 2000). The aim of anti-oppressive ethics is to retain the concept of autonomy, which seems fundamental to any account of personal freedom, but to strengthen and reinterpret it within the multilayered context of concrete social relations, where ethical values are learned and practised. Without the support of social relationships at differing levels, it becomes impossible to nurture, develop and maintain the ethical values of respect for persons. Parents need to teach and practise respect for each other and their children for those children to understand what it means in everyday life, and to be able to value for themselves that culture of free self-determination. Organisations and societies need to develop and maintain cultures of respect if they are not to facilitate institutional forms of discrimination. Anti-oppressive ethics thus requires consideration of the impact of interacting social systems on the lives of individuals at micro- and macro-levels and questions the roles of both actors and systems in the generation and resolution of moral issues.

4   Personal and social histories

In Elsie's case there are economic, physical and psychological factors that emanate from her past, especially the complex relationship between herself and her two daughters. An obvious difficulty for the social worker is that there are bound to be differing interpretations of that past. The two daughters will inevitably see things in diametrically opposite ways, with their rival claims to understanding their mother's best interests and true wishes. The opinion of Elsie herself about her own past – how well she has been able to manage and how she sees that continuing – is going to be a critical factor in the social worker's assessment. However, the case study indicates that her capacity to grasp the issues surrounding her ability to cope is itself a matter of dispute. This may be also an issue for Jean, who, as an adult with learning difficulties, may be reciprocating the care she has in the past received from her mother – an increasingly common situation with the growing number of people with learning difficulties and other disabilities living longer and gradually becoming carers for elderly parents without their caring roles or their feelings being fully appreciated (Gant, 2008). Carole, the elder daughter, is able to use the consultant's diagnosis to call into question her mother's cognitive ability, and therefore the appropriateness of any decision she may come to. This is a powerful argument, drawing on clinical expertise that has to be respected. However, medical opinion needs to be complemented from a social perspective: the social worker has a responsibility to assess whether Elsie has any conception of her own past or understanding of her own identity. Fliss will be able to use her social work skills to talk to Elsie about her experiences, and come to an assessment of how much or little she can understand about herself. Even if she is not fully rational, she may be able to make some contribution to the decision if the first sister is right, or not, if Carole is right. Either way the combined histories of the service users and the differing carers, combined with information from different agency files constitutes a body of empirical evidence that also has to be interpreted and triangulated with the medical perspective. The interaction between the changing histories and perceptions of individuals and agencies constitutes an important context for understanding the ethical potential in social situations.

5   Reflexivity

The Kantian concern with rationality and universality means that the idea of reflexivity has little relevance to ethical issues, except in a residual sense. The individual has a personal decision to make, but to be moral in the Kantian sense it has to be within the clear guidelines of rationality and universality. The basic choice is whether to be moral or not: the individual's social location in relation to significant others is not important.

However, in the above case study the position of the social worker is not one in which she can ignore her own social location. Her relationship with the service users and the carers is considerably influenced by their respective memberships of the various social divisions, their relative powers and histories. Fliss has a specific role to play and expectations to fulfil. Her limited ability, time and resources to understand the complex and disputed perspectives of those involved is filtered through her own experience and personality. Who she is determines how she approaches the ethical issues, and she must take this into account as well as she can, rather than take it for granted. An anti-oppressive ethic treats reflexivity as a basic component of ethical deliberation. The moral act is not one that can simply be deduced from an ethical principle or principles. Such rules have to be interpreted and applied to concrete situations, and the participation and presence of the actor itself changes the nature of the situation.

AUTHORS' PERSPECTIVES: DIFFERENTIAL POWERS IN THE CASE STUDY

Elsie's case is similar to many cases dealt with by hospital social workers, and one of the authors has experience of being both carer and a hospital social worker (at different times). However, the principles concerned are of wide relevance, and not only applicable in hospital settings. They need the addition of the anti-oppressive dimensions before appropriate ethical discussion is possible, one of which is the reflexive position of the actor illustrated here by the authors' own perspectives – against which you can compare your own.

We are both younger than Elsie, and of a different generation. Nor have we experienced the difficulties of being as old or as ill as Elsie, nor lived through the troubled times of the mid twentieth century as she has. There is thus an experiential and social gap between us. We are relatively powerful simply through being younger, able-bodied professionals. We have it in our power to sympathise with the carers rather than the service user, as we have to take on responsibilities and concerns for our own parents. We would need to listen especially carefully to the potentially hidden meanings in the muted voice of an older, frail and relatively powerless woman. We would additionally reflect upon our own specific social location either as a white male or as a black female engaging with an older woman whose ethnicity is not given. It would make a difference in how she would see us and be able to relate to us, and that difference would be refracted through her and our experiences of these social divisions – and possibly others that we might need to consider. Would she expect white professionals to collude with her in relation to a black social worker, supporting her relatively powerful position in relation to minority ethnic social groups? Or would she prefer to speak to a female social worker, seeing a male as another authority figure?

In addition to our different membership of social divisions we would need to consider our location within a professional bureaucracy, and its relative power *vis-à-vis* other professions – as well as towards service users and carers. This would be a complex issue in a hospital environment where the various health professions would be on 'home ground' and confident of their advice – regardless of social work or service user views. The 'medical model' that underpins hospital care would be a potential source of misunderstanding in our relationships with both medical and nursing professionals. In addition, our individual membership of social divisions would interact in different ways with those of the particular professionals we met.

On the other hand, our own social work management would be expecting us to process service user requests efficiently in the light of service policies and priorities. We would feel under some pressure from all directions, and in our thinking we would need to take into account, but go beyond Kantian ethical considerations. We have multiple concerns about ethical choice that a simple universal rule would not easily resolve. The process of reaching an anti-oppressive ethical decision would require us to pay a lot of attention to our own particular social location, the differing kinds and levels of powers involved, including our own personal and agency powers, and their impact on the situation. In the end we would need to make an ethical and a political decision about which powers needed to be positively used, and which reinforced or resisted, in dialogue with the individuals involved, and mindful of the vulnerability of the least powerful.

CHAPTER SUMMARY

In this chapter we have looked at the problems that can arise for a social worker who is trying to act ethically in relation to an older person who may not have the capacity to make difficult decisions. We have argued that anti-oppressive concepts help to reinterpret ideas about autonomy and respect for persons so that this traditional ethical view is made more meaningful and can be applied more effectively and systematically.

FURTHER READING

This case study discusses the crucial issue of consent, which is particularly important not only in social work practice but also in research practice (see especially the Department of Health reference).

Clifford, D.J. and Burke, B. (2001) 'What practical difference does it make? Anti-oppressive ethics and informed consent'. A practical discussion by the present authors of a similar case of informed consent.

Department of Health (2001) *Seeking Consent: Working with Older People.* The UK National Health Service guidelines offer a succinct summary and suggest that the issues of consent for research are the same as consent for treatment and care.

Kant, I. (1993) 'Fundamental principles of the metaphysics of morals'. An extract from Kant's original study of ethics.

McLeod, C. and Sherwin, S. (2000) 'Relational autonomy, self-care and health care for patients who are oppressed'. A study of relational autonomy in health settings by feminist ethical theorists. (Compare the discussion of feminist ethics below in Chapter 8.)

O'Neill, O. (1993) 'Kantian ethics'. A brief introduction to Kantian ethics.

Preston-Shoot, M. (2001) 'Evaluating self-determination: an adult protection case study'. A detailed analysis of a comparable case study involving complex ethical issues in autonomy and informed consent in elder abuse (compare the decision-making guidelines below in Chapter 9).

Chapter 4

Confidences and Consequences: Good Outcomes and Social Histories

KEY IDEAS
Consequentialism: the idea that what makes an action ethical is that there is some good consequence that is the outcome of the action.
Utilitarianism: the idea that what makes an action ethical is that it has a particular kind of good consequence — one in which the amount of happiness is the greatest for the greatest number of people.

In this chapter we discuss a case study of a young person giving information in confidence which apparently has serious consequences for a third person. The importance of keeping a confidence can be regarded as a matter of respect for the person whose confidence has been given to you. This can be seen as an important ethical principle derivable from the Kantian ethics discussed in the last chapter. However, in this chapter we will examine what the implications are for a utilitarian view of ethics, which focuses on the consequences of action, rather than on whether it is consistent with any rule of ethical conduct. We will be exploring what difference an anti-oppressive ethic makes to this scenario, and what it might gain from, or add to, a utilitarian approach, with a particular focus on the importance of personal and family social histories to anti-oppressive ethics.

The importance of good outcomes in social work is consistent with the utilitarian orientation of many contemporary governments and global corporations, where the empirical assessment of processes and outcomes is regarded as the 'bottom line' in measuring success. Social work ethics has also had an interest in ensuring that workers operate in an effective and competent manner in order to facilitate good outcomes for service users, as well as promoting the reputation of the profession and the employing agency. The international commitment to social work values agreed by the International Federation of Social Workers (IFSW) and the International Association of Schools of Social Work (IASSW) includes the idea that the social worker should work competently: 'Social workers are expected to develop and maintain the required skills and competence to do their job' (IFSW/IASSW, 2004, 5:1). In the UK the Codes of Practice also support the importance of 'working in a lawful, safe and *effective* way', and to this end 'undertaking relevant training to maintain and improve your knowledge and skills' (GSCC, 2002, paras 6.1 and 6.8).

Part of the requirement to work competently to ensure good outcomes includes the idea that keeping confidences is part of the professional worker's responsibilities, and helps to ensure trusted relationships from which good outcomes can be developed: 'Social workers should maintain confidentiality regarding information about people who use their services. Exceptions to this may only be justified on the basis of a greater ethical requirement (such as the preservation of life)' (IFSW/IASSW, 2004, 5: 7). The idea of keeping confidences is also endorsed in the UK, where workers are specifically instructed to 'maintain the trust and confidence of service users', and this is said to include 'respecting confidential information and clearly explaining agency policies about confidentiality to service users and carers' (GSCC, 2002, paras 2 and 2.3). It tends to imply that it is organisationally as well as personally important: it is not enough to intend to do your duty or to be of a good will – what matters are the consequences, and whether they do in reality add to the safety and welfare of service users, and the effectiveness and reputation of the agency. A utilitarian approach to ethics is at the basis of this kind of thinking, and the idea of confidentiality may be based (but not exclusively so) on the understanding that in most circumstances it helps to ensure a good outcome.

CASE STUDY: JONNY AND HIS GRANDMA

Jonny is a 16-year-old school truant who is already misusing drugs, and rapidly getting into petty crime in order to feed his developing habit. He lives with his grandma who is unable to control his activities, and who is herself receiving social work support – a package of care to support her in the community where she wishes to remain, despite her increasing illness and infirmity. Jonny has been given a Final Warning by the police officer on the local Youth Offending Team. He is befriended by Sally, a young and newly appointed social worker whose role is to pick up relatively low risk cases, with a view to doing some proactive preventive work. Sally is in the early stages of building up her relationship with Jonny when he says he wants to tell her something, but on condition that she does not pass on the information. She agrees to this, but saying that her promise could not include anything that could be harmful as it was agency policy that all information is confidential unless there is a clear risk of harm to himself or others. He tells her that his grandma has multiple sclerosis, and has started taking the cannabis he is using. He does not want anyone to interfere with his grandma because he has nowhere else to go, having been thrown out of his parents' house 15 months ago, but he explains that it is not just his fault that he has to thieve to find the money for drugs – he is also supporting his grandma's 'habit'. Jonny claims that his grandma is frequently depressed, and has 'overdosed' twice already. Sally is concerned about grandma's health and welfare, but her primary consideration is to help protect Jonny from further involvement in drugs and crime by diverting him into local youth alternatives, and offering him support and advice in relation to school and career. However, Sally contacts grandma's social worker expressing her concern, but decides that at this early stage, uncertain of the truth of what Jonny is saying, it is neither advisable nor necessary to yet pass on the specifics of his allegations about shared drug use. She has promised to keep Jonny's confidence, and breaking that promise would jeopardise their developing relationship. She realises that further investigation may lead her towards breaking that confidence. However, two days later she receives a phone call from the same social worker, who is irate. Grandma has died from a cocktail of drugs, drink and medication, and on discovering the source of the drugs, she has been told by Jonny that it was not his fault: he had told Sally all about it over two weeks ago.

THE PROBLEM

Workers often get told lots of personal information, and sometimes there are clashes of interest involved where the information might be more significant for one person than another, and sometimes also clashes of principle. It is fairly apparent these days that in large organisations personal information is passed round very freely, especially with the aid of computers. Given Sally's social work values, she is likely to be influenced by the classic Kantian ethic discussed in Chapter 3. The principle of respect for persons clearly implies that when someone gives you information in confidence and asks you to promise not to disclose it, then you should not do so. A principle of duty is involved which means that anything less than full observance of this promise constitutes lack of respect for the individual who has offered the confidence. You would hope to be treated yourself in the same respectful way. Similarly, although grandma is not her primary responsibility she would also wish to offer her respect as a person with the right to make her own autonomous choices.

However, Sally has also been professionally responsible in warning Jonny that she cannot keep promises that would involve her in keeping a confidence that would result in harm to himself or others. She works for an agency that itself has corporate responsibility for its services, and it is an agency policy that service users should be told about these limits to confidentiality.

She is sympathetic to the idea that avoiding harm and trying to maximise the happiness of service users is a good ethical objective. However, the problem is that she is not sure whether there is any potential harm to grandma or to Jonny that realistically could be affected or exacerbated by keeping this confidence. Sally needs to consider (a) the seriousness of the possible harm, and (b) calculate whether the agency requirement to report, even if a possibility, could be overruled by calculation of the total harm in this case. She also needs to consider whether the agency *rule* is an acceptable way of maximising happiness in this case. She therefore needs to consider the possible consequences of breaking agency rules if that is what she decides to do. Does the rule give her enough guidance as to what to do? Or should she make a calculation based on this *particular act*, with the agency policy regarded as only one of many factors to be taken into account? When making the decision she could not predict the awful aftermath, and when she eventually found out, she was uncertain whether the grandmother's death was a 'consequence' or a coincidence.

SALLY'S SOLUTION

The case study details suggest that Sally's solution was not simply a matter of her keeping a promise, and respecting the privacy of the information that had been given to her in confidence. She had another motive. She wanted to avoid any undesirable *outcome* that would defeat the whole purpose of her work. She aimed to divert Jonny into alternative social activities and networks – a course of action that was planned to produce good outcomes not only for Jonny, but also for the rest of the community, including his own family, who might otherwise continue to suffer from his developing criminal career.

Whilst acting in accordance with a Kantian rule of respect for confidences, Sally was actually using a different kind of ethical principle – one that looks not just at actions or at basic rules of behaviour for their own sake, but at their *consequences*. She wanted to justify her decision to maximise the possible good outcomes of her decision to keep a confidence, when there was the opportunity to pass on information. She judged that the news would get back to Jonny, and then there could be unfortunate repercussions in either his ejection by a grandma angry at being betrayed or, if he could avoid that, his certainly being angry with Sally and thus ruining any chance that she might be able to influence him away from a criminal career. On the contrary it would only reinforce his suspicions about social workers and their so-called 'help'. He would not be able to trust her again with any confidences, and their relationship would be seriously harmed. She regarded the uncertainty of any harmful consequences either to Jonny or to grandma of keeping the confidence as helping to justify the decision. It was not clear at this point (when she spoke to the community care worker) that harm would accrue to either granny or Jonny if she kept the confidence. It was clear that harmful consequences *were* likely if she 'told', so she didn't. In this case the agency rule about confidentiality and the calculation of outcomes of the proposed course of action seemed to reinforce each other.

COMMENT: ACHIEVING BEST OUTCOMES

This approach to ethics, concerned with consequences of action and trying to ensure a 'happy' outcome, is called '*utilitarianism*' and is associated with some of the greatest names in British moral philosophy such as Jeremy Bentham and John Stuart Mill (see further reading at the end of this chapter). It can be seen as part of the British empirical tradition of observing and measuring outcomes, but it can also be linked to other ethical traditions. For example, although Buddhist ethics does not see pleasure as the main objective, nevertheless the Buddha was 'described as a person concerned with the well-being and happiness of mankind' (De Silva, 1993, p62 – and see Chapter 5 below for a different interpretation of Buddhism). Other religious ethics – such as in Islam – will have similar general aims, often with a concern for virtuous action to achieve this end (Nanji, 1993, pp114–15). More prosaically, it is also part of the 'modern' agenda for social services that we should always attempt to achieve 'best outcomes' for social work intervention, evaluating our work, and ensuring that the needs of service users are met as far as possible. Closely related is the requirement to achieve those best outcomes through 'best value', thus meeting service users' needs without costing taxpayers too much money, and therefore *maximising the happiness of all* – the classic utilitarian ethical imperative.

The long ethical tradition of utilitarianism supports this type of decision-making and it has to be a serious contender for the consideration of all social workers, entrenched as it is in contemporary law, policy and ethics. It certainly has advantages that are demonstrated in this case by the calculation that Sally made. Despite the unforeseen effect on grandma (in fact because of this event), she has certainly shown Jonny that she did not in fact pass on this piece of information: she respected his confidence. Her relationship with him has been protected, and she can continue to work with him, and safeguard the community whilst improving his life chances in the process. She can indeed now offer him support in any bereavement issues that arise for Jonny (issues that might well have arisen anyway given grandma's age and ill health), and build further her good relationship with him. Without this good relationship of trust his grandma's death could well have triggered Jonny into an emotional spiral of anti-social behaviour.

Achieving best outcomes thus involves making a calculation about what the consequences of a decision are going to be, coolly working out what in the long run will be best for all concerned. That is then the basis for making a real 'moral' decision – one which relates to the needs of individuals and communities in the real world. It means that workers have an obligation to do good assessment, research and evaluation, using evidence to support their calculations about 'what works'. Utilitarian ethics demands no less. It means that professionals should always attempt to avoid doing harm and positively try to achieve good outcomes, understood as those that maximise happiness for all. In medical ethics two closely related principles, 'beneficence' and 'non-maleficence', sum up what the aims of professionals should be. They do not necessarily have to be understood in a Utilitarian sense, but they are an essential part of the aims of a Utilitarian social worker. As long as 'good' and 'harm' are understood in terms of maximising happiness and minimising pain, then they are exactly the general rules that underpin a Utilitarian approach to any professional intervention in people's lives, provided they are combined with a rule about the limits to professional interference in people's lives (see below). It was clear that the rule of confidentiality (and the agency rule modifying it) was designed to maximise good outcomes, and the breaking of confidentiality in this case would certainly be the occasion of harm, whereas keeping it would have clear benefits and no definitely discernible harm.

KEY IDEAS
Beneficence: One ought to do or promote good, and prevent harm.
Non-maleficence: One ought not to be the cause of harm.
Individual freedom of action: There should be no right of the state to interfere in the lives of individuals provided that their actions are 'self-regarding', that is, they only affect themselves, and are not 'other-regarding', that is they have no significant detrimental effect upon other people.

BUT WHAT ABOUT GRANDMA?

There are two ways of coping with any possible effects on grandma, whilst staying within the framework of 'achieving best outcomes', and 'maximising happiness'.

Solution 1: including others in the calculations

It is not necessarily the case that Sally ignored grandma's problems – or the possible effect of not passing on information to someone who could have intervened in ways that might have been to her benefit. As a newly qualified social worker she was concerned about grandma, despite being herself employed in a youth justice role. Therefore, in addition to calculating consequences (for Jonny and the community) of disrupting her preventive programme with him, she also calculated (and set off against these benefits) the possible harm that would occur to grandma as a result of not telling the social worker about grandma's use of Jonny's drugs. The fact is that at that point in her relationship with them it was impossible to be sure what that outcome would be. In addition grandmother was entitled to decide for herself how to live in the way she wanted – as long as it was not harming anyone else. This is another key principle of utilitarianism, which also applied to Jonny and his use of drugs. John Stuart Mill advocated that individuals should be free to do whatever they wanted as long as they did not interfere with others: people should choose for themselves what their own pleasures and desires were. However, as a juvenile Jonny might be regarded as a young person in need, including the need to protect him from some of his own risky decisions. On the other hand, if grandma chose to abuse alcohol or drugs whilst taking medication, then that was her right to choose – as long as she was actually capable of making a rational decision. If she was taking too much in an accidental way, then Sally could advise Jonny about storage of his drugs, and about monitoring his grandma's medication. The fact that grandma died might have occurred whether or not this information was divulged to the community care worker.

This solution simply widens the calculations to ensure that as many people as possible are involved, and uses the argument that people who appear to harm themselves (by using alcohol or drugs or in other ways) have the right to make their own choices in life, however sad or misguided they seem to others, as long as they do not directly harm other people, and as long as they are judged to be able to make their own decisions. As far as Sally could judge, the evidence suggested that the overall outcome favoured her *not* breaking her promise at this stage, so she was right not to do so.

Solution 2: making use of rules about what works

Another solution would be to take the view that being realistic in social situations it is not always possible to prevent harm to someone. Thus although it may be very sad when there are outcomes that harm individuals, the only sensible way to work with individuals and groups in society is to develop rules which should not be broken, because they are usually to everyone's benefit in the long run, even though occasionally that may not be true for an individual case. These rules sum up what is generally thought to be the most advantageous courses of action to take, and may be tested out or re-framed in the light of evidence and research (and are therefore not absolute in the way that classic ethical rules are sometimes thought to be, or in the way that Kantian ethics is meant to be). This is known as a 'rule-utilitarian' approach to ethics (see further reading, below), since the maximising of happiness is calculated in terms of the effects of having the *rule*, whereas the calculation of the consequences of an individual act is known as 'act-utilitarianism'.

The notion of confidentiality in this case could be seen as a useful maxim, which is not an absolute requirement, but helps you to make a sensible ethical decision without having to continually recalculate all possible outcomes. It *also* has the considerable advantage of helping to develop a culture of acceptance as a norm which will be to everyone's benefit if people generally abide by the rule. In this agency the confidentiality rule is itself modified by the agency rule that confidentiality *can* be broken if there is clear evidence of the potential for harm towards the service user or others. In this case the rule was applicable with no definite countervailing outcomes that could be safely predicted. Therefore the course of action that Sally actually took was correct, and was in accordance with both act *and* rule utilitarian considerations. The unfortunate occurrence to grandma may be very regrettable, but not an outcome that necessarily resulted from her inaction, nor from the rule (which supported consideration of third parties such as grandma), and not one therefore that Sally should feel guilty about.

On the contrary she has followed the local ethical guidelines which enjoin workers to 'strive to establish and maintain the trust and confidence of service users and carers' (GSCC, para 2). This is something that is highly valued by the service users themselves. It is listed as one of their prime concerns in a 'Statement of Expectations' of service users and carers concerning social work training – social workers should: 'Respect confidentiality' (Training Organisation for Personal Social Services, 2004). These codes could also be properly regarded as rules which are ethically obliging precisely because they are based on human experience and evidence that abiding by them is to the benefit of society as a whole. The support given to them by the service users suggests that they are well founded. Even if there was some doubt in Sally's mind about the need to inform another professional, she considered that the importance of the confidence rule (as modified by the agency), and its obvious justification in relation to maximising good outcomes in this case, was a matter of overriding importance at this point in time.

An alternative utilitarian rule or a utilitarian decision about an act?

In effect the agency has already supplied Sally with an alternative utilitarian rule that overrides or modifies the simple standard of confidentiality. However, it has qualified this principle in *two* ways: first by laying down the requirement that workers inform service users in advance that confidence will not necessarily be kept if harm accrues to individuals, including the service user; secondly, by requiring workers to provide records, and share information on service users to other members of the agency (especially supervisors), and also where appropriate liaise with colleagues in other agencies. The well-known lesson of many tragedies in social care is the failure of professionals to communicate with each other. Sally is thus faced with the moral dilemma either of calculating the overall consequences of keeping the confidence, including failure to meet her own agency standards, or alternatively following this other agency policy on sharing information even though she thinks it will ruin her developing work with Jonny, and despite the fact that she cannot be sure that the confidence needs to be broken at this stage. She is aware that grandma is taking cannabis along with prescribed medication to ease the discomfort and pain that result from multiple sclerosis. She regards this as a decision that grandma is making in full control of her faculties, as far as she is aware, and wishes to respect her decision. She has followed agency policy in giving advance warning to Jonny about the limits of confidentiality. She is not yet ready to regard the situation as coming clearly under the agency's policy about sharing information with colleagues, and anyway, she argues even if it did, her own calculation of the overall outcomes would still *in this case* favour keeping the confidence for the time being.

Sally has at least three utilitarian alternatives:

1 Should Sally make a decision based on a utilitarian calculation of the outcomes of the proposed action concerned at this point (when she meets the community care worker): should she break the confidence or not? This is the 'act utilitarian' solution, which requires the use of professional calculation and judgement every time a decision is made.

2 Or should she adhere to a utilitarian ethical rule of confidentiality (which includes the proviso about harm), that has been laid down to

guide her? This is the 'rule utilitarian' position which allows the worker to simply apply agency policy, and she regards the case as falling under this rule in the absence of clear evidence that harm will accrue.

3   Or should she consider instead that the rule of confidentiality is limited by another utilitarian rule about sharing information with co-workers and colleagues. This requires the worker to make a professional judgement about conflicting rules, and which one should be prioritised.

In all these cases empirical research evidence would be relevant (in theory) to inform the judgement being made. In practice there are inevitable complexities arising from the availability of research evidence and its relevance and applicability to the peculiarities of the given case. In fact the social worker thinks that the first two alternatives are compatible in this case, and reinforce each other to the exclusion of the third possibility. She regards the calculation of overall utility resulting from the proposed act as uncertain, but tending to indicate the usefulness of keeping the confidence. This is exactly what she is supposed to do according to the rules – and the Codes of Practice for social workers. In addition the rule about confidentiality can be regarded as being of somewhat *higher priority* than the rule about disclosing information to others (see Loewenberg and Dolgoff, p63, and Chapter 9 below). This is consistent with a utilitarian view, which would only value the principle of truth-telling and information-disclosure as long as it was consistent with overall happiness. But how far do you agree with this? In retrospect have we the right to assume Sally was wrong?

INTERDISCIPLINARY ISSUES

A further consideration here is the complications for utilitarianism that arise from the interdisciplinary issues. These arise at two levels for Sally. First, the team she works for is interdisciplinary: there is a policewoman on the team, and the involvement of the grandmother in the use of prohibited drugs is something that needs to be considered. If Sally discloses this information too readily then her credibility with Jonny will certainly be low, especially in view of the medicinal reasons given for the drug use. However, the functioning of the team must depend on a level of trust and sharing of information. There is therefore a difficult issue for her to decide. Much will depend on what agreement the team have arrived at concerning disclosure. Previous experience of this kind of situation will have occurred before. The existence of agreed utilitarian rules will certainly help her to make a decision here.

However, the judgement will be a fine one which may depend on some intangible factors such as Sally's attitude to drug use; the police colleague's attitude to it and the relationship between them, as well as developing team culture in relation to the relevant law. However, at a different level there is an interdiscplinary issue about the disclosure of information about granny both to the social worker and to health workers who are caring for granny in the community. These colleagues may not be in the same team, but to what extent should Sally take responsibility for health and care issues which are not her prime concern? Equally, there are education workers not only in her Youth Offending Team, but including teachers at Jonny's school with whom she needs to liaise. How much information about Jonny should she divulge, and what effect would that have? How far will utilitarian rules help her in this regard?

ANTI-OPPRESSIVE ETHICS AND SOCIAL HISTORIES

An anti-oppressive ethical perspective would be additional to the ethical codes and legal framework required of the social worker, and would support a more rigorous ethical examination of the issues than would be possible within a utilitarian calculation of benefits accruing to individuals or even to social collectives consisting of individual actors. In this section we will briefly indicate some of the implications of an anti-oppressive framework, with a focus on the concept of social histories as a key aspect of understanding individuals' and groups' experiences in life during specific time periods and in specific places. We follow this with brief outlines of the other concepts in the anti-oppressive framework in relation to this case study and the utilitarian ethics applied to it.

I Personal and social histories

The personal histories of the actors are a key influence on their current behaviour, not only in the conventional sense of psychological development, but also in their membership of the communities and social divisions to which they belong. Their identity within these social groupings and the interleaving of their own histories with organisational and social changes will help to determine which ethical possibilities are still open or about to open, and which have been foreclosed by previous decisions or developments. There has been recent family history involving the separation of Jonny from previous carers, in his move to grandma's. Additionally he will have had a history of relationships with the various agencies – and they with him. The onset of puberty and adolescence has apparently coincided with a family crisis. Grandma herself will have a lot of information about her own and the family history. What these personal, family and social histories make possible or constrain will help to determine the nature of an anti-oppressive response sensitive to changing social and political dynamics, and the meaning that users and carers make of their own past, their values and perspectives. The moral dilemma faced by Sally is affected by user and carer histories, but also by her own past experiences and the history of the culture, personnel and practices in her agency. It is also critically affected by the changing circumstances of the current situation. Understanding their life stories needs to be a critical part of Sally's strategy, even if there are practical problems about achieving this end: the attempt to apply utilitarian principles without a dialogue about their understanding of their own past will not provide a satisfactory basis for ethical reflection or action.

The ethical importance of putting human situations within a dynamic socio-historical context draws on feminist and black feminist evaluations of appropriate ways of understanding women and black communities. It also draws on other more basic considerations common to men and women. Having respect for a person entails knowing something about that person. This is particularly important for women, as a feminist ethicist has noted: 'Our self-understanding is morally significant and respect requires us to know each other in our self-defined specificity' (Porter, 1999, p23). Clearly our biography, understood in its broadest sense as comprising the interleaving of personal, family, community and wider social histories, is a critical part of our self-understanding – and of our understanding of others.

Feminists have strongly supported the movement towards reviving all kinds of biographical and autobiographical methods across the social sciences (Clifford, 1998, ch. 4). In the 1990s there was a particular emphasis on the value of oral history, precisely because of the liberating nature of the method itself, and its 'inherent' compatibility with ethical, anti-oppressive values: 'the telling of the story can be empowering, validating the importance of the speaker's life experience' (Gluck and Patai, 1991, p2). It was clearly a moral impulse which encouraged feminists (and many others associated with subordinated social groups) to use the method to uncover 'hidden histories', and to listen to 'muted voices' (Anderson and Jack, 1991, pp16–17). However, the ethical issues are complex in that the person 'doing' the understanding *also* has a specific history, and for that reason 'the feminist oral historian's mission to "give women a voice" is conducive to discomposure rather than composure, if it is actually accomplished' (Summerfield, 2000, p101). This is precisely why respecting the 'other' is in itself a moral enterprise that involves both engaging with the specificity of the history of the other as a person, *and* the reflexive history of the self.

However, ethical interest in life stories is not confined to feminists. Postmodernism and related theories in the social sciences have encouraged a growing concern with narrative issues generally, and this has been reflected in medical ethics especially with a concern with the relevance of narrative to understanding cases. A recent paper uses this background to argue for the importance of narrative and life stories to social work ethics, claiming that 'in asserting the centrality of narrative in the construction of our identities, it moves beyond the feminist approach' (Wilks, 2005, p1250). Wilks contrasts the narrative approach to ethics with the 'narrow confines' of utility, arguing that our current principle-based structures for ethical thinking fail to convey the richness and complexity of real decision-making. In particular he argues (consistently with the position presented here) that understanding a person's life stories helps to address the complexity of identity formation and its variability over time. In particular, it provides a space for service user and carer life stories to be regarded with the respect that is widely recognised to be their due.

However, personal life stories have to be seen in the context of broader social divisions and wider social histories. Wilks' conclusion that the 'localised temporal sphere' of narrative ethics is a sufficient basis for integrating diversity and care issues in social work, and that this approach supersedes a feminist or anti-oppressive approach, is dubious. First, the particularity of the moral voice (especially of subordinated social groups, such as women) has been a significant theme of feminist ethicists for a long time. What marks the 'different voice' of women (Gilligan, 1982) is its attention to particular others in actual contexts: 'The moral self is "thick" rather than "thin". The "thick" self implies that there is substance, deep meaning and history attached to people's identity' (Porter, 1999, p10). It therefore follows that: 'Responding sensitively to the narratives of different people is crucial to moral agency' (Porter, 1999, p11). A recent example quotes a service user and carer who could be echoing the probable thoughts of service users in the case above: 'What upset me in particular about the response of paid workers was their apparent lack of interest in finding out about Mum – what her life had been like, the nature of her relationship with me and my sisters' (Barnes, 2006, p20). But this does not mean that the personal life stories are detached from wider issues, and must remain primarily on the local plane. Barnes points out that it is 'the *wider* service user and carer movements that have provided spaces within which identities can be articulated separate from the construction of such identities by welfare professionals' (Barnes, 2006, p138, my emphasis). She also uses feminist theorists to support the view that redistributive notions of justice such as those based on utilitarian ethics are desirable but inadequate in the context of diverse societies, in which opportunities for participation and voice are essential 'for the development and exercise of individual capacities *and* collective communication and cooperation' (Young, 1990, p39, our emphasis).

Even more emphatically, recent discussion by women concerned with the ethics of particular times and places also emphasise the wider – not just the local – parameters of narrative and identity. Tronto argues that ignoring the past can be positively dangerous, and may be a symptom or tactic – 'to escape or to ignore the structures of power and privilege that have, in the past, proved oppressive' (Tronto, 2003, p133). It is therefore not enough to see the narrative approach in ethics as limited to personal local encounters in which fragmented lives negotiate a respectful moral understanding. The feminist argument has always been to reject 'either-or' solutions, and rightly to assert the importance of both the particular – *and* the commonalities of the experiences of subordinate social groups: the personal and the political.

Finally, the ethical significance of both the particularity of personal life stories and the wider structures to which they connect is clearly supported by a black female writer who reasserts the position in no uncertain terms. It has long been a matter of great importance to many black authors that the identity of the individual is not only a matter of their personal life stories, but also of histories of their families, extended families and communities, and their wider cultural and historical experiences. However, although the post-modernist grasp of diversity is appreciated, the idea of a post-modernist narrative ethics would attract the comment that: 'postmodern theorising as a whole tends to suppress and exclude collective experiences and histories of black people' (Graham, 2002, p12). The author is aware that whilst 'it is important to be mindful of totalising experiences of oppression, it is equally important to recognise the shared and collective expressions of social and political thought that emanated from black social movements and that continue to empower black peoples in their struggle for social justice' (Graham, 2002, p89). As she points out, the 'notion of community speaks to the interdependence of people, their sense of collective history, loyalty and commitment' (Graham, 2002, p10). Experiences of enslavement, diasporas, struggles for social justice, and survival in hostile communities all provide wider social contexts that are simultaneously significant for individual and shared lives, and are also part of individual identity.

The feminist and anti-oppressive concern with wider social divisions and histories supersedes narrowly narrative approaches rather than the other way around. The claim made here is that an anti-oppressive ethic draws on feminist and other concepts of life histories, but only within the context of all the other concepts in this framework. This implies that the individuals' life stories are connected to wider social systems, including families and communities, but also to the political and economic parameters – the social divisions and power structures. These wider factors will both connect and divide service users and carers from an interviewing social worker – depending on who that person is, and what their life experiences have been – and their current vested interests, and status.

2 Social divisions

The differing social divisions which are involved in this scenario are an important factor in forming the moral landscape within which critical decisions are being made, and are at the centre of an anti-oppressive ethic, rather than being an incidental consideration in a utilitarian calculation. There are some obvious social divisions at work – and some less obvious ones. The issue of age is obvious in the case study, with Jonny being a young person subject to various legal, economic and social constraints. His social worker Sally is not identified by age, but it is certain that she is an adult, and very likely of a different 'generation'. Evidently grandma is also of a different generation from either of them – although she might be a 'young' grandma. The gender identities are clearly given, but the social class of the service users is not so apparent. The stereotypical assumption would be that they are likely to be 'working-class'. Whether this assumption is justified in this case may be relevant to establishing trust with Sally, but it will also depend partly on her own social class background and current status. The case example does not mention 'race', culture, religion or ethnicity in relation to any of the actors – ethical case examples about utilitarianism often don't. There is no discussion of relevant disability issues, although it seems likely they are relevant to grandma – and possibly Jonny or Sally as well. The nature of the sexuality of any of the participants remains hidden (as it often is) even though as a possible contributing factor to the human interaction in this case study it should not be ignored.

Anti-oppressive ethics question the impact of differential membership of social divisions on the nature of the moral issues. This does not mean that Sally should automatically ask questions about some of these sensitive issues, but she should certainly consider whether and how they might be relevant, and whether more information about them would be helpful *and* justifiable to try to obtain.

3   Power dynamics

The nature of power in this example is fluid and complex. Its existence needs to be considered in relation to the basic ethical opposition to the impact of oppressive forms of social relationships. The social worker herself has both personal and organisational power in relation to Jonny, but is subject to the power of other individuals and agencies, such as her supervisor, the agency she works for, and the law. She may find herself vulnerable to Jonny if he is a verbally or physically aggressive male, but as a middle-class adult woman working for a state agency she has considerable organisational and social power, which she can exercise in relation to either Jonny or grandma. There are different kinds of power involved, and they do not flow in one direction, yet there are also clear imbalances of power.

There is also a complex power dynamic between Jonny and his grandma, the details of which we do not fully know. As an older woman who is in ill health and partially disabled she may well be vulnerable to a young and fit teenage male (assuming he is not disabled), even though he is relying on her help for accommodation. She may also depend on him for assistance with errands and other household chores, but whether this 16-year-old male would willingly perform them remains to be seen. A utilitarian discussion of consequences does not usually consider the implications of the differing kinds of powers unless it is of immediate relevance to the meeting of individual needs, or is relevant to a socially beneficent rule.

4   Social systems

The state and the agency which employs the social worker make available various opportunities as well as constraining the actors through legal, economic and administrative means, even though the actors may not be fully aware of the factors influencing them. Jonny has involvement from educational and social agencies concerned about his truancy and behaviour, of which he is certainly aware, but he might be less familiar (say) with the local and national politics of funding for drugs initiatives. These large organisational systems are reinforced by informal systems that impinge differentially on all the actors. One would certainly expect to find a peer group or groups affecting Jonny's behaviour, whilst grandma's informal social networks may be dwindling – or perhaps not: we need to know. Their extended family systems are not mentioned but there clearly remains a significant issue with respect to the reasons Jonny lives with his grandma. All these various social systems at their different levels provide the social context within which actors construct their lives. They have complex implications for anti-oppressive ethical possibilities depending on which social systems are perceived to have relevance by the actors, and which may limit or facilitate action with or without the actors' perceptions.

5 Reflexivity

The dialogue between the worker and the service user is a key site for the examination of anti-oppressive ethics. The worker has to take account of her own powers, values and strengths, as well as her limitations in reaching out towards a young person who is obviously of a different gender, and may be of a different social class and culture. His perspective, and his grandma's perspective, on the ethical dilemma may be very different. Her adult professional persona constitutes not only a strong barrier to trust and dialogue, but also a real threat to Jonny achieving some of the ends he may desire for himself, in so far as some of them will almost certainly conflict with the ends she is willing to support or allow. Sally's specific age, gender, culture, organisational position and social experiences will be factors in their interaction. Her relatively short history as a social worker will undoubtedly have both positive and negative implications for her approach to this case, moulding what she can see as an ethically acceptable range of responses to a possibly aggressive and apparently anti-social male. Does she have in her own family history any experience of drug-taking, and consequently a hidden agenda of sympathy, or conversely, has she suffered the impact of drink and drugs differentially because of her gender? Does she have a feminist concern for an older woman struggling to cope with a young male, or does she have an equally feminist concern to modify anti-social male behaviour? Perhaps she regards accountability to her own agency as the main ethical issue.

Utilitarianism assumes the possibility of an objective and 'expert' account of the nature and availability of happiness for a service user. It tends to assume the possibility of expert professional assessment of needs, aided by the expressed preferences of the consumer of services. Anti-oppressive ethics insists that this is limited by the partial and participative position of the social worker, and the nature of the dialogue between worker and service user, involving as it does, muted voices and dominant discourses.

AUTHORS' PERSPECTIVES: DIFFERENTIAL HISTORIES

To work effectively with Jonny and his grandma we acknowledge that we bring to the situation a number of socialised reactions from our different backgrounds and life stories. Our different ethnicities, class position, gender, age and family experiences of older and younger relatives – including one who misused drugs – will direct our relationship with Jonny and his grandma in unique and different ways, influencing our views of the ethical issues involved.

One of the challenges of practice for *one* of the authors in this situation is that of being able to genuinely empathise with Jonny's position. Personal family experiences from the past may lead one of the authors to over-identify positively with the older woman, and less so in relation to the potentially disruptive male presence of Jonny, as in relation to Jonny, grandma appears to be emotionally and physically vulnerable. The decision in relation to maintaining or breaching confidentiality has to be well thought through in order to balance Jonny's rights and needs with that of his grandma.

Some of the expectations for young working-class males to 'stand up for themselves' would resonate with the other author's male experiences of past youth. For a male worker attempting to befriend Jonny, the effect of breaking his already fragile trust in adults could have serious consequences for the community and for himself. In this case, there would be a danger of having greater understanding of Jonny, and prioritising the keeping of his confidence: it would then become important not to focus on this ethical commitment at the expense of grandma, or of accountability to the agency.

'Expertly' maximising happiness is not enough to help us with the dilemmas caused by the limited experiences of our own histories, in relation to the specific histories of service users. Anti-oppressive ethics sensitises us to these complexities, including the importance of finding ways of listening carefully to the life experiences to which we do not 'naturally' relate, and which may be muted by dominant social discourses.

CHAPTER SUMMARY

In this chapter we have looked at the problems that can arise for a social worker who is trying to act ethically in relation to a complex situation where there is more than one service user, and it is not entirely clear who is caring for who. We have argued that anti-oppressive concepts help to reinterpret ideas about outcomes and consequences so that this utilitarian ethical view is made more meaningful and can be applied more sensitively in the light of the particular personal and family histories relevant to this situation.

FURTHER READING

This is a case study which draws on utilitarian arguments. This approach to ethics can be further studied in many publications, websites, textbooks, commentaries and in original texts by moral philosophers. The following is a very brief selection of useful papers:

Goodin, R.E. (1991) 'Utility and the Good'. A paper which distinguishes between different versions of utilitarianism.

Hooker, B. (2002) 'Rule-Utilitarianism and Euthanasia'. An explanation of rule utilitarianism, and its application to euthanasia.

McDonald, G. and McDonald, K. (1995) 'Ethical Issues in Social Work Research'. A paper which argues a utilitarian case for research ethics.

Norman, R. (1998) 'Utilitarianism and its Rivals', Chapter 4 of his book, *The Moral Philosophers*, pp179–202. A review of contemporary utilitarian arguments compared with alternative current ethics.

Pettit, P. (1993) 'Consequentialism'. A paper which argues for the importance of consequence in ethics (of which utilitarianism is but one example).

Thompson, M. (1999) *Ethical Theory*. A brief explanation of Mill, Bentham and utilitarianism can be found on pp74–83.

Chapter 5

Virtues, Realities and Reflexivity

KEY IDEAS

Virtue ethics: an approach to ethics that concentrates on the integrity and character of the actor rather than on rules or actions.

Virtues: aspects of the character or dispositions of an actor regarded as good, such as courage or helpfulness.

Vices: aspects of the character of an actor in so far as they are disposed to be evil: the opposite of the virtues

In previous chapters the approach to resolving ethical questions and dilemmas have focused on ethical theories which claim that certain types of actions are inherently right or good as a matter of principle. Virtue ethics, unlike the deontological theory of Kant and utilitarian ethical theory, focuses on the moral agent and their lives, rather than on discrete actions or rules. Virtue ethics, with its focus on the internal moral world of the individual, prioritises and examines the motives of the individual, their disposition and their character. Moral action then is a consequence of having a moral character rather than whether an action conforms to abstract moral rules in relation to action or consequences of action. In summary, 'virtue ethics sees the morality of an action as emanating from the character of the individual performing that action and not in the outcome that is envisaged as a consequence of following particular procedures' (Lloyd, 2006). For a virtue ethicist the central moral question is not 'What I ought to do' but 'What sort of person am I to be?'

In this chapter we consider what virtue ethical theory can contribute to our understanding of working with vulnerable people. What are its strengths and what can anti-oppressive ethics add to this perspective? How far is it understood as part of existing practice, and reflected in codes of practice and ethics? In particular how far does it help us to act in a reflexive way consistent with anti-oppressive ethics?

In the Preface to the IFSW/IASSW ethical statement there is the assertion from the start that 'Ethical awareness is a fundamental part of the professional practice of social workers' (IFSW/IASSW, 2004, Preface). There are also numerous statements about professional practice which demand that social workers globally should display various character traits in the way they conduct themselves, such as 'integrity', 'competence', 'compassion' and 'care' (IFSW/IASSW, 2004, section 5). There is no explicit emphasis upon the development of good character, but it is assumed that the good social worker will possess such a character. Another section asserts that: 'Social workers should uphold and defend each person's physical, psychological, emotional and *spiritual integrity* and well-being' (IFSW/IASSW, 2004, section 4:1 our emphasis).

In the UK, the GSCC Code of Practice also makes statements about the character of the professional worker: 'Professional practitioners should be honest and trustworthy' (GSCC, S2.1), they should be 'reliable and dependable' (GSCC, S2.4). There is a clear indication in the code that our actions should be informed by good internal motives, in short a good social worker is someone who not only acts well but is also a certain type of person. In a profession that is characterised by relationship-based interactions between practitioners, service users and carers the importance of practitioners being, reflective, reflexive, emotionally aware and engaged cannot be understated (Morrison, 2007, p258).

CASE STUDY: NATASHA'S STORY

Natasha, a 26-year-old black woman with an interest in mental health, recently completed a degree in social work. A year into her first job Natasha's confidence in her abilities as a social worker is severely tested. The agency is in the process of developing and implementing new policy and practice guidance in relation to the assessment of need. This has resulted in the eligibility criteria being reviewed and tightened. Reductions in staffing levels, policy and practice changes has placed the team under a great deal of stress.

At a team meeting some staff talk about various coping strategies that they have had to develop over the recent months because of the pressure of work. A couple of the staff talk about contacting the union and taking industrial action if things get any worse – but so far that step has not been seriously considered by the majority of the team. Other suggestions are put forward such as limiting the areas of work that the team covers so that current staffing levels could be more effectively used. Another member of staff Anita, an experienced worker, objected to this idea as she felt that it would send out the wrong messages to people in need of a service. She argued from a Christian Evangelical perspective, and was known as a strong advocate of personal rather than political responses to situations that arose. What was needed, she asserted, was for workers to be more effective: resources were always finite and therefore it was the duty of social workers to ensure that they used them effectively. It was not her role to make judgements about management who had their own duties and responsibilities to discharge. She further contended that stress was a normal part of life, especially in social work, and the team as individuals and together needed to develop their spiritual resources to cope with situations rather than offload their troubles onto service users or managers. She suggested more regular team development days and proposed a discussion of the place of spirituality in direct work with service users. She requested a team vote on her proposal. As an agnostic and an activist, Natasha found it hard to agree with Anita's approach.

NATASHA'S DILEMMA

Natasha reflects on her position: she wants to be a good and effective social worker, but she is unsure as to how to manage this in the current climate (cf. Lymbery, 2004). It appears that being a good social worker is not consistent with being a good employee and there are different perspectives about the purpose of social work held by her manager, colleagues, other professionals, service users and carers. There are a number of questions that she feels that she needs to answer for herself, which relate to the role and purpose of social work and the contribution that she feels she can make to the profession. Natasha wonders what challenges she can make to a system which is becoming increasingly bureaucratic, technicist and prescriptive in its orientation? How does she regain her professional autonomy and creativity as a practitioner?

Natasha feels that she is at a particular juncture of her professional career: her aspirations regarding her practice do not match the reality of her current employment. She is concerned that if she does not take some control and responsibility for her personal practice then she could easily drift into working in ways that may well satisfy the agenda of the agency but would not meet her aspirations as a practitioner or meet the needs of the people that she works with (cf. Charles and Butler, 2004). Natasha believes that the managerialist perspective that is currently directing the actions of many of the workers is undermining the fundamental principles that underpin her practice. Equally she is concerned about the relationship that may exist between a team member holding a particular strong religious belief and how this will influence practice within the team and the agency. Natasha is aware that her view of the world is one of many. There are a number of religious and cultural beliefs which challenge as well as reaffirm her professional identity and debates in the team about the meaning of 'spirituality', and the relationship between Christian values and social work's moral base and anti-oppressive ideals have at times tested her ability to be tolerant (see Chapter 9 for a more detailed discussion). Previous debates between team members have led to improvements in practice and the delivery of appropriate services. Natasha is aware of growing interest in 'spiritually sensitive practice', but is not sure how far it is possible to distinguish between that and 'religious moralism and religious absolutism' (Gray, 2008, p177). She is not convinced that a religious solution is for her, but she accepts her own moral responsibility for being a good social worker, and addressing herself to the whole person, rather than exclusively managerial goals.

NATASHA'S PERSONAL VALUES

Natasha considers it important to ensure that the needs of mental health service users drive the assessment strategy and that the uniqueness of the individual is not lost in the process. She believes that social work services should be offered and given in a manner that is 'honest, open, truthful and transparent to users' (Clark, 2000, p51). Collaborative working with service users and other professionals has enabled her to work effectively, especially in the area of mental health, where service-user organisations have been rapidly developing greater partnership with social work (Beresford and Croft, 2004). For Natasha, failure to adhere to these principles would lead to the development of routinised and defensive practice: for her social work is a creative activity and her ability to practise is linked to her capacity to be reflective and reflexive (see below for further discussion of these terms).

Natasha's practice is informed by a commitment to a person-centred philosophy, encapsulated in the idea of being 'a congruent, genuine integrated person' (Rogers, 1957). She believes that if you are to help individuals to face the truth of what are often painful situations then it is important to be self-aware, to be emotionally available, to care and feel compassion and be able to empathise with the other. As a practitioner her guiding principle when working with people was that of valuing the individual for who they are. For Natasha person-centred practice was about listening with the 'whole of yourself' (Jordan, 1979), because working with others requires that you engage with the other person on a number of levels: emotional, cognitive and behavioural.

The concepts used within person-centred practice, such as unconditional positive regard (valuing the person for who they are), empathy (accurately understanding the person's awareness of their experiences), being genuine and respectful can also be identified as virtues, and in particular the virtues of a good social worker. These virtues she believes are relevant to the practice of a profession that has always occupied a contested space between the individual and the state. The social worker is able to see at close quarters the realities of people's lived experiences, their individual distress, and assist and support that person to develop their own potential in their own way.

NATASHA'S SOLUTION: A DIFFERENT WAY

Natasha is aware of how policies and procedures are impacting on her practice. She feels increasingly that she is supporting and sustaining practices and social conditions which are shaping practice in undesirable ways. One way of challenging this is for her not to be afraid to engage in critical dialogue with her manager and colleagues about the impact of agency policy on team practices and on service delivery. Her philosophy of engagement with the distress of individuals who are trapped in unyielding structures and organisations needs to be extended to managers and colleagues as well as service users.

Ethical perspectives based on 'rule following' attempt to be objective and to provide rational solutions, but have a tendency to reduce the complexity of the human condition to one-dimensional terms. However, social divisions and inequalities distort social relationships, and are part of practice in social services organisations as much as part of life. Since social work practitioners and managers are not 'rational automatons' (Gallagher, 2004, p199) they require an approach that does not just focus on right or wrong action but which enables the worker to engage in a meaningful dialogue with others. Working from an ethical perspective informed by virtue theory means acknowledging that social workers are moral agents who are engaged in relationships with others within the social world. The 'virtuous' social worker is able to empathise through the use of the self to develop dialogical relations.

Natasha's solution to the dilemmas of managerial practices and resource limitations is therefore seen by her as a 'middle road' between the ambitious enthusiasm of entrepreneurial social workers on a career ladder, and the conservative trade unionism of other colleagues devoted to past ideals of public service. It focuses on active engagement with service users, colleagues and managers, seeking to find practical solutions for particular dilemmas, and working with a good will to support the development of all. She does not accept Anita's religious interpretation of this, but sees her own ethics in terms of the 'middle' path of Buddhist and Aristotelian ethics – not a complacent compromise, but an active and fluctuating path derived from the stable disposition to engage with all sorts and conditions of people, and involving both the intellect and the emotions, but avoiding extremes (Keown, 2001, pp207–10). As a black woman, she can also appeal to the African ethical tradition of 'Ma'at', with its emphasis on 'a balance in all things . . . caring for body mind and spirit' (Graham, 2007, p204). It requires good professional judgement, and is compatible with her own personal values and with the complexities of the job. Natasha reflects on the possibility that circumstances might become so constrained that there is little or no opportunity for discussion, empathy and engagement. If it comes to that, she thinks she will resign and seek employment elsewhere – possibly in the voluntary sector as a counsellor, where she believes that she will be able to develop into the social worker that she wants to be.

CHARACTER AND VIRTUE IN SOCIAL WORK

Virtue ethics, through the work of Anscombe, MacIntyre and others has become part of the ethical theoretical landscape in contemporary moral philosophy. As long ago as 1958 Anscombe argued that modern ethics 'should relinquish its preoccupation with moral rules and moral obligation and instead concern itself with philosophical-psychological investigation of what it is to be human' (Anscombe, 1958, p18, cited in Feary, 2003). MacIntyre further developed this idea in his book *After Virtue* (1981) in which he posits the view that virtue is a learned quality necessary for achieving various standards in human activity. MacIntyre sees virtues as relative to culture and role, and by locating an understanding of virtues within a social context MacIntyre has made the study of virtue ethics particularly pertinent for the social welfare professions (Banks, 2004; Gray and Lovat, 2007), faced with the complexities and uncertainties of both contemporary theories and practices.

Being virtuous is a matter of character – something that is distinctive and predictable about a person's behaviour. It is a part of what we are – an aspect of our identity. In short most people want to be seen as a person with some moral integrity, and to be able to have respect for themselves. Virtue ethics focuses on the character of the individual making the moral decision as opposed to the action, and is sometimes called an 'agent-focused' ethic (Banks, 2004). However, it would be wrong to see virtues as 'private possessions reflecting personal purity' (Lafollette, 2002, p251). To be a virtuous person involves you not only instinctively and intuitively knowing the right way, the moral way to behave, but also requires a social context which will support the expression of the virtue: a way of life, tradition or 'social practice' (MacIntyre, 2002, p666). Virtuous character and action are developed through communication and interaction with others. For example, within social work the virtues of respect, honesty, tolerance, reciprocity, empathy, care and compassion are able to flourish because of the continual engagement with people who are vulnerable and in need of support, assistance and guidance. By listening to their stories of loss, pain, violence, trauma, resilience and recovery we begin to understand what it means to have a critical awareness of injustice, care and compassion. Practice informed by these virtues has the possibility of contributing to changes within situations of adversity. It is through developing relationships with others that we develop our understanding of what it is to be virtuous. Working with other professionals, engaging in professional training, and working within a supportive agency will also help to encourage and develop particular virtues in practitioners. Virtue ethics has a focus on the capacity of the individual to be reflective, self-aware and to engage in 'emancipatory knowing' (Gray and Lovat, 2007). Through knowing oneself and owning one's values the individual will act according to their moral beliefs. The identity of the individual changes through time and textures the nature of relationships that are made with others; therefore it is important for the practitioner to continue to make good moral judgements. They not only have to have certain personal qualities but they need to clarify and own that identity as much as possible – developing their own moral character through time.

Problem-solving and decision-making within social work is a complex interplay between knowledge, practice experiences, ethics and values. The decision to engage in particular action is informed by a creative act of imagination and interpretation of difficult social problems. Practitioners attempting to find solutions to difficult social situations draw on a range of resources – however, a main resource is 'the person that they are'; their biography, character and personal dispositions (Clark, 2007). The practical wisdom of the practitioner enables them to understand situations as they are presented, and to make decisions in less than ideal circumstances, where emotions are charged, where time is limited and resource constraints add to the complexity of the professional task of making informed judgements and ethical decisions. The complexities and the messiness of life require an ethics which is not rule-based but an ethics which acknowledges the important role and abilities that the individual brings to situations. In comparison to Kant's imperative or the utilitarian calculus, 'in virtue ethics the individual is concerned with being "good" and acting well rather than "doing right" or following "obligation" and "duty"' (Begley, 2005). It is assumed that the virtuous person will act appropriately in any situation as the individual's right action is based on their personal and professional experiences, maturity, intellectual and moral capacity (Begley, 2005). The practitioner is psychologically equipped to lead a good life and to engage in right action.

However, the very conditions in which social work is offered can transform what should be an ethical act into one that is viewed by service users as unhelpful. For example, Natasha's concern regarding the needs of her service users is motivated by her genuine concerns and good character. However, if she was acting from a concern mainly with good outcomes, that is to effectively meet targets and work within limited resources (as social services are increasingly directed to do), rather than from the integrity of her own character in her relationships with others, she could become overprotective and paternalistic, increasing dependency rather than promoting autonomy and self-development. If Natasha was concerned only with duty, according to relevant law and policy, she could be seen as judgemental in her thinking and advice. To be virtuous is not about following prescribed rules about how to behave, but is about making good, sensitive ethical decisions in conditions of uncertainty and complexity (McBeath and Webb, 2002).

Virtue ethics is informed by an 'expressive-collaborative conception' of morality: a view that is shared by some feminist ethical theorists (e.g. Walker, 1998). Virtue ethics, like some feminist theorising, emphasises the importance of interpersonal relationships in a social context (Feary, 2003, p7). It emphasises the role of emotion, relationships, feelings and personality in guiding moral action (cf. Rachels, 2002, p701). This approach is also shared by some eastern philosophies, for example Buddhism. Keown suggests that in spite of their different social and cultural contexts there are many formal parallels between Buddhist and virtue ethics (Keown, 2001). Within classic Aristotelian virtue theory the possession of virtues are the means by which an individual can achieve meaning and fulfilment in life. In Buddhism 'virtuous' choices are rational choices motivated by desire for what is good and deriving their validation ultimately from the final good for man, described as 'nirvana' (Keown, 2001).

An obvious question about virtue theory concerns the nature of the specific virtues involved. What are these virtues? Homiack (1999) suggests from her reading of Aristotle's work that the virtuous person is not overly dependent on others, has self-esteem and confidence, challenges views, and in classical Greek times was a politically active person, and intellectually able to engage in decision-making processes. Such a person is hard-working, compassionate, has passion, commitment, and drive, is justice-orientated, authentic, empathetic, caring and truthful. It has been pointed out, however, that such a person is also usually male: Aristotle, along with other classic moral philosophers, thought women were inferior in their 'deliberative faculty' (Feary, 2003, p11). Clearly, the issue of which virtues are to be prac-tised is critical. Beauchamp and Childress (2001) make some important observations regarding virtues and health care professionals, which can be usefully transferred to a discussion of the social work profession. They argue that the model that one holds of the role of health care professionals within society will suggest different primary virtues. If one held a paternalistic model, then the virtues of benevolence, care and compassion are dominant; if an autonomy model is ascribed, then the virtue of respectfulness is more prominent. If the social worker's role is one of advocacy, then the virtues that such a worker would need to have/display would include 'respectful-ness, considerateness, justice, persistence and courage' (Beauchamp and Childress, 2001, p32).

Husband (1995) proposes that the following virtues are consistent with the development of social work practice that is moral: care of others, the courage to accept responsibility for one's actions, scepticism about the claims of authority, self-criticism. Other writers talk about the virtues of honesty, a commitment to egalitarian relationships, perseverance, and clar-ity of thought. For example, two recent authors put forward the view that the role of a virtuous social worker is one that necessitates appropriate appli-cation of intellectual and practical virtues such as justice, reflection, percep-tion, judgement, bravery, prudence, liberality and temperance (McBeath and Webb, 2002, p1016). However, feminists emphasise the virtues associated with caring (e.g. Feary, 2003, but see Chapter 8 below). Virtue ethics relates the rightness of actions to the character of the individual who acts, so a good social worker is one who not only acts well but also is a certain kind of person. However, as the above lists of suggested virtues indicate, there is no agreement on exactly which virtues should be practised in which context.

VICES OR VIRTUES?

Virtue theory sets out an ideal model of excellence for professionals to aspire to and aim for in their relationships with others. However, what does virtue theory have to offer in relation to ethical problems or decision-making? How does Natasha reconcile making decisions about the needs of her service users with the demands placed on her by her agency to work in a particular way? Why should a worker care at all about the development of their own character in the context of work? Realistically it is primarily a form of income, and the job is to be done as defined by the employer. Attempting to define what we mean by 'good practice' and, by extension, what makes a good social worker is beset with difficulties. It depends very much on who is engaged in the process of defining virtue and vice, and the purpose of the definition.

A wide range of virtues have been identified within the literature, and some have been specified for social work as suggested above, but which are the ones that should be demonstrated by a good practitioner in this *particular* case? Are some virtues more important than others? Is there a hierarchy of virtues? How are the issues of identity and difference accounted for within virtue theory? Does it always diminish the action of a social worker if the motive for action is informed by a desire to *appear* good rather than action that arises out of the good character of the worker? It could be argued that it is possible for practitioners to act as though they 'care' and as if they possess the virtues of respect, reliability, honesty and justice. However, being a good social worker requires 'self-knowledge' and 'self-discipline' (Jordan, 1979, p12), and learning to care is a painful and difficult process, which requires you to be open to being changed by the experiences of others. Caring is a relational act. At times social workers will work with people who are challenging and in situations where it is difficult to demonstrate virtues such as empathy and respectfulness. These situations require on the part of the practitioner 'emotional labour' (Gallagher, 2004). It might therefore be emotionally dangerous to act as being virtuous on a day-to-day basis: following the rules may be easier on the worker and more effective for the service user.

A criticism of virtue ethics is that no blueprint for action is provided: to be told to be a good person is one thing but how is this to be achieved? Virtue ethics does not provide universal rules to guide moral action because ethical right action within this framework varies from context to context, from culture to culture and from relationship to relationship. There is no universal right or wrong so therefore there are no objective grounds for absolutely ruling out certain actions and behaviours. Ethical decisions informed by virtue theory are dependent on the specific social and cultural context. So how is it possible then for virtues to be demonstrated in an organisation such as a social services department? Louden (1984) suggests that because virtue ethics is concerned with the questions that relate to the character of the moral agent, it is particularly weak in the area of 'casuistry and applied ethics' – it is unable to provide answers to specific moral dilemmas. However, Hursthouse (1997), from a neo-Aristotelian perspective, argues that virtue theory does offer a set of rules and principles. She points out that every virtue 'generates a positive instruction (act justly, kindly, courageously, honestly, etc.) and every vice a prohibition (do not act unjustly, cruelly, like a coward, dishonestly, etc.). The social worker when faced with a particular situation just needs to ask the question of herself: 'If I were to do such and such now, would I be acting justly or unjustly?' (Hursthouse, 1997, p221). But this offer of a solution does not rule out the fact that it is still possible for virtuous individuals to interpret acting justly according to their own beliefs and experiences. Because virtue theory is not a problem-oriented approach to ethics it relies very much on the individual demonstrating moral maturity and independence within situations – which begs the question of when can someone be said to be a 'self-actualised virtuous person', who is able to evidence in their practice moral insight and virtuous action? How realistic is it to expect individuals to demonstrate at times a range of virtues?

Experienced social workers on a daily basis make a number of professional decisions in areas of risk and uncertainty, and most decisions have led to a positive outcome. Yet we are aware that social workers have made decisions that have been judged to be wrong, and have had fatal consequences for those who needed to be protected. Having the right virtues, acting from the best of intentions does not guarantee that the right decision will be made. A limitation of virtue theory is its over-reliance on individual character in interpersonal contexts, and its failure to address adequately the wider social context in which the individual operates.

The concept of character also has to be considered. Louden (1984) suggests that the concept of character within virtue theory tends to be viewed as a permanent fixture, rather than an aspect of the individual that is subject to being changed over time, and is influenced by a range of experiences and external realities. A weakness of virtue theory is its failure to sufficiently take into account the role of social divisions in the formation of character. Society reflects a number of competing interests, and consequently different virtues will be seen as important by different groups, sections or classes of society: character is significantly formed by the experience of social divisions. Such social divisions and differing character formations occur within and between organisations as well as between services and service users. As social service departments merge with other organisations, such as housing, health and education, a different identity may be taken on that is not always consistent with the values of social work. It is well known that workers within health and welfare organisations increasingly feel marginalised as different management systems are imposed on them rather than negotiated with them. Practitioners feel devalued, disenfranchised and angry. Given this situation, social workers (including Natasha) have to be honest about how organisational difficulties and the emotionally and morally demanding nature of social work influence the way they are able to manage the decisions they make. Part of this honesty has to be around acknowledgement that the delivery of effective services and development of emancipatory practices requires critical analysis of the different levels of interactions that take place between practitioners, service users and managers. A personalistic, character-based approach to ethics seems necessary but insufficient for this task.

ANTI-OPPRESSIVE ETHICS AND REFLEXIVE AWARENESS

I   Reflexivity

Whilst we would acknowledge that virtue theory has considerable relevance for social work and other human service professions, viewing it through the critical lens of anti-oppressive ethics reveals aspects of virtue ethics which can be criticised, particularly in relation to reflexivity. Working with people is not just a matter of 'personal ethics and psychology but also of sociology, history and politics' (Clifford and Burke, 2005). Actions which demonstrate respect, care and concern are emotionally and intellectually challenging and require more than having the right disposition or virtue. To understand another's need and to respond to them appropriately and ethically requires that the practitioner is able to understand how they contribute to the social relationships in which they are engaged, as well as how they themselves may be changed by the nature of those relationships.

D'Cruz, Gillingham and Melendez (2007) have concluded from their critical exploration of the diverse meanings of reflexivity that there are some significant variations. One variation regards reflexivity as 'an individual's considered response to an immediate context and making choices for further direction' (D'Cruz *et al.*, 2007, p76). Reflexivity in this sense is seen as the capacity of the individual to engage in life-enhancing actions through the process of critical reflection. Within this variant of reflexivity, 'social and political causes of the problems of individuals are downplayed while the knowledge and skills of the individual are emphasised' (D'Cruz *et al.*, 2007, p76). This approach appears consistent with a virtue theory of ethics, where the motivation of the individual and the reflective acting out of their characteristic values are the prime focus of ethics. Another variation of the term according to D'Cruz *et al.* is a dynamic process in which the individual engages in a self-critical approach to understanding the social world which involves questioning how knowledge is created and how they may 'be complicit in relations of knowledge and power that have consequences for inequality, privilege and power' (D'Cruz *et al.*, 2007, p86). This understanding of reflexivity informs our thinking in relation to the concept.

An anti-oppressive ethical principle of reflexivity (see Chapter 1) reminds practitioners that their personal biographies, their social identities and their values will affect their relationships with others. The virtues assumed by social workers are not in fact necessarily universal but related to the social context in which they have been brought up and educated. They come to any relationship with a particular social identity which will be expressed in the differences in power which exist between each of the players who are located within a particular context at a specific point in time. Within practice situations it is important that differences in power on a structural and relational level are not only acknowledged but are acted on. An anti-oppressive understanding of reflexivity takes this into account and will add to a 'virtue ethics' approach to practice. 'The overly personal perspective of the virtue tradition and the excessive contemporary focus on individual psychology' (Held, 2006) is both a strength and a weakness of virtue ethics. It is a strength in that the moral agent is an active participant in the process of ethical decision-making – the individual is seen as potentially self-aware, analytical and reflective, who through dialogue and reflexive interpretation makes appropriate moral judgements (as in Natasha's case above). However, its focus on the moral agent as an autonomous individual fails to give enough credence to the relationship between macro- and micro-social relations and the constraints of the context in which the moral agent is located. By not explicitly acknowledging the relational and structural contexts in which decisions take place, it tends to assume that moral decision-making is not complicated by issues of power and fails to appreciate that the relationship between practitioners and service users is not neutral: it is a space in which different aspects of vulnerability and domination are played out in the context of formal and informal systems of power.

There may be a 'natural' inclination to care if a social worker indeed has a caring character, but this will be tested and found wanting in situations where demonstrating care and concern is constrained by factors such as conflicting interests, power, social divisions, and other people's values and motives. Whilst virtue ethics examines the dispositions of the social worker, and the ways in which her character informs her action, it does not sufficiently raise the issue of the social location of the actor in relation to that of others interacting with her. It omits the element of a critical social auto/biographical awareness, and how that should be taken into account in the way moral problems and ethical actions are considered. The virtuous dispositions are seen as being developed by the individual as part of her personality, and as a project for the development of her life, and as part of her particular cultural tradition, but without a critical view of herself as having occupied a particular (changing) position within the range of social divisions. An understanding of one's own values and character with reference to social location and the impact of social inequalities and diversities is a prerequisite of reflexive engagement with others. In short the abstract values of respect and self–determination, for example, 'are necessarily coloured by local community and tradition and by the biography and character of their exponents' (Clark, 2006), but also crucially by membership of the different social divisions. Equally, an assessment of the different kinds and relative degrees of associated powers, and their implications for strengths, needs, and vulnerabilities, requires that the worker should analyse the nature and limits of *her own* powers, and their impact on others. Anti-oppressive ethics would question the impact that the practitioner's own membership of the various social divisions would have on their view of the nature of social work, their own role and character within the profession, and their interaction with service users, carers and other professions.

2 Social divisions

In this case Natasha can draw on a variety of experiences of oppression – as she has survived and thrived in difficult circumstances. She is still a 'junior' in terms of the agency hierarchy, and probably also in relation to its age structure, and a newly qualified worker who still has a lot to learn, and is vulnerable within the agency. However, she is also a representative of a powerful agency, and she herself is now employed, and on a career ladder: she is young black woman becoming 'middle-class'. Compared to others in the community (her own community and that of others), she is relatively well-off, with security, education, and good prospects. She is also an adult, with formal and informal powers and responsibilities towards younger and older people. She needs to appreciate how her own character and dispositions will be perceived by the socially different persons and groups with which she interacts. They will impact differentially depending on their membership of differing cultures and social divisions. She needs to be aware that the impression of 'virtue' may not only be misread but may have counterproductive effects. Virtues vary across social groups, and social workers are inevitably involved in various kinds of cross-cultural dialogue where virtues can be misunderstood. She also needs to be aware of her changing character and dispositions as she moves from her family and culture of origin, and experiences differing influences from the social work profession, from other disciplines, and from public perception. Anti-oppressive ethics should alert workers to the fact social situations are textured by changing social differences upon which character and integrity will impact in different ways and be interpreted differently in different cultures and social divisions.

3 Power dynamics

Virtue ethics does not explicitly address the issues of power and inequality that critically affect relationship possibilities, since it concentrates on the character and intentions of the actor. Service users, the supposed 'beneficiaries' of the social work relationships and good character, may still experience that relationship as powerful, and potentially threatening – however 'good' a character the social worker may have. The worker has access to power vested in them due to the professional role that they have, and all that this confers on them in relation to authority and status, to which is added membership of at least some dominating social divisions – as mentioned in the previous section. Practitioners need to be aware of the vulnerability of service users, and that even if care, compassion, and empathy inform their practice, they can still be experienced as demeaning and oppressive. The friendly and helpful disposition of a worker may have an immediately beneficial effect, but may also have longer-term negative results if the service user, for example, feels encouraged to reveal too much too soon, and later feels betrayed. Similarly, a warm, sensitive disposition towards managers and elite individuals, particularly on the part of minority ethnic women in white male-led organisations, may lead managers to exploit the worker's benevolent disposition, unintentionally or not, at the cost of the worker's morale or mental health. One solution to this is the development of a range of *other virtues*, including courage, and intellectual acuity. However, we would argue that no matter how comprehensive a range of virtues possessed by a social worker might be, the worker needs to take account of the way that character and virtue may be exploited and commodified by the powerful (including themselves), and overridden by social and economic change. Virtue ethics presumes that it is possible to be virtuous in any situation; however, this does not adequately take into account how much the differences of power and inequalities between people will direct behaviour and initiate responses which are not always 'virtuous'.

4 Social systems

Virtue ethics emphasises the importance of context, relationships, feelings and personality in guiding moral action. It is useful in its attention to the character of the actor in so far as duty and rule-keeping are not enough in social work – nor in many other professions. It is also useful in its attention to the relationships within which integrity and good character are displayed. However, it fails to acknowledge the full impact of social systems on the lives of individuals – the variety and levels of social practices that impinge upon them. It tends to concentrate on the micro-social systems of interpersonal relationships – areas of life which form character, such as the family, friends and work colleagues (Pence, 1993, p257). In the above scenario Natasha is embedded within the agency system but also within the wider social systems – systems that do not necessarily concern themselves with the needs of service users, despite the official rhetoric. Her actions as a 'virtuous' social worker are not always supported by the organisational systems of which she is a part and which impact on her, directing her role as a social worker. It could be argued, on the contrary, that the needs of service users are created and exacerbated by those systems, which enmesh, impoverish and alienate them (cf. Ferguson and Lavalette, 2004). An anti-oppressive ethical position requires that Natasha's commitment to values should transcend the specific context of practice and reflect wider alternative practice discourses. The focus on individual character pays too little attention to mezzo- and macro-social systems, and too little interest in the outcomes of systemic relationships at these wider levels for those groups most in need. An anti-oppressive ethic requires a consideration of the impact that interacting social systems at *all* levels will have on service users and practitioners and how both parties need to take account of the influence of structured social and economic systems upon moral situations.

5 History and process

Virtue theory takes account of the development of relationships and the skill of the virtuous actor in making judgements relevant to a particular situation as it develops through time. However, the importance of time and history in anti-oppressive ethics is more radical than virtue theory allows. The process of time has its impact on the social worker, through the influence of their particular family and character and her experiences of inequalities and diversities. Her virtues come from a changing personal and family history, and the particular cultural milieux into which she was socialised. The continuing development of her character and values in the present is part of that historical process. In addition, the formal context of the agency with its changing personnel and policies also has to be understood as a historical cultural context into which the worker is socialised at a particular point in its development. Meanwhile, the broader social history, for example the emergence of user movements and organisations, and the development of managerial and consumer-oriented services have to be seen as part of the historical backcloth, with important implications for current action and ethical reflection. Against this context individuals make life-changing ethical decisions, with consequences for the service users who may depend on them, as well as for themselves and their families. Anti-oppressive ethics requires an historical understanding of the development of character, in personal, family and social life, as well as of the changing historical constraints which affect how integrity and good intentions can be undermined or supported within agencies.

AUTHORS' PERSPECTIVES: DEMONSTRATING REFLEXIVITY

We provide the following reflexive perspectives to begin to demonstrate the anti-oppressive principle of reflexivity in relation to the case study. For the purposes of this chapter we decided to reflect separately on two different aspects of the case study. Beverley's response is concerned with the question of managerialism and bureaucratic practices. Derek's response is concerned with Anita's challenge to the team on the issue of spiritual values and individual responsibility. Both are linked to the central issues in this chapter – the nature of reflexivity in the context of virtue ethics and anti-oppressive values.

Beverley's perspective

I empathise as a black woman with Natasha's position. She is clearly struggling with the conflicting imperatives of being a 'good and effective social worker' and being a 'compliant employee'. If I were in Natasha's position I would want to be true to myself, having made a conscious decision to pursue a career in social work so that I could engage in work that would contribute to improving the life chances of people requiring a service. I would have to very consciously think about how far I was able to engage in practice that might be antithetical to that commitment. I would also have to consider the grounds on which I may reconsider my commitment to working from an anti-oppressive perspective. A number of questions would have to be carefully considered. Is it acceptable to remain in post because of financial necessity? Is it possible for me seek out and maximise the opportunities available to me to work in ways that I find acceptable? What are the possibilities of making alliances with other workers who also wish to challenge current practice and policy? What are the possibilities of working with other organisations such as trade unions, professional associations and service users' groups? How far am I willing to risk not being true to myself? Does compromising put me at risk of being involved in practice that is defensive, reactive and morally insensitive? My decision would be based on an intellectual as well as emotional response to these questions. My decision would have to ensure that I did not engage in work that would be harmful to others; it would have to be a decision that was achievable and one that I could live with.

For me the procedural and bureaucratic responses to social problems have to be counterbalanced by a commitment to engaging in social action, contributing to the process of change and a belief in the possibility of equality and justice. By working in partnership with others who have similar concerns within and external to the profession locally, nationally and even internationally I will hope to continue to develop my personal understanding of practice, sensitive to the needs of socially excluded people, as well as making links with others who wish to question and change current practice realities.

Derek's perspective

Having a concern for one's own character and integrity in the face of managerialism is not only something for 'virtuous' and/or religious people. It is about having some respect for yourself. As someone like many other social workers, whose values have made it possible to see social work as a potentially satisfying career expressing some of the values I hold, I would also want to have respect for the integrity of colleagues and service users, as suggested in the international codes of ethics (IFSW/IASSW, 2004, section 4:1) – even though they may have very different foundations for their values. However, I would want to go beyond an individualistic focus on my own or others' basic or 'spiritual' values and I would not see respect for people's character and integrity as being exempt from critical assessment. Both my own and other people's values need to be reviewed in the light of anti-oppressive concepts. For example, I would want to be critical of any approach that focuses on individual psychology, character and meaning with little reference to the organisational, social and political context. Any perspective (for example) that promoted inequality and injustice would be justifiably open to criticism.

An important issue here therefore is the degree to which Anita's religious approach is either tolerable or acceptable, *and* the extent to which it raises questions that I need to consider. In Natasha's position, I would want to respect Anita's right to her own values, but consider how it impacts upon service users. If understanding and providing an outlet for service users' 'spiritual values' (whether these are religious or not) is something they express a need for, and it is relevant to the social work task, then Anita should be congratulated on raising the issue. A team discussion could be a helpful event, with a focus on the practice of the team and members' ability to facilitate service users in this regard – especially but not only in the event of death and bereavement. However, if it means that Anita is using this as a way of infusing the team and service users with a particular religious interpretation of 'spirituality' then I would be critical of her proposal. Nevertheless I would need to think seriously about the challenge of her views about spirituality in a reflexive way – relating it honestly to my understanding of my own values and prejudices. How far am I able to facilitate discussion of basic values with service users when they need to talk? In particular how would I deal with people who have religious values – or secular perspectives – that are so different from my own that I might not understand them? Service users from particular cultural backgrounds would know instantly if I demonstrated false sympathy, especially when I am ignorant about their beliefs.

CHAPTER SUMMARY

In this chapter we have looked at the problems that can arise for a social worker who is troubled about how to maintain her self-respect and act ethically in the face of bureaucratic pressures to conform to questionable practices, and challenges from her colleagues. Her approach is consistent with the virtue theory of ethics which places great store by the good character of the actor, who should practise with integrity those virtues, such as courage, honesty, and care, which are part of her way of life, negotiating with others the best ways forward in respectful dialogue. We drew out some of the strengths and weaknesses of this perspective from an anti-oppressive perspective.

FURTHER READING

Cahn, S.M. and Markie, P. (eds) (2002) *Ethics: History, Theory and Contemporary Issues.* A collection of papers about virtue theory, including an extract from MacIntyre's *After Virtue* on pp693–734.

Feary, V. (2003) 'Virtue-Based Feminist Philosophical Counselling'. An online paper that uses virtue theory as a basis for therapeutic feminist counselling.

McBeath, G. and Webb, S. (2002) 'Virtue Ethics and Social Work: Being Lucky, Realistic, and Not Doing One's Duty'. An application of virtue theory to social work.

Pence, G. (1993) 'Virtue Theory'. An introduction to virtue ethics.

Rachels, J. (2002) 'The Ethics of Virtue'. An introduction which argues that virtue theory is best used in conjunction with rules and ideas of duty.

Statman, D. (1997) 'Introduction to Virtue Ethics'. A critical introduction to virtue ethics.

Chapter 6

Politicising Ethics: Justice, Fairness and Interacting Social Systems

This chapter discusses radical approaches to ethics in the context of a case study involving child protection. It deals with both Marxian and (to a lesser extent) classic feminist positions, both of which focus on the social, economic and political determinants of human behaviour, and the unacceptable consequences which flow from them. It also discusses the contribution of John Rawls to ideas of justice and equality with particular reference to equal opportunities and human rights, a contribution plausibly described as 'the most developed liberal egalitarian view in the field' (Nagel, 2002, p63). These are important aspects of an anti-oppressive ethic, as it is concerned with minimising unequal social powers and their use and abuse in the interests of some but to the disadvantaging of dominated individuals and groups. Such themes are also arguably inherent or implied in differing ways in the various versions of most feminist and Marxist writers.

SOME KEY DISTINCTIONS
Justice as the distribution of goods fairly between individuals on the basis of equal opportunities.
OR
Justice as the elimination of institutionalised discrimination and oppression.

Equality as the starting position from which individuals are equally free to make use of opportunities without discrimination

OR

Equality as the end position, where outcomes such as goods and services are shared fairly between individuals and groups.

There is of course a range of positions here – from liberal to revolutionary. What they tend to have in common is that they see ethical ideas as contextualised by political, economic and social systems, and are concerned with ideas such as 'equality' and 'justice', even though these terms are themselves often questioned or rejected by Marxists and feminists as too reflective of, and enmeshed within, capitalist and/or patriarchal systems. It is the existence of multiple interacting social systems which causes concern, and is also a key guiding concept within anti-oppressive ethics in this book – and one which will be the focus of attention in this chapter. It emphasises the way ethical issues are themselves political in that they are related to arguments about human need, and how fairly resources and powers are distributed throughout the various social systems that constitute a society, and how they interact to constrain or facilitate the lives of individuals and groups. How exactly is an anti-oppressive ethic relevant? How does it differ from or add to radical approaches to ethics? How far can large-scale issues such as social justice and equality be related to specific ethics of personal action? How far are human rights necessarily anti-oppressive? A fundamental issue in this chapter is the nature of justice, rights and equality – concepts with both ethical and political dimensions – in the context of the social environment.

The function of official codes of ethics tends to be related to system maintenance, rather than reform or revolution, and radical concepts of justice may not always feature strongly in them. It tends to be assumed by professional codes that individual ethical values are shared within a general consensus. However, the international social work statement of ethics places a considerable emphasis on 'social justice', including concepts of distributive justice, discrimination and diversity, and advocating the duty of social workers to: 'challenge social conditions that contribute to social exclusion, stigmatisation or subjugation, and to work towards an inclusive society' (IFSW/IASSW, 2004, Principle 4.2.5). The statement is also prefaced with references to United Nations conventions on a range of human rights. The approach of this body, often reflected in national social work organisations, implies a range of human rights and concerns about equality, justice and diversity. However, the international statement clearly leaves open the question of exactly how 'inclusive' any society should be, and how much equality, justice and human rights should be applicable in any particular society. So we return to the point that these ethical ideas may involve a range of interpretations. We shall refer to some of the different versions below.

CASE STUDY: EVVY'S CHILDREN

Evvy James is a 28-year-old single parent of Jason (10) and Donna aged 2. She is a black British woman of Jamaican origins with mild learning difficulties, her parents having arrived in the UK in the early 1950s. She lives in an old terraced property, and is unemployed. She encourages her son to 'defend' himself, and expects him to act as substitute father for Donna whenever necessary. Unfortunately neither James nor his mother are seen as being able to guarantee safe care, but they are nevertheless a family with close ties.

Pete, the area social worker to whom the case was allocated, is in a childcare team that received the referral from a GP. Donna has been seen by health visitors since her premature birth, and has failed to gain weight satisfactorily. There has been a recent report from neighbours about Evvy leaving the children unattended, and most recently the baby was seen at the local health clinic with fingertip bruising to the upper arms. The doctor is concerned about the slow rate of growth, and the level of care, but Evvy suggested angrily that if the authorities were so concerned then maybe they should take the baby into care. Pete is worried about Evvy and her family, and he is a new social worker, recently graduated from the local university. Evvy is 'known' to Social Services, and some previous social workers tell Pete that she basically needs support and advice. Pete's senior, however, wants him to consider the potential risk to Donna very seriously.

THE PROBLEM

Child care workers are faced with difficult decisions to make about the care of children. Who can tell whether the indicators for abuse are sufficiently serious in a given case to warrant taking action? It is sometimes not very clear. Even when it is clear that action is needed to ensure the child's safety, what kind of action should there be? Is it enough to support the family, or does the child need to be looked after away from home? And if that is the case then how is the social worker to weigh up the longer-term future of the child? Does the child need a fresh start, and should a 'clean break' adoption be part of the plan, or should the links to extended family and community be preserved as an important priority? In offering respect to service users, and in advocating for their justice and rights, is there a possibility that this type of ethical approach may undermine a clear view of the child protection dangers?

The moral dilemma for Pete is that he knows that Evvy is herself a vulnerable young woman who is probably doing her best for the children despite her overt aggressive style. He also knows that in order to assess the situation with any sensitivity and accuracy, *and* in order to facilitate any possibility of long-term contact between Donna and her birth family (if it turns out, as his senior suggests, that the only way of ensuring her safety is to remove her), he needs to make as good a relationship with Evvy as he can. He has to consider planning to take Evvy's child away from her *at the same time* as he tries to gain her confidence – just what she fiercely does not want him to do.

Pete also suspects that many of Evvy's problems in caring for Donna could be alleviated with the right kinds of support – especially from family and social networks, better childcare advice and support in the community and more resources at school to assist with her older child, not to mention better housing. Evvy would certainly benefit from a better income, which would allow her to avoid debt repayments at high interest rates, and generally ease her personal situation. Pete is sympathetic to radical analyses of social work in general and childcare in particular. He agrees with the critics who suggest that much of childcare social work is about controlling the behaviour of working-class women, rather than trying to change their appalling circumstances. He is also concerned about the possible discrimination that may arise against Evvy because she is black.

The interprofessional issues were an additional key element in his discussion with his senior. The family doctor had indicated that the immediate symptoms were not indicative of deliberate harm, and had requested further support for them. However, the health visitors with whom Pete was in close contact held different views. Their focus on the individual child tended to encourage them to take the senior's position in this argument. They saw reasons for multi-professional action designed to protect the child. They did not share Pete's social analysis, and were critical of his supportive style with parents. After a preliminary assessment, and after liaison with the health and education services, reviewing the evidence with his senior he manages to persuade her that the case should be regarded as a prevention case. He therefore decides to do as much as he can to support

Evvy, to prevent Donna from being 'looked after', and to make sure she is safe with her birth family.

PETE'S SOLUTION

The case study details suggest that Pete's solution was very debatable because there are some indications of the risk of abuse, but it is possibly also in line with some welfare policy thinking that regards social workers as too quick to draw children and their parents into the 'heavy end' of social services intervention. By their heavy-handed intrusiveness social workers may make bad situations worse. They may leave children in the community with no more services or resources than they had before, having traumatised and stigmatised them for no good purpose (Dept of Health, 1995). Pete's determination to support Evvy is set in a context of scarce resources and heavy caseloads, but he has a small area of discretion in how he uses his time, and he is determined to use it to network, liaise and advocate to the best of his ability to support Evvy and keep the family together.

It is part of a modern agenda for social services that social workers should ensure that service users get services of sufficient quality. Not only should the taxpayer get good value for money in so far as costs are kept to a minimum, but that the services on offer do in fact achieve the objectives laid out for them. In this case the services which should be available in the community should ensure that a single parent and her small family should be able to survive, and the children's welfare and development be supported, without the need for their being looked after by the local authority – a more expensive option.

Pete's radical view is that the official line ignores the levels of deprivation, poverty and powerlessness that exist, and that available support hardly addresses the reality of people's lives. He personally feels that some cases require a commitment on the part of the social worker which is over and above the official requirement. His ethical perspective is therefore based on the premise that whilst the market economy exploits and abuses many working-class women, especially from minority ethnic backgrounds, there is still the possibility of intervening in families and communities to make a positive difference in people's lives. As a matter of social justice and fairness it is a strategy that he sees as an important ethical commitment, advocating for the rights of Evvy as a black mother to be supported in keeping her family together, and also supporting the rights of her children who, when asked, clearly indicate their loyalty to their mother. Such a position is clearly consistent with IFSW/IASSW values, based on United Nations conventions about the rights of children and families. It is also consistent with the policy of working in partnership with service users, respecting their values, and supporting their efforts to determine their own lives.

However, his senior social worker and line manager Suzy, who has similar radical perspectives, has a very different view of the ethics of this case. Her argument's conclusion is similar to that of the health visitors who are critical of Pete, but her reasons are different. She feels that Pete is taking a risk with Donna's welfare which is difficult to justify in view of the limitations to resources – the financial and other kinds of support that he can possibly muster. She agrees wholeheartedly that it is a feminist issue, and that Evvy may be the subject of discrimination at a personal level, and also suffers from wider oppression because of her gender, class, disability and ethnicity. However, she regards the (post)modern state as having a very limited function, and social workers as having a very limited mandate to interfere in family life. The dominant policies of agencies remain that of protection of the child – and secondly protection of themselves as a frequently criticised organisation. They require workers to take appropriate investigative and remedial action to ensure the safety of the child, whose interests must be placed first. There is a vast amount of support for Evvy that is ideally required but is simply not available within the limits set for social work by current policies. The right thing to do therefore is *not* to set yourself and the service user an impossible task, with possibly dangerous results. The aim should certainly include the avoidance of any kind of undue discrimination against Evvy – she should get her fair share of support as compared with any other service user – little though that may be. However, this aim should be set within the primary agency objective – protecting the welfare and safety of the child. The latter should therefore be the prime focus of intervention – in partnership with the parent as much as is possible, and working together with the other agencies. The social worker's commitment to Evvy as a black working-class woman should be transferred to political and other welfare initiatives *outside* the immediate work environment, where more structural changes – at local and national levels – might be achieved which would more effectively benefit Evvy and others like her. The senior uses legal and ethical arguments about the paramount rights of the child, and the duty of care to children that takes precedence over the rights and wishes of the parent.

<table>
<tr><td colspan="1"></td></tr>
</table>

KEY IDEAS
Oppression as a function of social structures If unjust social structures significantly determine people's lives, it is the social worker's ethical role to apply the rules fairly, but as citizens and workers they may collectively try to change the structures. Only then can they apply new and different rules. Individuals are seen as bound by the dominance of powerful systems. *Agency: justice in personal actions* If unjust social structures oppress people then the social worker's ethical responsibility is to take action – to help service users fight against structures and to reinterpret and re-write the rules in whatever way they can, including going against the rules if that is necessary. Individuals are seen as active agents of change. *How possible is it to reconcile the difference?*

RADICAL ETHICAL PERSPECTIVES

1 How far should a social worker actively engage with and support a service user, knowing that their professional befriending might come to a bitter end?

If the measures taken do not succeed in a relatively short space of time, despite the natural parent's protests, a care order may be made. The child is then looked after by a social services department, and a foster or adoptive placement is sought. Even if rehabilitation is not ruled out, current 'twin-tracking' procedures mean that adoptive carers may be lined up even as the worker is discussing the chances of rehabilitation – just in case that option fails. The child will then be permanently removed, with no guarantee of continued contact. Natural parents resent social workers' apparently duplicitous and uncaring attitude towards them (Charlton *et al.*, 1998). Therefore which approach is the most ethically appropriate? Pete's solution is to emphasise the importance of a partnership which aims to prevent reception of Donna into care. Although he explains honestly to Evvy that part of his role is to protect children, and that this includes removing them from dangerous situations, he concentrates on the message that his aim is to support the family. Only if and when he becomes aware of any issues which seriously undermine this objective will he begin to consider the longer-term future of Donna, and the need to take action to provide alternative care options.

2   How much should a social worker allow his/her own views about the wider social factors impacting on children's lives to influence his/her decision to engage closely with a carer, offering *supportive* services, or to keep their distance, concentrating more upon the assessment of welfare and protection issues?

A radical analysis suggests that poverty, structural and community factors might indicate that prevention strategies should be used much more seriously, and this analysis can be supported by the UK government's own research data (Department of Health, 1995). The latter research criticised social workers for too much emphasis on 'heavy' investigation, and not enough on preventive and supportive work. In view of the risk of family breakdown as a result of institutionalised oppression of families like Evvy's, it is surely an ethical decision *as well as* part of a measured assessment for Pete to commit himself to supporting Evvy? His ethical perspective is based on considered views which he can support with social theory and empirical research.

In terms of the dilemma at a personal level, there is no doubt that much social work is done with natural parents who come to the notice of the local authority because they are poor and usually have a series of other additional disadvantages stacked up against them. They are very likely to be depressed (Sheppard, 2002), and will become even more so in the course of their interaction with social services – even to the point of suicide (Charlton *et al.*, 1998). A significant proportion will have learning difficulties (Holland, 2000), and others will have physical and/or mental health problems, which will overlay persisting forms of oppression based on social class, gender, and ethnicity.

Taking these matters into account, we can see that the above two options (i.e. Pete's and Suzy's) are *both* logical conclusions to draw. They are both examples of radical ethical thinking at work: they are both concerned with social justice and the inequalities which condition people's lives. In Pete's case the optimistic radical conclusion is based on the assumption that individuals *can* make a difference in the workplace despite the overarching structural factors which impact on people's lives. It is therefore ethical for Pete to put his shoulder at the point where support is needed most. This does not necessarily imply the *imposition* of his views on the service user; at least no more than any other worker imposes their views. What he is doing is making a broad assessment of the social situation, including the immediate family circumstances, and contextualising them within the framework of local and national social conditions.

In Suzy's case her argument would be that it is unethical to implant false hope in the minds of service users, and therefore more ethical to be more explicitly distant but more objective and more honest from the start. The worker's role is to ensure that the interests of the child are paramount – as set out in the legal frameworks for childcare social work that are common in many countries across the world. The possibility of a childcare tragedy arising from too much reliance on and respect for parent carers of children is very real and has guided the necessity for such legislation. The emphasis here is upon working in partnership with other professions to ensure the safety of the child. There is no guarantee that Evvy can be supported, and any commitment in this direction might be seen as an unwise deployment of scarce resources. It may also mean that other vulnerable children on the worker's caseload are neglected on the (doubtful) chance of a significant recovery in Evvy's parenting and social skills. The ethical course of action is to lobby for a radically different approach to social welfare provision outside work hours, making sure at the same time that there is no discrimination against specific individuals within the work environment (Wise, 1995). This radical view is based on the premise that a sexist, market society structures people's lives so much that there is little chance of escape, except where a child can be given a different start with a new family.

These two positions are not necessarily polar opposites, but may be more like positions on a continuum, where one tendency is given more weight than the other. But they are of course not the only ethical positions that might be taken. In both cases the radical nature of the ethical position is engendered by the close connection with a radical analysis of social history and social structure. In both cases there is a concern with the conflicting interests and powers of differing social systems and structures that affect individual lives. Other ethical approaches either place much less emphasis upon the connection of the individual with the social environment or else deny that the significant feature of that environment is conflict and oppression, thus undermining the importance of justice, rights and equality.

ALTERNATIVE APPROACHES: INDIVIDUALS ACTING ETHICALLY?

In previous chapters we have seen ethical arguments proposed that would see this case in a very different light. The third chapter discussed the importance of basic respect for individual persons, and how that could be translated into moral action in social work practice. The treatment of Evvy,

Donna and Jason should on this account be primarily a case of abiding by appropriately respectful rules of conduct, particularly in relation to confidentiality or privacy. It would also include the important rule of treating Evvy as a person able to make her own moral decisions: especially relevant to a woman with learning disability who may sometimes not be treated with such regard. This approach will stress the importance of honesty in spelling out the goals, and in delineating the repercussions of her own decisions. However, we have already seen in Chapter 3 that this approach has some weaknesses which anti-oppressive ethics tries to overcome.

In the fourth chapter we saw the value of an approach that tried to measure as accurately as possible the balance of pain and pleasure, and then opt for a course of action that would maximise the most desirable outcomes. The advantages of having a good character and making an honest decision, and treating people with respect, are not seen on this account as being an adequate basis for an ethical decision, although it might help to facilitate one. What really matters is: what has been shown to work and what evidence is there relevant to this case? In this case it would certainly have something important to offer in that the social worker who does not take sufficient account of research and clinical evidence about this situation is not doing the job properly, and can be regarded as ethically and legally in breach of their duty of care.

In the last chapter we examined the view that the character of the social worker was the key ethical issue. In the case of Evvy, it could be argued that the very uncertainty of the moral dilemma involved means that all anyone can or should expect is for the social worker to be of good character, and to act with integrity and honour. Being as genuine and as honest as one can, whilst still unsure what the real outcome of an assessment is going to be, is all that anyone can ask. Or is it? In the last chapter we also used the anti-oppressive ethics checklist to analyse this argument and suggest a more rigorous approach to ethics.

In all three of these approaches to ethics, the focus is upon the individual actor and the effort to make morally acceptable decisions, or to behave in an ethical way or to develop their individual character. What plays much less importance in each is the social environment, and the way in which that environment is characterised. In an anti-oppressive perspective the social environment is a crucially significant factor. It highlights the way that social systems continually interact to reinforce the powers of some and undermine others, affecting the life chances of individuals before they are even born. It is also the way that individuals' values as well as their needs are moulded by that unequal social, cultural and economic environment. This brings ethics closer to politics and the need to consider much more seriously the concepts of rights, justice and equality.

However, social work has traditionally been a subject where the social environment has been seen as an important factor. In social work theory 'systems theory' was once popular, and remains influential through so-called 'ecological' approaches. The biological analogy implicit in these approaches may facilitate assumptions that there are shared values and self-adjusting social systems in which individuals will prosper if they only play their allotted roles well enough. The crucial issues here are whether the social environment is understood sufficiently well in terms of the unequal powers and conflicting values of different social groups and organisations.

JUSTICE FOR SERVICE USERS

To some extent principles of justice motivate both Pete and his senior, but they view them in different ways. The recently deceased philosopher John Rawls is famous for supporting a moderate liberal idea of justice as an ethical and social principle which can be derived – like Kant's ethics – from a consideration of what rational individuals can be expected to choose. Pete could use some of these arguments to support his position that justice would be served and an ethical principle upheld if he were to act as effectively as possible in ways that would help the service users in this case live a better life with a better share of the resources available. Distributive justice concerns how we should distribute the products of social cooperation among the people, including economic goods. It should be noted that there are other aspects to justice, for example, when it is in relation to offences that individuals have committed. Here the concepts of retributive, restorative and compensatory justice come into play (see Clark, 2000, pp148–52, for a discussion of these different concepts of justice in social work ethics). Rawls holds that problems of justice cannot be resolved by decisions individuals make separately. Justice can be achieved only through something like a collective social contract, in which we all autonomously agree on rational principles. He contends that we should arrive at these principles from behind what he calls 'a veil of ignorance'. That is, we should ask: what principles of justice would I adopt if I were ignorant of my present position in life, and had to assume that everyone was basically equal? He argues that certain principles of justice are justified because they would then be agreed to in this hypothetical initial situation of equality. We would be likely to select principles of justice based on *fairness* between free and equal individuals, and there would then be an agreement that these principles should be the basis for a just society. Distributing resources equally to ensure a minimum standard of safe care could well be seen as a rational distributive principle of justice – though not necessarily a very radical one.

Rawls' own first principle of justice is about the guarantee of free choice to individuals, in order that they can reason together and agree on a social contract at all. Thus the first responsibility of government is to guarantee equal civil liberties for all citizens. However, his second principle of justice is that the state should distribute economic goods to maximise the advantage of the least advantaged members. This means that inequalities are permissible only if they increase the good of all – particularly those with the least – and it especially means that the opportunity to acquire goods and employment should be equally open to all. In his hypothetical thought experiment, it may be that *you* are one of the least advantaged – or you may be better off. This principle of justice implies that you should have the same fairness of opportunities to acquire goods and positions, but that the inequalities that then occur should not be so damaging to society that those least able to thrive are further disadvantaged as a result.

This view of the principle of justice asserts the rationality of providing minimum conditions of life for everyone, and equal opportunities for all. The ethical course for a professional is therefore to support a disadvantaged service user who clearly needs to be able to claim a reasonable minimum of resources. This fits well with the justification for distributing resources to maintain a state of safe care for all children. This principle of justice is a moderate ethical position since it does not necessarily require revolutionary social change, and is not compatible with collectivist or authoritarian societies where individual free choice is not valued. However, it could be compatible with a liberal or moderately 'radical' social work position in so far as it clearly justifies a concern with fair distribution, and supports the moral demand to act in accordance with that principle.

Suzy is concerned about justice, but she feels that the impact of social structures on people's lives is so strong that it is not a helpful strategy to confuse individual practice with social justice at a political level. Only the latter will make a significant difference to people's lives, and genuine feminist initiatives may only be possible outside statutory work (cf. Wise, 1995). She may nevertheless draw on Rawls' argument to a limited extent, to justify her concern to apply the rules fairly. She may also draw on classic Marxian and feminist arguments which tend to see individualist ethical principles in terms of ideologies of either (or both) capitalism or patriarchy. After all, it is in the interests of those in power to convince those who are dominated that the social system does in fact operate fairly – especially if it doesn't! Marx is famous for suggesting that ethical principles are screens behind which hide the financial interests of the holders of economic power, and that unequal distribution is the symptom and not the cause of oppression (Wood, 2002). The pretence of 'justice' at the individual level would therefore be unethical as well as ineffective for Suzy.

Another contemporary feminist writer also rejects the principle of distributive justice along similar lines. For Iris Marion Young what matters where justice is concerned is not just what we own (i.e. distributive justice) but what we do, and what we are allowed to do (Young, 2002). Social justice in her view means the elimination of institutionalised domination and oppression. A focus on the distribution of material goods and resources inappropriately restricts the scope of justice, failing to bring social structures and institutional contexts under evaluation. She contends that for a social condition to be just, it must enable people to meet their needs and exercise their freedom; thus requiring them to be able to express their needs. This extends the principle of justice in ways that Pete might think service users deserve – not only the right to a fair allocation of resources, but a voice in the decisions that are made, and how they are made. However, Suzy might still feel that both distribution of resources and the right to participation in decision-making would not in practice make a significant difference to where the power really lies, or who in reality will have most access to material goods and services. So even an extended feminist concept of justice is subject to debate about how it applies in specific circumstances, and what the ethical implications are for professionals – or indeed whether it is just an ethical issue. Suzy would argue that it is essentially a political issue. However, what seems to have been widely accepted is that some concept of justice is an essential part of the considerations that social workers ought to bring to bear in their dealings with service users, but with an awareness that there are political as well as ethical issues involved. Even so, this discussion indicates that there are serious differences about the nature of the concepts involved; how they should be applied, and the political context of ethical decisions.

Similar qualifications need to be made about the use of concepts such as equality, equal opportunities and human rights, including the rights of parents, children and minority ethnic groups, and the rights of immigrants. The notion of human rights has become an increasingly important part of global considerations in social work. The UN Convention on Human Rights has been translated into the national legislation in many countries, and there are a range of rights to be considered, including rights very relevant to this hypothetical case. For example, the right to family life could be cited by Pete as a good reason to protect Evvy from unduly intrusive interference. If this had been a family recently arrived in the country, then the rights of immigrant families (or asylum seekers, as they might have been) would also have been relevant – another area where Pete would be concerned about the rights and justice for the service users.

The broader emphasis in recent times on the rights of children challenges the assumptions of all adults about how children can be both respected and protected, and families supported or controlled (Fox Harding, 1997). The rights of children to be safe from harm, and for their health and education to be promoted, are obviously of central importance, and are enshrined in the international convention on the rights of the child (United Nations, 1989), but the justice and fairness of intervention is a complex issue. It has been argued that children's rights are in any case conditional, and subject to parental veto: they are 'best understood as duties owed to the children by the parents' (Frost, 2003, p55). Children are not allowed the right to opt out of educational or health support systems: for their own long-term good they are subject to the decisions of parents and social workers. However, precisely how this is managed in relation to the need to respect a child as a person, whilst doing justice to the competing claims of children and parents to 'rights', is difficult.

If Evvy's children wish to stay in a risky situation, at what point does that become unacceptable for the social worker, and how far is it just to expect children to be responsible for far-reaching decisions that they know will impact both on themselves and on parents and siblings (cf. Smith, 2005, pp167–8)? These classic childcare dilemmas are reflected in changing social policies, driven by politics and social affairs. Their focus may shift (for example, as it has in the UK), from trying to 'balance' child protection and family support, towards a greater emphasis upon child protection and state intervention, with ambitious plans to use communications technology to monitor the progress of all vulnerable children to ensure their safety and welfare (Smith, 2005, p190). Smith's suggestion, drawing on Fook (2002), is that workers need to identify their own value positions in relation to childcare, and proceed systematically, avoiding superficial judgements, and recognising the various alternative perspectives of child, parents and the differing professions. This is salutary for both the social work professionals in this case study. Does Pete have an 'optimistic' perspective which, applied insensitively, can lead to disastrous consequences for the child? Does Suzy have a personal interest in her agency position and a white(?) feminist suspicion of 'family' values which incline her too much towards intervention at the expense of a black service user?

ANTI-OPPRESSIVE ETHICS AND INTERACTING SOCIAL SYSTEMS

In this section we will briefly indicate some of the implications of an anti-oppressive framework, with a focus on the concept of interacting social systems as a key aspect of understanding individual and group experiences in life during specific time periods and in specific places. We follow this with brief outlines of the other concepts in the anti-oppressive framework in relation to this case study.

I   Interacting social systems

Radical ethical perspectives are often seen as emphasising the large-scale ('macro') social systems which control our lives. They are regarded in contemporary parlance as 'structuralist' and 'modernist' views of social explanation – as against 'post-structuralist' ideas which contemporary social work texts tend to advocate, where the fractured, contradictory and plural factors affecting social life are stressed. The classic Marxist argument about ethics is that the 'fair' price of labour (for instance) is whatever is dictated by the *economic market system*, regardless of what your actual needs are for a living wage. There is no question of using the concept of fairness to question the system itself because the social system defines what fairness means. Thus individual behaviours, including the use of ethical concepts, are to be explained by the interaction between large social groups within a macro-market system – between the owners of capital, and those who own only their own labour. Feminist logic can apply in a similar way to *patriarchal social systems* which assume it to be a 'natural' and inevitable role for women that they should service the needs of the family. These social norms are a given part of the dominating patriarchal values which also cannot be questioned since they reflect assumed natural gender roles in society as a whole, dictating what can be defined as acceptable moral behaviour.

However, ethical theories are traditionally oriented towards individuals making conscious decisions about their lives. The implication of 'ethics' is that individuals may choose to act in certain ways or not. The influence of macro-social systems upon them is not always regarded as being a relevant consideration – unless it is to encourage individuals to resist external influences which might deflect them from an ethical path. On the other hand class-based and/or feminist analyses make the assumption that exploitation between social groups is indeed a powerful source of human thought and action; that it is unacceptable, and that growing consciousness of this leads to action by individuals and groups. There is consequently often an underlying tension between, on the one hand, regarding the 'ethics' of oppressive social systems as being presented (falsely) as 'natural' by powerful groups which individuals *cannot* significantly resist, and, on the other hand, a varying impulse to *actively* attack those values as unacceptable, ethically and/or politically. In the case study we presented two workers tending to take opposing positions on this issue, and in the subsequent discussion we analysed the difficulties in applying differing concepts of justice and rights to family situations. Neither approach can demand unqualified respect, yet they do raise issues about justice and rights which should not be ignored.

Feminist ethicists have laid much emphasis upon this social, relational context of ethics. The notion of the individual making moral decisions and judgements independently of any social relationships is seen by them as obviously male in its construction, and women have understandably pointed out that all ethics and values are *first* nurtured within the *relational* context of a micro-social system – the family, where women usually play a critical role (Held, 2006; see also Chapter 8). In particular, feminist views of social relationships as a basic constituent of moral obligation emphasise the point that 'The ethics of care builds relations of care and concern and mutual responsiveness to need on *both* the personal and wider social levels' (Calhoun, 2004, p69, our emphasis). Interacting social systems are not reducible on this account to a collection of independent individuals, and the abstract individual of the liberal state is an inadequate basis for understanding how ethics is both constituted and constrained by the immediate and more distant social relationships that change and develop in interaction with other social systems: 'Ethics do not emerge in the abstract but in daily life dilemmas like sexual relations, parenting, friendships, work relationships' (Porter, 1999, p5). The family, community and surrounding organisations and social systems that contextualise the lives of Evvy and Pete mould their identity and values: they are a significant part of who they are and what they care about. Conversely, the feminist argument also attempts to retain the 'personal and political' elements within the sphere of family, organisational, political and economic systems: 'The ethics of care provide a way of thinking about and evaluating *both* immediate and the more distant human relationships, with which to develop morally acceptable societies' (Calhoun, 2004, p69). Individuals respond to and in their turn affect the various social systems through their interleaving and continuing relationships: the politics of human relationships runs through the different interactive levels as well as the ethics.

Building upon this, an anti-oppressive perspective requires consideration of the impact of interacting social systems on the lives of individuals at micro-, mezzo- and macro-levels and questions the roles of *both* actors and systems in the generation and resolution of moral issues. Neither the individualistic human rights and obligations of a liberal model nor the political reductionism of a deterministic radical model is adequate to understand the complexities of justice and equality. From the radical model an anti-oppressive ethic takes the insight into inequalities of power between significant social groups, and the way that influences individuals' perceptions and actions – but not without recognising complexity and personal agency. From the liberal model an anti-oppressive approach takes the emphasis of human rights, but contextualises it within interacting and unequal, often conflicting and oppressive social systems. Sensitivity to these concrete social contexts is a feature of the feminist ethical theories which inform an anti-oppressive approach. *Both* the 'personal' and the 'political' dimensions of the circumstances need to be factored into any consideration of what the social worker ought to do. Social workers have to develop skills of listening; negotiation and advocacy, networking *across* micro- and macro-social and organisational systems if 'relational autonomy' is to be progressed effectively. For further discussion of feminist relational ethics in relation to an anti-oppressive perspective see Chapter 8.

2   Social divisions

In this case the social divisions of age, gender, ethnicity and social class are all obviously present. There are also disability issues because of Evvy's learning needs. The radical ethics of Pete and Suzy do take into account social class and gender, and this makes an important contribution to understanding the complexity of the ethical issues in this case. The problems of radicalism identified by an anti-oppressive ethical approach partly consist in the identification of *some* social divisions – but not others. The focus on class and gender may have the effect of excluding adequate consideration of other social divisions – in this case particularly age (especially in relation to the child), ethnicity and disability, and the ways that all the social divisions, including sexuality, culture and religion cut across and overlap each other in the life of this family. Although the issues of gender and social class have strong radical indications because of the structural factors which profoundly impact on service users' lives, the specific way that the social divisions inter-relate in a particular case is crucial to the assessment, and therefore the ethical implications. This may not necessarily dilute the radical views espoused by Pete and Suzy, but will certainly add to the complexity, subtlety and adequacy of their positions.

In addition to being a working-class woman, Evvy is a black woman with mild learning difficulties. It would be advantageous to investigate the degree to which the 'mild learning difficulty' label is a significant factor for her parental functioning and self-care, without either trivialising or overplaying the importance of gender or class. It is possible that her particular family has a history of low academic achievement because of her specific inherited limitations. Another possibility is that she has been mislabelled, possibly because of racist assumptions about black people by white professionals: to what degree does she really have learning disabilities, or are cultural and linguistic factors interfering with a fair estimation of her ability? It would be important to understand *her* perspective on her place in the community, and how far she is able to access support that might be offered. Do the inter-connecting social divisions in her life combine to make insuperable difficulties, or are there countervailing factors in her personality or in her social networks that offer hope for change? She has been able to survive for this long, so what strengths has she been able to draw upon, and are these strengths diminishing or increasing over time?

Similar complex issues about membership of social groups would need to be considered about Evvy's children. The nature of childhood as a social division is itself an important issue in this case, leaving both Jason and Donna differently vulnerable to specific adults in their environment (as well as to powerful adult groups), and in Donna's case to her own brother. Their ethnic background cannot be assumed to be the same as Evvy's, and their gender clearly has important implications for safe care and welfare within and outside the family. We would contend that the tendency of the classic radical traditions in social work ethics, whether socialist or feminist, has been to 'read off' the ethical implications from a political analysis, without always paying sufficient attention to the intervening variables. Anti-oppressive perspectives systematically question the qualitative impact of differential membership of social divisions on the nature of the moral issues in specific circumstances.

3   Power dynamics

Radical ethical perspectives take power issues seriously, as do anti-oppressive ethics. However, the (perhaps stereotypical) radical approach has traditionally tended to see power as 'top-down'. The oppression of women and/or the working class by men and/or the upper and middle classes expressly portrays the abuse of power by those 'above' over those 'below'. Anti-oppressive practice requires a thorough examination of power as *both* unequal and multidirectional. The nature of power in this example appears at first sight to be unidirectional, and matches the tendency of radical ethics to assume that the representatives of powerful groups exercise power over dominated groups of people. A radical ethic therefore tends to take the view that the professional is in a continual moral dilemma – working both in and against a state dominated by powerful elites. Pete takes the view that it is more ethical to resist the state, whilst Suzy takes the pessimistic view that only political and economic change can alter the underlying structures. In the meantime it is ethical to work for the state where objectives such as child protection can be justified.

An anti-oppressive ethic learns from radical perspectives the importance of accounting for inequality and power on community, national and international levels, and envisioning how this shapes the lives of the powerless. However, it also regards the nature of power as complex, not only because of the cross-cutting impact of different social divisions, and not only because of the intervening effects of intermediate sources of power such as organisations or families. It also recognises that power can be wielded by the most unlikely sources – even if only for short periods of time or with limited impact, and that it is produced in social interactions between people whose power will not be static but will vary with the changing situational specifics.

Thus Pete's solution tends to downplay the significance of Evvy's power as an adult over both her children, and arguably also the moral power that she can exert over him. As a white male he may exert his conventional power over Evvy, by assuming the objectivity of his knowledge over hers. But if as a liberal white male he tries to actively take her side, the power relationship can be inverted at critical points. She may take advantage of his defensive attitude and offer explanations of her parenting that convince him of her 'cultural' ethnic approach. This may lead him to misperceive the dangers in the situation. The same is less likely to be said of Suzy, who may be sceptical of cultural explanations, and more focused on the dangers. However, she may not be reading accurately the different relationships of power within black families, and may also be wielding the power of the state with questionable complacency. There is no easy solution to this dilemma: thorough analysis of power is crucial to the anti-oppressive ethics of the situation, including the relative powers of the professionals themselves, and those of service users.

4   Personal and social histories

In Evvy's case there are bound to be numerous psychological factors that emanate from her past. Experiences of family relationships in her family of origin, and in her current family, need to be related to changing social and historical circumstances, including personal, organisational and political forms of racism. Changing attitudes towards women and to learning disability will also have made their mark, refracted through the particular circumstances of her life.

Pete's relatively optimistic view of the possibilities for positive support for Evvy stem from his assessment of her as a working-class woman whose poverty is a key issue in relation to her parenting abilities. He may tend to neglect the complex histories that have helped to form her character. However, some of these historical and developmental factors may be *strengthening* her life, such as her survival skills in the face of various forms of oppression and discrimination, but the same factors may also have damaged her ability to cope. The specifics of her own psychology and family patterns of behaviour have been changing, and the current state of play has to be assessed alongside the factors of social division. For example, how far is her aggressive behaviour understandable as a survival skill which she has under control and is able to deploy when needed to defend herself and her children? How far is it a personality trait developed out of her own unmet needs and personal frustrations? What then do these differential possibilities imply for intervention? Has Suzy overlooked the survival skills, personal strengths and family ties that Evvy has developed over the years? Has Pete been too sanguine in his focus on the social factors, and is she placing her children at risk when she loses her temper?

What is the evidence concerning the child's social and psychological development, and what are the children's views about their own life stories? The obvious danger of a concern with macro-social factors is that you don't analyse sufficiently the personal and family histories of the micro-social world. Both the large-scale issues of social history with their impact on individuals, and the small-scale social and psychological details need to be integrated into any assessment that is holistic and could claim to be anti-oppressive.

5   Reflexivity

The problem with radical perspectives in relation to reflexive issues is that the concern with wider social issues tends to neglect the role of the actor. If people's lives are mainly explained in relation to social divisions such as gender, class or 'race', then the mutual interaction between the service user and the professional worker, and their respective social locations is not such a key issue. However, at the level of social work practice it cannot be ignored, and to reduce individuals (including the service user and the worker) to puppets of a system cannot possibly yield sufficient guidance for ethical assessment and intervention.

In Suzy's case, there is insufficient acknowledgement of her own role, not merely as an agent of the state, but as a line manager in a local organisation with a particular history of relationships with Evvy and the community in which she works. She herself is a white, able-bodied, educated middle-class woman, and the agency is white, with male senior managers. From Evvy's perspective, the social worker and his boss are authority figures to be feared in view of their social location. As a manager, Suzy needs to review the possibility that there is an issue of institutional racism because of the difficulty she has in offering Evvy anything like the support she needs. Suzy compounds this herself by taking a pessimistic view of the role of the agency in childcare. Even if there is something to be said for Suzy's view (and there certainly is in the light of concerns about the limitations of child protection agencies), she needs to take reflexive account of her own actions and her agency to judge how far she is adding to institutional racism and oppression, rather than resisting it. How much is she really concerned with protecting Donna, and how much is she protecting not only the agency but her own position within it?

Pete's optimistic support for Evvy can more readily be characterised as anti-oppressive and 'empowering'. However, he also needs to take account of his own social location and history. There are many issues for him to consider. For example, he may have good intentions as a liberal male, but he is working for an agency with a reputation and a history. He is not just a person but an employee and representative of the power of the local and central authorities, which Evvy may have learnt to fear. He may wish to work in partnership with Evvy, but will she really want to work with him? He has some understanding of the discrimination that Evvy may have suffered, but how well will he be able to see it from her perspective? How will he counter his own prejudices in relation to a woman with learning disabilities, whose use of language and ability to express her ideas will be very different from his own? What kind of dialogue is going to be possible: how well will he be able to access her views and involve her in 'partnership'? He is also a new social worker dealing with a case that may become very clearly and quickly a child protection case. How far do the strengths and weaknesses of being fresh and keen help or hinder in this case, and how well has his course prepared him to work with black families? How well has he been trained to work with children? These are also issues for his supervisor, and they need to be raised by both of them. Taking account of the personal perspectives of the actors in this situation (service users, carers and workers) and how they will interact is an essential constituent of anti-oppressive ethics. How they can best be supported through advocates or community support will be part of this reflexive consideration (cf. Houston, 2003). Anti-oppressive ethical perspectives require the interrogation of the worker's social position, personal history, behaviour and motives, in addition to and in conjunction with the service user's and carer's perspective.

AUTHORS' PERSPECTIVES: PARTICIPATION IN INTERACTING SYSTEMS

Evvy is a first-generation young, black British woman whose family originally came from Jamaica – these factors provide some points of contact, for one of the authors, but points of difference for the other. We would both, however, have in common our status as employed social workers in an organisation with links to a myriad of other formal and informal social systems. The differences between us will also have a significant impact on relationships between individuals and systems, including the informal networks that all individuals are enmeshed within, including service-user family and community systems, and our own continuing experiences of networks at home and at work.

Evvy herself would have to make a rapid assessment of the situation. In one case she has to make sense of the incongruity of a black worker working for a system that has offered little in terms of service provision to individuals and families from black communities. In the other she has to assess whether a white male would be willing or able to make the effort to understand her circumstances, given her probable (?) understanding of the authority often wielded by white males in formal organisations. Her story to date has been silenced and reinterpreted through various professional discourses set within powerful organisations. A worker's personal experiences of being female and black in black community systems, combined with black feminist ideas facilitates the hearing of a different story – of challenging social systems, of growth and survival in a hostile and contradictory environments. A white male may not be able to elicit such narratives so easily, or if told, be able to 'hear' them.

We would both want to make a careful assessment of strengths, needs and risks, and possibilities for change, prioritising the youngest child's needs as the most vulnerable and powerless service user. We would both wish to balance the rights and needs of parent and children, and whether they would see the need for a black advocate or friend, seeking justice for the parent and balancing that against the priority of a vulnerable child, and the demands of both black communities and formal agencies. We would need the advice of supervisors about child protection, and want to consider where our own strengths and weaknesses would come into play in following or challenging system expectations. We would in our different ways use the anti-oppressive framework, but, placing ourselves within it, come to our own conclusions about how ethics and good practice can best be resolved in this case.

CHAPTER SUMMARY

In this chapter we have looked at the problems that can arise for a social worker who is trying to act ethically in relation to children and parents living in difficult circumstances. We have drawn attention to the distinction between social democratic arguments for justice, equality and rights which in recent times are based on the work of John Rawls, and more structurally oriented concepts of exploitation, alienation and inequality which are drawn from classic Marxist and feminist writings, and are reflected in Young's work. We have argued that anti-oppressive concepts help to reinterpret ideas about justice and equality so that they can be applied more fully and ethically, focusing in particular on the importance of interacting social systems and relationships.

FURTHER READING

Cahn, S.M. (2002) 'Two Concepts of Affirmative Action'. A paper on justice and equality in relation to equal opportunities practice and policy issues.
Jewson, N. and Mason, D. (1992) 'The theory and practice of equal opportunities policies: liberal and radical approaches'. A paper describing different approaches to equal opportunities.

Rawls, J. (2002) 'A Theory of Justice'. An extract from Rawls' writings about the concept of justice.

Scanlon, T.M. (2002) 'The Diversity of Objections to Inequality'. A paper that discusses the varied grounds both for opposing inequality, as well as objections to equality.

Wise, S. (1995) 'Feminist Ethics in Practice'. A paper that puts forward a feminist case similar to the one presented in the above chapter.

Wood, A. (2000), 'Marx against Morality'. A short paper that explains Marx's classic critique of morality and 'justice'.

Young, I.M. (2002) 'Displacing the Distributive Paradigm'. A brief extract from Young's critique of distributive justice.

Chapter 7

Uncertainties, Decisions and Social Divisions

This chapter uses a case study involving group work to illustrate issues for post-modern and existentialist approaches to ethics. It also focuses upon the existence and nature of social divisions. Can anti-oppressive ethics add anything to the sophisticated social awareness of post-modern perspectives where uncertainty and the diversity of perspectives is emphasised?

KEY IDEAS

Uncertainty: The view of post-modern philosophers is that there can be no universal foundations for knowledge – or for morals.

Diversity: What exists are networks of different meanings, languages and cultures which everyone views from a particular social position in a specific local place and time.

Identity: Not only are individuals socially different from each other, but even their own identity is itself changing, fragmented and constituted by the effects of social variability and social interaction through time.

As part of an ethical outlook on social work, post-modern ethics can be regarded as being reflected in a number of ways in the international codes of ethics, as well as in national codes. One most obvious point of connection is right at the beginning, where the preface enjoins social workers to have respect for the range of international human rights declarations and conventions, including those dealing with cultural rights, the elimination of racial and other forms of discrimination, and the convention on indigenous and tribal peoples. Such diversity of cultural perspectives has always been a critical issue, but in a (post-modern) globalised world where travel, communication and immigration are so important, the opportunities for misunderstanding, discrimination and uncertainty are obviously multiplied. Social workers are thus enjoined to: 'recognise and respect the ethnic and cultural diversity of the societies in which they practise, taking account of individual, family, group and community differences' (IFSW/IASSW, 2004, 4.2).

Recognising uncertainty is *also* directly represented in the IFSW code in its recognition that social workers have an obligation to reflect on how general ideas may be locally applied because of the inherent ambiguities of the social work role, for example:

> The fact that the loyalty of social workers is often in the middle of conflicting interests.
>
> The fact that social workers function as both helpers and controllers.
> (IFSW/IASSW, 2004, section 3)

The code therefore explicitly recognises that differing accountabilities may lead to uncertainty:

> Social workers need to acknowledge that they are accountable for their actions to the users of their services, the people they work with, their colleagues, their employers, the professional association and to the law, and that these accountabilities may conflict.
> (IFSW/IASSW, 2004, 5.8)

The social world is clearly understood as a place where there is a degree of risk and uncertainty, and where workers therefore have to recognise and use their powers responsibly, engaging in ethical debate and reflection with colleagues. In other words they have to make decisions and take ethical responsibility for them in conditions of diversity and uncertainty. This could be seen as a post-modern vision of ethics.

CASE STUDY: BECCY AND JANE

A social work team decided to run a group for adolescent girls who were in danger of being received into care. Jane C, a 30-year-old lesbian social worker, was particularly keen to try out her groupwork skills. The agency aim was prevention of reception into care, along with prevention of other undesirable outcomes such as prolonged truancy; teenage pregnancy; sexual and physical abuse, all of which were factors in the lives of these young women.

The ethical issue that arose in the process of the groupwork concerned her involvement with a young woman of 13. In addition to a variety of group activities focusing on the needs and interests of young women, they had group discussions in which participants shared their experiences. These were regular semi-structured events, usually at the end of the session in which the discussion was based on questions arising from the topic of the week, but was discussed in terms of their past experiences and present circumstances.

Gradually the young women became confident about expressing themselves. One such session concerned domestic violence, and at the end, Beccy the 13-year-old asserted that she knew all about it – the group session had taught her nothing. Jane commented defensively that the value of the group session was to share some of our knowledge. Recalling her own experiences, Jane said she did know personally about domestic violence. But Beccy was by now angry and getting up to walk out. Spurred by an earlier confrontation, she refused to discuss it in a quiet room with another social worker (as previously agreed with the group), and made to leave, knowing that Jane had promised to return her to her foster parents. Jane's dilemma was how to handle a potentially volatile situation, balancing her responsibilities to Beccy, her foster parents, her natural parents, the agency, her colleagues, other group members, and other members of society who might become involved if Beccy was allowed to run off. Beccy tried to push past her, cursing as she went.

THE PROBLEM

Jane was confused because there were several legal, ethical and practice issues swimming round her head all at the same time, and she had to make a rapid decision, and try to retrieve the situation, as best she could. She had been trying to treat the service users in this group as young women who were entitled to the utmost consideration and care because of their multiple needs. At the same time she recognised and accepted that their own perspectives were of crucial importance, and she valued their opinions and their independence. She wanted to treat them as equals making their own way in life, perhaps with some friendly guidance from responsible adults. She had become aware of rapidly changing group dynamics – as she and her three colleagues had expected. But the concrete details of the developing relationships, and what they had mutually shared about their experiences had been a kaleidoscope of feelings. Jane had disclosed *some* of the details of her own life, convinced that there needed to be some reciprocity about personal information.

The group included three other co-workers, and together with the service users they had agreed some ground rules for behaviour at the start. This had included the provision of a quiet room for counselling and for cooling down when there were upsets. However, Beccy had no intention of being counselled, nor of quietening down. She wanted out.

Jane was faced with an immediate dilemma. Should she treat Beccy like a naughty child: raise her voice; call for reinforcements; ensure that the young women knew she and her colleagues were in charge, responsible, accountable, and in so doing ensure their safety? Or should she accept the assertiveness of a young woman who was capable of finding her own way home, respecting her wishes and opinions, allowing her to make her own decisions, and thus helping to prepare her for independence? In walking out, Beccy was disrupting this process; disturbing the feelings of other young women and ignoring their contribution to the discussion. Should Jane use her social work understanding of Beccy's disturbed background to interpret this behaviour as unrepresentative of her 'normal' feelings, and use her authority to stop her leaving, or should she accept that Beccy disliked the groupwork, despite all the effort that had been put into it? Should she also take into account the confused feelings that had arisen between them following on from earlier events? How far did she need to think about her own relatively vulnerable position, and the conflicting perspectives held about sexuality by colleagues and parents?

JANE'S DECISION

Jane knew it was a risky and *uncertain* decision. She was also very aware of her position as the only lesbian worker in the team, and although she had *not* publicised her sexuality, and had been careful to behave in a professional way towards the young women in her care, she also felt she had the right not to be in denial of herself as a whole person. She had therefore been honest when questions of sexuality had (very occasionally) arisen in relation to herself, and thought that at least some of the group members, and the staff, were aware of that part of her identity. In addition she was conscious that although the recent history of public attitudes towards gays and lesbians appeared to be towards more tolerance and acceptance, there were still many people, including some religious people in her own agency, who disapproved of her sexuality, and were not happy about her openness or her values in working with teenage girls.

The incident with Beccy had been preceded by work with the group about their own identities, and deliberate and positive valuing of social differences within the group. There was the 'usual mixture' of young women from backgrounds where poverty was combined with other forms of social division arising from gender, age, ethnicity and religion. Her own position had changed within the group as a whole and in relation to individuals within it. This did not come as a surprise to her at all. She was well versed in the changing, fragmentary nature of individual and group identities, having experienced in her personal and professional life a number of significant changes, particularly, but not only, in relation to her sexuality and her age.

Jane was also informed by her recent educational experience of qualification as a postgraduate social worker. She had relished the opportunity to study recent developments in the social sciences, and welcomed the recognition of the plurality of identities, and their change over time, and the shifting relations of power between people and groups that was influenced by post-modern ideas. She felt that this helped to make sense of the confusion and multiplicity of change that she experienced, and she recognised that her own identity and power to act in the group was complex.

Jane's solution was to consider the options in the specific context, using her education and professional experience to make an existential decision, though informed by knowledge of her legal responsibilities. She understood well the post-modern insistence on the importance of being prepared to assess particular and local claims, and, accepting the relative, situated nature of her own understanding and ability to make a moral decision: one that recognised the legitimate claims of others. She would accept the consequences of that decision, without making a narrow utilitarian calculation about the outcomes. Her personal involvement was not a contingent but a necessary factor in the groupwork process and she either acted with integrity and lived with it, or she did not. After brief consideration of relevant local issues, such as distance from the foster home, transport, and Beccy's intelligence and reliability, she decided to let Beccy go home, but with an admonishment that what she had said was offensive, and she would be visited by one of the other staff with a view to discussing what now needed to be done.

KEY IDEAS
Reflexivity: You should take account of your own participation in discourses at a particular time and place, relative to that of other persons and other discourses.
Responsibility: You should have a sense of your primary ethical responsibility for other people capable of resisting the prevailing influences of socialisation or of government, organisations, or peers.

COMMENT: MAKING A MORAL DECISION?

In Jane's view the fluid nature of her relationships with the various people to whom she related, the continuing reassessment of her own identity, and the changing situations in which she found herself all meant that she had to make decisions that were 'true' for herself, resisting the pressure to conform only to departmental procedures or standard professional ethics. She did not believe that she could make them true for anyone else. This is a kind of argument that is typical of post-modern thinking which insists that there is no universal basis for ethical theory or ethical concepts (or for that matter any general concepts in the social sciences). The most important feature of the social world is the way in which we use words to convey all kinds of different meanings without anyone being in a position to determine which concepts are the 'best': 'there is a rejection of the modernist idea of universal principles or laws' . . . and a 'focus on the self as the source of morality (Hugman, 2003). In this uncertain situation Jane has to make her own moral decision (Baumann, 1998).

This is in great contrast to some of the ethical theories that we have come across in social work contexts in this book, and it questions some of the most basic assumptions that are commonly made. It implies that there is *not* a rational foundation for ethics as the Kantian would have it. Common human rationality does not exist – it varies from place to place and across time: reasoning is extremely variable between people and cultures, and is not equally valued. If respect is relevant it can only be because of the existence of human diversity which demands recognition of the 'other' as a feature of human society. Respect cannot be based on a universal rationality which doesn't in fact bear close examination. For example, feminists see the notion of universal human rationality by classic moral philosophers as a pretext for the affirmation of male values (see Chapter 8).

Jane is faced with a dilemma of ethical action in which she can take a protective but authoritarian role, or she can take a constructive but risky decision. It is not clear to her which way she should go, because she can see reasons for doing both. She knows that the social work ethics code encourages her to 'respect and promote people's right to make their own choices and decisions, irrespective of their values and life choices, *provided* (our emphasis) this does not threaten the rights and legitimate interests of others' (IFSW/IASSW, 2004, 4.1). The point, however, was: how she could be sure of doing both in this particular situation? She has to choose, and postmodern ethics encourages the idea of taking personal responsibility for your choice, rather than relying on a code which in any case has to be interpreted and applied.

This is important especially to an ethicist and sociologist like Baumann, whose study of the Holocaust led him to view with grave suspicion the power of social and moral regimes over the individual (Baumann, 1989). His view is that many ordinary German people were socialised by a modern state into accepting the ultimate evil of the Holocaust. His conclusion is that an ethical decision is one made by the individual in the light of his or her responsibility to the 'other', and that decision is in a sense *pre-societal*, that is, it is made by the individual as an existential choice, one for which the individual takes responsibility: 'moral responsibility . . . is the first reality of the self, a starting point rather than a product of society' (Baumann, 1992, p13). This is similar to earlier existential philosophers such as Sartre, for whom ethical questions are 'the most important questions to which all others are merely preliminary' (Warnock, 1967, p53). It also 'draws particularly on the existentialist philosopher Levinas' (Hugman, 2003, p1027) for whom the moral ambivalence of human life demands individual ethical responsibility in the face of the 'other'.

Jane felt she had to make her own decision – one that could not be reduced to the formulaic rationale of Kantian or utilitarian ethics. Nor could it be deduced from a foundational theory of society such as marxism or feminism. It could not even be easily drawn out from the supposed virtues of a good social worker, because that did not tell her which of the options she should take, and it left unresolved the different views about what a good social worker should be like.

Ethical choice on this kind of view is one that must be able to stand the test of being able to resist socialisation into moral codes and systems, and the forces of social and governmental agencies. This is similar to the existentialist insistence on choice: the individual is a free moral agent and, 'is wholly responsible for creating his [*sic*] own world' (Warnock, 1967, p54). Equally, more recent support for an existentialist approach to ethics in social work advocates the importance of authenticity and self-overcoming, albeit with awareness of the socio-cultural environment (Thompson, 2008). In making this choice the post-modern condition of diversity and fragmentation requires Jane to take *reflexive* account of the way she herself is located within a web of different and changing perceptions. This concern with the agency of the self within a fragmented social environment is also characteristic of Foucault, another post-structuralist writer who is regarded as contributing significantly to a 'post-modern' ethic (cf. Hugman, 2003, p1027). As we ourselves have noted elsewhere, 'Foucault . . . advocates the 're-animation of an aesthetic relation to the self' (Lloyd, 1997, p82) in which there is a much greater emphasis upon personal choice and self-creation' (Clifford, 2002, p31).

Jane has indeed become increasingly aware that the multiple aspects of her identity have been gradually revealed during the course of the group. She has been one of the leaders of the group and taken on a protective and accountable role as an adult with professional and agency responsibilities. She is still a young woman, and varies between sisterly and motherly roles in relation to the teenage girls in her care, perhaps not aiming at either. She is a relatively new colleague for the other leaders of the group. She is also an academically minded practitioner, interested in developing policy and practice, and has needed to get the cooperation of staff and group members. She is a lesbian who has seen her identity, her friendships and relations change significantly in recent years. In the group her lesbian identity has become known at least to some, and this has also been a factor in how some of the young women have reacted to her – including Beccy. The powers inherent in these various positions are themselves varying and Jane sometimes feels strong, but at others, vulnerable. She feels that a post-modern interpretation of her position is indeed apt, and as a lesbian she has also taken some interest in 'queer theory' – the application of post-modern ideas to gay and lesbian lives. The disparate writers associated with queer theory have in common the view that 'notions of fixed or shared identity [are] confining and exclusionary' (McLaughlin, 2003, p147, cf. Spargo, 1999). They support the idea of 'transgression' – the breaking of social rules and expectations – and inevitably the concomitant ethical responsibility for so doing.

She decides to make a choice that is influenced by her perception of herself as a multiplicity of identities, realising that other people's expectations will vary. She regards herself as someone who is aware of the professional and legal framework for the groupwork, and she does not ignore the reality or the importance of that. However, she makes a brave choice in response to the 'ethical demand to recall and live with our responsibility for the other' (Smart, 2000, p518). She has decided that her ethical responsibility to a young teenager is to allow her to similarly develop her own capacity for making an ethical choice and living with it. She regards this as part of her maturing into adult life, and also as an episode in their developing relationship within the group. It is to treat Beccy as a responsible human being, to recognise that she is old enough to recognise her own choice and take responsibility for her own actions in the same way that Jane is doing: she reflects on the possibility that Beccy may not go home, even though she lives nearby. But that decision could also be made at any time outside group hours, and would again be Beccy's decision, not one for which Jane feels she is responsible. But will her senior managers agree, she ponders, if Beccy does not go home? But that's the point, she tells herself, that's the *ethical* decision as far as I am concerned. But is it the 'right' decision? Should the care of a 13-year-old young woman mean that she is allowed to wander the streets, and will Jane's decision be accepted by other interested parties, including her own agency, and Beccy's foster and natural parents?

ANTI-OPPRESSIVE ETHICS AND SOCIAL DIVISIONS

There is no denying the valuable contribution that post-modernism has made to ethics, epistemology and research in ways that are very relevant to social work. Within social work, there has been 'the emergence of a "critical postmodernism" [which] allows for the integration of structural analysis with diversity' (Hugman, 2003, pp1035–6). A recent paper cites Baumann, a leading post-modern sociologist, as supportive of social work's moral responsibility (Bisman, 2004, p117). This might be read as suggesting that there are no significant problems about post-modernism which prevents such an integration. However, there has also been a healthy debate between feminists concerning the extent to which feminism can incorporate post-modern ideas (cf. McLaughlin, 2003, ch. 4). We suggest that feminist reservations about post-modernist ethics in research and social work are important, and both post-modernism and these feminist reservations contribute towards an anti-oppressive ethic.

I   Social divisions

The issue of social difference is central to both post-modern and feminist thinking. Post-modernist ideas are based on assumptions about the fragmentary and partial nature of multiple discourses. On the other hand feminism begins from the basis of recognising the significance of the major social differences between genders, and then continues by recognising the multiple social differences between women. Both perspectives clearly militate against the idea of monolithic categories of social difference as a sufficient basis for social explanation or for an ethics that can be sensitive to the nature of fragmentary social discourses. An early feminist example of this approach can be seen in Stanley and Wise's critique of sociological research, which was directed against monolithic foundational assumptions made by both feminists and Marxists (Stanley and Wise, 1983). They asserted the importance of multiple social differences and discourses explicitly because of their own experience of them as lesbian (and thus minority) members of the women's movement of that time.

In one sense, there is no problem for a post-modernist in recognising the social differences in the case study in this chapter. There would be recognition of the different meanings, different perspectives and identities throughout, and that is what attracts Jane to this approach, as she herself has experienced, and continues to experience, changes in her own position. Indeed, the problem associated with a post-modernist position from an anti-oppressive perspective is that it is in danger of dissolving away the categories of social difference so thoroughly that there is hardly anything left except individuals with multiple changing identities situated in local contexts. Indeed, the categories of social division are themselves challenged by postmodernism as exclusionary devices which portray a false coherence.

The category of 'woman' for instance, upon which feminism has historically been based, ignores or downplays both the extraordinary variations between women, as well as some of the sexual and social overlaps between men and women, as in transgendered individuals or transvestites, for example. This is no small issue and has exercised feminist thinkers for many years: they have been well aware of the opening up of a chasm of social differences once the gender difference has been exposed (Ahmed,1998). It has also been an issue for lesbian feminists to destabilise notions of male and female, 'butch' and 'femme' (cf. McLaughlin, 2003, ch. 6). This tendency seeks to appreciate the variety of meanings as well as the variety of differences between people. Nevertheless, as many feminists have pointed out, not only is it a political necessity to critique categories of social difference, but it is also methodologically and politically important to also recognise continuing commonalities, and to retain the basic category of 'woman' (and equally other categories of subordinated and oppressed social groups) as an active subject in history, both individually and collectively, with an emancipatory project that is as yet only partially fulfilled.

It has taken hundreds of years for women to battle against being treated merely as the objects of male dominance in history. In particular, an anti-oppressive ethic, along with some contemporary feminists, will emphasise the importance of the material aspects of social division such as the unequal distribution of resources. It requires recognition of the importance of maintaining an analysis sensitive to the complexities that arise from specific social, historical and cultural variations, overlaps and interconnections, but also no less sensitive to the material, cultural and political inequalities between the major social divisions. There is therefore a need for the reappropriation of the concept of 'women' as a significant social category, in spite of the complex and contradictory experiences of and between women, and the theoretical objections of post-modernism to the categorisation of social groups. Stanley's initial awareness of the multiplicity of social difference (and the contribution of anti-foundationalist, post-modernist ideas towards it) did not prevent her from *also* asserting the importance of retrieving the category of 'woman' as a significant concept in history (Stanley, 1990). She recognises but critiques the implications of post-modernism in her advocacy of a 'fractured foundationalism' (Stanley and Wise, 1994) in which *both* the multiplicity of social difference and the significance of broad social categories are recognised.

Equally the struggle of gays and lesbians to be accepted has taken a long time to get to its present level of relative tolerance (at least in some countries) and there is in many ways still far to go. The central issues relating to sexuality therefore also need to be seen in terms of both multiple difference and also in relation to broad categories of social division in which enduring inequalities continue to have a significant impact on the lives of individuals and groups. The broad category of social class and its associated enduring inequalities would also be subject to the same approach – both accepting of the need to re-examine the enormous impact of broad class differentials in contemporary market societies and the significance of this in individual lives, but also aware of the multiplicity of class differences and their complex intersection with other social divisions.

Both of the major social divisions highlighted in the case study (relating to gender and sexuality) would impress themselves on Jane – possibly above all others, and the text makes it clear that she is aware of both, and aware of some of the ethical implications of her position resulting from these social differences (including in relation to her managers and peers, as well as to service users). However, there are other social differences that impinge on her actions, some of which relate to major social differences about which the text is relatively silent: but that does not mean they can be ignored. The narrative does indicate some of the issues resulting from age differences, but there is no mention of social class, ethnicity or disability. It cannot be assumed that these *or other* social differences are not highly significant variables in this scenario, and this is why it is important from an anti-oppressive ethical perspective to think through the potential implications arising from multiple social difference even if those differences are hard to assess. Using these broad categories may not sit well with a post-modern account of difference, but exploring the commonalities of inequality is just as important as being sensitive to the complexities.

An anti-oppressive approach to ethics questions the impact of differential membership of social divisions on the nature of the moral issues. It requires Jane to be aware of the commonalities as well as the differences between people, and that may require some ethical and political judgements about which are 'the differences that matter' (Ahmed, 2000) more than others. These differences will be structured by enduring inequalities between social divisions such as the major social divisions indicated in Chapter 1. Their overlapping and intersecting in peoples lives lead to complexities which have to be thoroughly taken into account. There remains a need to be responsible for one's own ethical actions in situations which may well be uncertain, but these reflections and actions are not outside society, or 'pre-social'. On the contrary, they are bounded by the historical impact of broad social divisions at the same time as they are refracted through the multiplicity of factors in individual lives, and need to be taken account of within an anti-oppressive framework.

2   Power dynamics

Jane is well aware of the fluid nature of power in this example, including her own varying deployment of it. An awareness of the ubiquitous and variable nature of power is one of the strengths of post-modernism and post-structuralism. Writers in these traditions have usefully criticised simplistic assumptions about power being held only by one half of a social division or by an individual over others. Social situations are more usually characterised by complexities in power relationships that alter in the space of time, sometimes very quickly. However, as feminists have pointed out, some individuals and some collective social groups simply do have a lot more power in most circumstances, than others. Jane's social work practice is going to be affected by who has most power to define situations, not only in the course of the group project, but also afterwards, when she may, for example, be called to account for her practice. Anti-oppressive ethics alert the worker to the variety and inequality of powers in social situations and their significant connotations for ethical action. It requires Jane to consider her own use of power; the powers that structure relevant law, resources, and policy, as well as the way the service user uses and experiences power and its absence.

3 Social systems

As in other chapters, various formal and informal systems, networks and relationships impinge on this ethical situation. Beccy's foster parents will be hoping that some good comes out of the groupwork. Colleagues in the agency have an interest in seeing it demonstrated that the groupwork is effective. The agency which employs Jane makes available various opportunities and has legitimate expectations, as well as constraining the actors through legal, economic and administrative systems. Beccy has both extended natural and foster families, and also peer groups at school and in the project to consider. Jane has her own family and friends to consider, and peers and colleagues at work. All these various social systems at their different levels provide the social context within which actors construct their lives. They have complex implications for anti-oppressive ethical possibilities, depending on which social systems are perceived to have relevance by the actors, and which may limit or facilitate action. Wider social systems will also impact on actors' lives sometimes regardless of their perceptions. Local and national authorities or voluntary organisations; local and national health and social service organisations; the legal and political systems all impinge on Jane. Anti-oppressive ethics require consideration of the impact of all these interacting social systems on the lives of individuals and question the roles of both actors and systems in the generation and resolution of moral issues. In the above example there are many types of system involved that would require serious consideration, not simply as an external restraint on the freedom of the actor, but as making appropriate claims on the ethical deliberation of the actor.

4 History and process

Post-modernists recognise the importance of process and change – especially discontinuity – in human social life, but the danger is to relativise it so much that it becomes less useful. Post-modern insistence on the specific local and changing historical nature of individual and collective lives has been an important antidote to static conceptions of people as belonging to fixed categories, and with fixed natures. People and groups change through time, and their histories are an influential and continuing part of the present. However, radical post-modern attitudes to history suggest that the past is indeed a different country, and in the present we can only create myths about it – narratives of our own lives that meet the needs of our present circumstances (Jenkins, 1995). Aspects of this argument are readily conceded by feminists, recognising the myths that dominant discourses have always spun about the past. Nevertheless, feminists are reluctant to concede that history is entirely reducible to present aspirations, or to disregard the painful realities that women have fought individually and collectively to overcome in various historical times (Stanley, 1990). Anti-oppressive ethics similarly requires an understanding of individual lives that is sensitive both to the mythic element of story-telling, and the material evidence of changing balances of power and resources. People's experiences of life are a critical resource for understanding both their uniqueness and their shared suffering and achievements. The history of groups and collectives, including organisations and wider social systems, are also important aspects of the conditions within which people live their lives. Appreciating these connections between the present and the past is a key factor in being able to understand the ethics of the present. An anti-oppressive approach to ethics adds a robust awareness of continuities as well as changes in social, family, organisational and personal lives to the post-modern emphasis on the variability and relativity of historical interpretation. Jane would need to be aware of both.

5   Reflexivity

Again, a post-modern position in ethics can be credited with offering insight into the importance of reflexivity in both practice and research, but tends to emphasise the local relative factors at the expense of commonalities which underpin shared identities. An anti-oppressive ethic similarly emphasises the importance of this concept, but interprets it in relation to the social location of the actor, in which the categories of social division play a significant role, as well as the local contingencies of place and time. This problematises the notion of interaction and dialogue between the actor and the 'other', because other people will almost certainly belong to different social divisions, and hearing across the social divisions can be very difficult. In this case we don't know much about the ethnic and social class background of Jane and Beccy, but the differences of age and social position are already significant and are clearly contributing to communications difficulties. Neither do we know about any hidden disabilities, and Jane's sexuality may either facilitate or hinder their interaction (or both) depending on Beccy's feelings and the quality of Jane's reflexive self-awareness. Anti-oppressive ethical perspectives require the interrogation of the worker's social position, behaviour, experience and motives, in relation to the service users' perspectives and the dialogue between them. Unlike some post-modernisms it does so with an awareness of the more distant and common, *as well as* local and variable factors which condition the discourse and understanding of both parties.

AUTHORS' PERSPECTIVES: EXPERIENCING SOCIAL DIFFERENCES

The case study is discussed above in terms of a worker influenced by post-modern ideas about social work. The ethical demands of post-modernism imply that the moral actor can and should be a critic of all social and political systems, customs and policies. This is an attractive stance providing a humanistic ethical standpoint as a buttress against bureaucratic, technological and social pressures, especially when managerialism can sometimes veer towards totalitarianism (Nellis, 2000). Both authors can appreciate the value of this approach but both are also aware of the reality for them of existing in a social world that conditions their values, rightly and wrongly, and the ethical issues would be different for each of us.

It is evident that Beccy is feeling a level of distress in the group which she has channelled into confronting Jane. If either of us were in Jane's position we would be very concerned that we had not been sensitive to the fact that Beccy was increasingly finding it difficult to function in the group and relate to us – but in socially different ways. A black woman would have to seriously consider if Beccy's behaviour is racially motivated. Is she finding it difficult to cope with someone who is black having power and authority? It is important to ensure that as a worker you are attuned to the various responses of the individuals within the group and that each member feels valued and listened to. Groupwork is a very demanding area of practice and requires a range of skills as well as emotional alertness so that the needs of the individual are not subsumed within the group. A male social worker would have had to consider carefully very different issues in relation to whether he had clearly set professional boundaries between himself and this young woman – as indeed would Jane in the case study. The reactions of the young women will be conditioned by age, gender, sexuality, position in the group and other factors, and a male presence in this group would obviously have needed careful thinking about before it began.

In critically reflecting on the situation we would be asking a number of questions: have we managed to maintain personal and professional boundaries? Did we unknowingly transgress the emotional and physical boundaries of group members and in particular Beccy's boundaries? How aware are we of the range of feelings, emotions and behaviours of all the group members? Discussing sensitive topic areas will produce a range of reactions in people – some of these reactions may be obvious, immediate and tangible whilst others may not be so concretely expressed. How competent are we to manage the reactions within this group? Have we allowed some individuals to express themselves more freely because they did so in a way that we found acceptable and manageable? Our own sexuality and socially different life experiences need to be examined in the light of the stories that we hear, and the reactions we are seeing. We would want to make sure Beccy was safe, and we would also want to respect her as a young woman, but we would take into account the above considerations about our own reactions, as well as our accountability to parents and to the agency before deciding what for us would be the right thing to do.

CHAPTER SUMMARY

In this chapter we have looked at the problems that can arise for a social worker who is trying to act ethically in a difficult situation in which her own identity and judgement are very much at stake. We have argued that anti-oppressive concepts help to deepen the post-modern critique, so that it maintains a clear connection to real material issues of power and inequality.

FURTHER READING

Baumann, Z. (2000) 'Am I My Brother's Keeper?'. A brief original account of post-modernist ethics specifically applied to social work.

Briskman, L. and Noble, C. (1999) 'Social Work Ethics: Embracing Diversity'. A paper suggesting that post-modern ethics in social work helps to deal with diverse perspectives.

Hugman, R. (2003) 'Professional Values and Ethics in Social Work: Reconsidering Postmodernism?'. A defence of post-modernism in social work ethics.

Lloyd, M. (1997) 'Foucault's Ethics and Politics: A Strategy for Feminism?' A feminist critique of Foucault with specific reference to ethics.

Norman, R. (1998) *The Moral Philosophers: An Introduction to Ethics.* This introductory text has a chapter on Nietzsche explaining the position of one of the precursors of post-modernism in ethics.

Smart, B. (2000) 'Sociology, Morality and Ethics: On Being with Others'. A brief account of the post-modern ethics of Levinas and Baumann, together with a study of earlier sociological accounts of ethics in Durkheim and Simmel.

Chapter 8

Feminist Relational Ethics and Anti-Oppressive Concepts

INTRODUCTION

Feminist relational ethics is a rapidly developing field of ethical theory that has emerged from the second women's movement of the late twentieth century. In relation to other ethical theories discussed in this book it is a very recent development. Virtue theory has also been recently revived but can trace its origins back to the Greeks. Other ethical theories also have long pedigrees. Whilst earlier women writers have had concerns about values and politics (famously in the case of Mary Wollstonecraft), the development of a body of work by a range of women interested in a feminist approach to ethics is a new and significant advance, especially for social work. Social work is one of the gender-segregated professions (with significant variations within and between countries) – like nursing and primary school teaching where women's alleged particular 'natural' talent for caring and nurturing is given expression. The role of women within social work has historically been central and remains so today, both on the provider side, and for service users and carers: they are the dominant social group giving and receiving care, and the relevance of feminist ideas has been well discussed by feminist social work authors (Dominelli, 2002b; Graham, 2002). Given that social work is thus socially constituted it is (perhaps) surprising that in the codes of ethics the importance of concepts relating to care and nurturing play only a small part. It is hardly referred to at all in the international ethical code for social workers published in 2004, where it is simply asserted that 'Social workers should be *concerned* with the whole person' (IFSW, 2004, Principle 4.1.3, our italics). It appears to be largely taken for granted that (mainly) female social workers will in fact care about service users, and be empathetic and compassionate towards their needs.

In this chapter we will use a case study to examine feminist ethics. However, we have referred in the title of the chapter to 'feminist relational ethics' because we wish to avoid what we see as a linguistic trap of associating feminist ethics with the 'ethics of care', despite the fact that the latter phrase is widely used, and for good reasons still thought of as synonymous with feminist ethics (e.g. Held, 2006). We take the view that feminist ethics is about much more than care (in its everyday usage) and the phrase, although understandable as a significant element in feminist thinking, is potentially misleading and liable to be used stereotypically. We think that feminist ethics has a lot to contribute to an anti-oppressive approach to ethics in professional social work practice, and in this final case study we will be looking at all the key concepts of an anti-oppressive approach to ethics to show how well they are exemplified in feminist ethical discussions.

The range of writing on ethics from a feminist perspective in recent years has been very wide, and we can only sketch out an overall view of some of the most common features of feminist writers in this area. We aim to present the main features in relation to the case study, and the commonalities with anti-oppressive ethics will become apparent. The differences will also be discussed. However, it has been suggested that there is little in common between feminist ethics except the broad aim of eliminating as much inequality between the genders as possible. Tong describes several types of feminist approaches to ethics, including the 'feminine', the maternal, lesbian, multicultural, liberal, psychoanalytical, cultural, global, ecofeminist and Marxist feminist, and there is thus little that can be described as *the* feminist perspective (Tong, 2003). Despite this variety, Tong concedes some commonalities entailed by a feminist ethical position such as the need to work and discuss within and between feminists, as well as with other social groups, to achieve change in the world that might alleviate gender inequalities for as many women as possible, whilst recognising the sometimes contradictory effects of policy on differing groups of women.

Feminist ethicists have laid much emphasis upon this social, relational context of ethics. The notion of the individual facing the world in a public context is so obviously male in its connotations, and women have understandably pointed out that all ethics and values are first nurtured within the family where women usually play a critical, but undervalued, patronised and oppressed role. Although the (now) classic work of Gilligan (1982) has been widely discussed and criticised, its effect (discussed below) has been important in requiring all subsequent writers on ethics to seriously consider the degree to which ethics needs to be seen in a broader, more inclusive context, and initiating a debate in social work about how the feminist insight into the importance of the relational aspects of ethics should best be understood (Clifford, 2002). The implication is that social workers have to develop skills of listening; negotiation and advocacy, networking across micro- and macro-social and organisational systems if 'relational autonomy' is to be progressed effectively. It cannot be solely the result of isolated individuals making rational decisions (nor indeed of private individuals acting in a caring, compassionate way): it is characteristically a dialogical process involving more than one or two people, within a social setting that involves difference, power and inequality. However, it is dangerous to assume that women's traditional caring roles by themselves must form the basis of such a commonality, if that ties women stereotypically to responsibilities from which they are not able to escape in sexist societies. We begin by describing some key aspects of the arguments in favour of care as a basic ethical concept in a feminist perspective. We then broaden this out into a feminist relational ethics that draws on concepts of care, justice, and discourse, and consider a case study in the light of these ethics.

THE ETHICS OF 'CARE'

Some contributions to ethics have been made in the self-conscious, explicit knowledge that they are made from a particular rather than a universal perspective – one which seeks to acknowledge the historic and continuing oppression of women. In her influential book *In A Different Voice: Psychological Theory and Women's Development* (1982) Carol Gilligan argued that women typically reason differently from men about moral issues. The positive contribution of Gilligan to an understanding of moral development in women is in striking contrast with the fact that 'Almost every canonised philosopher up to the 20th century has explicitly held that women are lesser . . . moral agents' (Walker, 1998, p20). The starting point for Gilligan's work was an examination of the work of Lawrence Kohlberg on moral development in children. He identified 'stages' in moral development, which could be analysed by a consideration of the responses children gave to questions about moral dilemmas. In fact, Kohlberg wanted to say that a specifically moral framework of reasoning was being attained as children grew into maturity. Moral dilemmas were resolved by an appeal to universal rules and principles – an understanding of morality based on traditional ethics such as Kant's. However, Gilligan's psychological research indicated that there were often differences between how women and girls approached ethical issues when compared with the ways that men and boys resolved such issues. A simple example of this is given in the case study of two children, Jake and Amy.

CASE STUDY: JAKE AND AMY

Jake and Amy were asked to respond to an ethical dilemma. A man called Heinz has a wife who is dying, but he cannot afford the medicine. Should he steal the medicine in order to save his wife's life? Jake's view is that Heinz *should* steal the drug, and he justifies his answer in relation to principles about saving life, and about stealing. Amy, however, suggested that Heinz should go and talk to the druggist and to his wife and see if they could not find some solution to the problem. Whereas Jake sees the situation as needing logical reference to abstract systems of law and ethics, Amy, Gilligan suggests, sees a need for mediation through discussion: 'a narrative of relationships that extends over time' (Gilligan, 1982, p28).

There have been many criticisms of the assumption that all women will share a common approach to ethics, but Gilligan was not the only person to suggest that male-oriented understandings of morality will be bound to misrepresent women's moral reasoning and set up a typically male pattern of moral reasoning as a standard against which to judge women to be deficient. Noddings (1984), for example, argues that a morality based on rules or principles is in itself inadequate, and that it does not capture what is distinctive or typical about female thinking. It cannot be a coincidence that these views were expressed after the Women's Movement of the 1970s. Feminists have pointed out that one of the commonalities of most ethical theorists up to the twentieth century and beyond has been that their theories 'mirror spheres of activity . . . associated with socially advantaged men' (Walker, 1998, p20). On the other side of this coin, the 'neglect of caring in the discourse of conventional moral philosophy is continuous with and provides support for the exclusion of experiences, interests, needs and desires characteristically associated with women' (Bowden, 1997, p185).

Gilligan set out a distinction between the typically male moral thinking which she regards as a *justice* perspective, as against a female view of moral thinking which she calls the *care* perspective (see diagram below). Typically, the 'justice' perspective draws on Kantian and utilitarian ethics, which can both be described in the 'justice' terms suggested below. Equally clearly the diametric opposition between these two categories sets up a stereotypical contrast which is not a useful basis for a feminist relational ethics. More recent feminists ethicists have taken a much more nuanced approach than this, but it is useful explanatory tool to begin with.

The Amy and Jake diagram is rooted in the view that the main traditions of ethics are based on common assumptions that represent right or 'justice' for men. These consist of a mixture of manly virtues, such as courage, rationality, individual responsibility and judgement, with another set of assumptions for women that are 'natural' rather than considered or chosen, including the usual stereotypes: tenderness, docility, innocence, domestic competence – and caring. However, the ethics of care takes women's concerns very positively and argues that they should be the central concern of ethical thinking – not peripheral or excluded as in the past. After all, it is argued, ethical issues do not emerge in the abstract, but in the realities of daily life such as in sexual relationships, parenting, friendships, and work. Consequently women have developed a different approach to moral reasoning: 'Whereas women, typically relying on a narrative mode of reflection, have an immediacy of moral response that is person- and situation-specific, men typically deliberate according to universal principles and abstract from concrete details about particular persons' (Porter, 1999, p4). Personal experience within a situated context related to time and place is central to feminist ethics.

Amy and Jake: Gilligan's Early Contrast between the 'Ethics of Care' and the 'Ethics of Justice'

	Characteristics	Conflicting Priorities	Ethical Practice
ETHICS OF 'CARE'	Specific nurturing practices, and gendered relationships. Particular social and historical contexts	Responsibilities to specific others versus Responsibilities to wider social groups	Meeting needs of the vulnerable through discussion trust and compassion
ETHICS OF 'JUSTICE'	General, universal, abstract and impartial principles such as individual autonomy	The individual's rights versus the rights of any other individual	Fairness between individual claims Rational resolution of competing rights and duties

Source: adapted from Porter (1999).

In practice, an ethic of caring places emphasis on the process of caring, seen as: 'an activity that includes everything we do to maintain, continue and repair our "world" so that we can live in it as well as possible' (Sevenhuijsen, 2003, p184). The same author, summarising recent ethics of care positions, argues that there are four basic dimensions of care, to which there are four corresponding values:

1 *Caring about*, recognising the need for care, for which the corresponding value is *attentiveness*.
2 *Taking care*, for which the corresponding value is the willingness and capacity to take *responsibility*.
3 *Care-giving*, for which the corresponding value is *competence* and the resources for caring in relation to what is needed.
4 *Care-receiving* for which the corresponding value is the *responsiveness* to ensure the care-receiver interacts well with the care-giver (Sevenhuijsen, 2003, p184).

One of the implications of this approach to ethics has been the suggestion that it can improve the practice of individual professionals involved in welfare provision – that the types of power inequality between professional and client can be reduced by care practices which focus on empathy, reciprocity and emotional connection (Porter, 1999, p67). Koehn argues that the specific concerns of a 'female' or 'feminist' ethic are akin to professional ethics in (for example) health care in the attempt to: 'derive guidelines for action from the character or essence of a single activity or virtue (e.g. care or trust)' (Koehn, 1998, p10). We have discussed this as a possibility in Chapter 5 above in relation to 'virtue ethics'. The danger of adopting such a positive approach to 'feminine' virtues is that it locks women into caring roles in the family as well as in the community, letting men off the hook – a form of compulsory caring that feminists have long argued to be the kind of caring demanded by patriarchal attitudes towards women.

KEY IDEAS

'Care' and 'compulsory altruism'
How far is caring a neglected but basic part of all ethical experience OR is it more a matter of 'compulsory altruism' mainly expected of women in sexist societies?

The 'personal' and the 'political'
How far is personal and private life the primary moral sphere where ethical behaviour
is nurtured and enacted, AND how far is it a 'political' arena in itself, and in dynamic
interaction with wider social, cultural and political systems?

FEMINIST RELATIONAL ETHICS

Feminists quickly realised that despite the importance of Gilligan's argument, and others like it, locking women uncritically into an 'ethics of care' was potentially a dangerous move, akin to stereotypical assumptions about women's role in society. It retains expectations that most roles in health and welfare, paid and unpaid, are carried out by women, and focuses on individual attributes of care without considering the wider aspects of the way arrangements for care and welfare are structured by the political and social divisions of society at large. The earlier 'ethics of care' is thus partly superseded (or at least further developed) in contemporary feminist ethical theory, which nevertheless takes seriously the importance of arguments about 'care' in the light of the history of male dominance of ethical theory, and the consequent neglect of care, and the 'private' areas of life where ethical relationships are developed – *and* where 'political' issues of justice are equally important.

Whilst Koehn wishes to develop a feminist ethic which can go beyond an ethics of care, she usefully sketches out the (then) existing parameters of feminist concerns in a way which illustrates the relevance of feminist ethics to professional social work concerns, and contrasting it with traditional male theories. She identifies six characteristics of women-oriented ethics as a baseline, summarising discussions since Gilligan. In Koehn's view this discourse emphasises:

1   the relational self, as against the individualist, ahistorical self;
2   a benevolent concern for the vulnerable (drawing on the model of the family);
3   the publicness of the private: the significance of intimate relations of caring;
4   the importance and the value of difference rather than consistency;
5   imaginative discourse, making conversants equal participants, rather than deductive reasoning;
6   power differences in historically situated circumstances, and making a difference by changing that world (Koehn, 1998, p5).

However, this baseline itself represents a move away from the simplistic contrast between a female ethics of care and a male ethics of justice. Another author expresses the concern that:

> there is a desire to find a way forward out of the dilemma: how to value ethical principles associated with caring, without romanticizing experiences of care, that justify the seclusion of women in the private sphere.
> (McLaughlin, 2003, p85)

There have been some key issues which have been discussed in varying degrees by recent feminist ethical and social theorists in relation to this question.

One general issue concerns the positive acceptance of uncertainty, and the tentative nature of its resolution in situated circumstances. One recent feminist ethicist recognises the danger of simply presenting an alternative in the grand theory tradition, as 'yet another universal and unitary moral concept' (Bowden, 1997, p2). She defends 'gender sensitive ethics' but 'advocates looking at caring from different angles, not trying to catch all the "facts" of the matter in a single statement' (Bowden, 1997, p20). Perhaps a more clearly sociological sense of uncertainty is the contribution of black women to an autobiographical sense of indeterminacy, drawing not primarily on post-modern roots, but on their distinctive feminist awareness of multiple difference and complexity in their own lives. British black feminists, for example, have recognised for a long time the complexity of social positioning, because in their own lives they have been acutely aware of the multiple and overlapping contradictions of social difference (hooks, 1982). Black women have written specifically about the 'uncertainty' of their own identities, linking ethics and sociology in their own autobiographical awareness of social differences within themselves and the implications that this has for their own social practice (Mirza, 1997). The links between the post-modernist celebration of indeterminacy and undecidability, and the perspectives of 'hybrid' women of 'mixed race' background are made explicit and the terms are reappropriated in a way that makes a positive ethical and political space for themselves (Ifekwunigwe, 1997, pp130–1). Such women celebrate the uncertainty of their identity and the richness of their heritage(s), making clear the connections between the ethics and sociology of personal identity within a complex social world. There is no assumption that one grand theory of ethics will meet all the requirements of such various and shifting positions, but there is an attempt to grasp some of the key elements as they are currently understood. This is exemplified in Graham's attempt to describe a black feminist ethics drawing on specific African themes, yet offering ethical insights from which others can draw (Graham, 2007).

An even more important move is to shift the focus away from caring relationships in the family. 'Ethics of care' arguments which concentrate solely on such relationships ignore the range of unjust social relationships within wider society, and the interconnections between private and public spheres. Gilligan's disciplinary area of psychology is complemented with a broader concern with the sociological parameters of behaviour. In particular, the existence of social divisions involving domination and subordination becomes more central to their thinking: the existence of 'caring' between strangers is important in wider society, and the state's role in providing or facilitating care also comes into the picture. This embeddedness of morality in a divided and unequal social world is a critical issue which distinguishes contemporary feminist ethics: 'what we need in order to understand specifically moral judgements or principles goes beyond specifically moral matters. We need to understand a social world' (Walker, 1998, p203). It has equally been a concern of feminist social workers to be interested in *both* care and justice in an unequal social world (e.g. Lynn, 1999).

A related aspect of recent feminist contributions to ethics is the attempt to take seriously the *range* of ethical principles, combining consideration of the ethics of caring with reassessment of principles of justice and respect. Some feminist ethics has *not* wanted to rely solely on a 'female' vision of 'caring' as the basis for personal behaviour, precisely because this altruistic and admirable quality is itself partly tainted by its association with stereotypical expectations of women. It is also a quality that can disguise the elements of control that so easily co-exist with caring. It is therefore equally important for feminists to draw also on notions of justice and autonomy, so that women and other dominated social groups can fully justify acting for themselves to achieve equality, rather than for ever be expected to provide models of consideration for others, which leads to the sacrifice of their own interests and self-respect. The latter strategy would leave them wide open to exploitation by dominant social groups. It would be ill-advised for social workers to take on board a feminist ethic of care which would leave them in a (traditionally) vulnerable position within their own relationships and organisations. Feminists therefore also want to draw upon the older concepts of morality such as Kantian and utilitarian theories – but they need to be 're-figured' within a feminist framework. This is exemplified in

Chapter 3 above where the concept of autonomy implicit in the rule of consent is reinterpreted in the feminist terms of 'relational autonomy' (Mackenzie and Stoljar, 2000). It is also one of the principles behind this book in its review of a number of classic and contemporary theories, in which ideas are reassessed in the interests of oppressed social divisions – including women.

However, exactly how feminist ethics related to older ethical concepts is a matter for continuing debate, and at least one recent feminist author continues to advocate the concept of caring as an organising ethical concept which is more fundamental than other ethical concepts precisely because it is based on a universal experience of nurturing that *all* must pass through in the process of (and before) becoming an autonomous, morally responsible adult (Held, 2006). However, she is also quite clear that the earlier narrower ideas about the ethics of care have been overtaken or further developed (Held, 2006, p22). She holds that other ethical concepts are not reducible to caring, and need to be attended to as appropriately relevant in their own fields. She is also well aware of the centrality of 'relational' ethics for feminist thinking, including both at its heart in the relationships of nurturing and also in wider social contexts, including, she argues, global arenas (Held, 2006, pp154–68). Caring is not simply about the virtues of care, trust and empathy: 'the heart of what goes on in practises of caring . . . is that they are caring *relations*' (Held, 2006, p33, original emphasis).

The following case study is discussed in terms of feminist relational ethics, drawing on Koehn's list of the characteristics of a woman-oriented ethics, but taking account of the re-figuring of other ethical concepts necessary for a feminist relational ethics. It will draw into consideration themes of justice, respect and virtue as well as caring. In particular we will demonstrate how all the key anti-oppressive concepts we listed in Chapter 1 are drawn into play in feminist relational ethics.

CASE STUDY: FEMINIST RELATIONAL ETHICS – SHEILA'S DILEMMA

Student social worker Carole was enjoying her placement at the SureThing Support Agency. It is hard work and colleagues are stretched to provide support for difficult teenagers with a variety of problems including homelessness, criminal behaviour, and drug and alcohol misuse. They are often young people with abusive past experiences, and can be violent or withdrawn. She is expected to work with Bob, an experienced social worker who specialises in work with drug abusers. He is very affable and gets on well with service users, but Carole becomes aware that he has been a drug user in the past. Carole is allocated some young women with which to work under his supervision, but after working with them for some weeks, is unpleasantly surprised to hear from a service user, Tina, that she has supplied Bob with heroin, and seemed to expect Carole to be interested too. Carole challenges Bob with this information, and although he derides Tina's story he does not actually deny it, but continues to give the impression that understanding and using drugs are not unconnected. He emphasises the importance of maintaining credibility and good relationships with young people, claiming that this often requires unconventional approaches.

Carole knows that the agency policy is that staff should avoid the use of drugs. She is frightened of the consequences for herself if she adheres to agency policy and reports what she has seen and heard. However, she feels that Bob is undermining her work and transgressing agency policy, harming rather than helping the service user. She plucks up her courage and goes to see the manager Sheila, who is faced with a difficult problem. Bob is one of her most experienced workers, and Carole is a temporary student. She knows about Bob's past, but has a responsibility for maintaining the reputation of the agency and protecting service users. She does not want to lose someone who has been a valuable worker, but must consider the possibility of a disciplinary hearing.

DISCUSSION

Sheila's position

The case study raises difficult issues in an organisational setting where personal and organisational ethics and politics come into play – a typical kind of scenario with which social workers have to contend. In this case we are looking at the situation from the perspective of the line manager Sheila, though the ethical options for Carole also raise some difficult issues for her. In terms of agency policy there is a need to collect evidence, and if sufficient to take a disciplinary course of action. Often the complications arise from interpreting the evidence and at the same time being pressed to take action: the political and ethical are mixed at micro- as well as macro-social levels.

The caring and nurturing of workers and service users is equally a responsibility for Sheila. Yet so is the need for justice, and the consideration of the various kinds of power that run through this scenario. Her own accountability to the organisation is underlined by the senior position she holds, yet she also has professional and personal allegiances and responsibilities towards the people involved and the wider social groups for which the agency represents a significant social service. Given the hierarchical nature of the organisational structure, and the legal and policy remit of the agency it would be easier for Sheila to justify from a Kantian basis a strict application of the rules. The evidence might be arguable, but the appearance of wrongdoing is in conflict with the job description and role for which the employee has contracted himself. To apply the rules strictly would be to owe the employee the respect he deserves as a rational person who has made a choice – one which conflicts with the promises he had earlier given when agreeing to the terms of the contract. Alternatively, she might take a Utilitarian position which could justify the possible breaking of rules, on the grounds that it does not appear to be harming the service user (who apparently takes the initiative in the transaction involved), and in the long run (from her previous experience of the worker) there are good reasons for believing that his unorthodox methods do sometimes maximise good outcomes.

Issues of justice also appear to be complicated, especially if there is any suggestion that the service user is not taking the initiative, but is being subtly coerced, and not sufficiently supported or protected. There are also issues of fairness in relation to the employee's position, especially if his previous record is good, and also justice in the larger sense towards the wider community of drug users who need a continuing viable service, and the wider public whose aims would appear to be to minimise the harm that drug and alcohol use is perceived to do. Sheila is certainly in a position to take responsibility for her actions here – though she could, if she chose, simply rely on the rules, or send the case to a senior manager to decide. However, despite her own management position she has professional and personal values, and would wish to express her own sense of integrity and probity in taking action which she herself can own. In other words she is conscious of a range of ethical concepts as having relevance to the case, and would want to act in accordance with her feminist values if she can.

KEY ANTI-OPPRESSIVE CONCEPTS AND FEMINIST RELATIONAL ETHICS

Reflexivity, difference and power

Sheila is well aware of her position as a manager and the expectations of the agency that she will ensure that the organisational rules are followed and that its reputation and effectiveness are maintained. However, she will also be aware of several other key issues about herself – that she has differing membership of the social divisions from the individuals with which she has to relate in order to settle this disputed situation. For example, she is aware of the gender difference between herself and the male employee – one which can raise issues of power and control. She has superior status within the organisation, but the drugs worker has a repertoire of male advantages that can be used against her, especially in view of the mainly male senior management, and the informal networks that link this worker to senior staff.

There is also the fact that there is a mainly male clientele, and this worker's insider knowledge of that culture can be used against her. There are other gender issues, but there are also other power and social divisions issues in relation to Tina the service user and Carole the student social worker. Sheila knows that her economic and organisational position and her older age will inhibit her communication with both of them, who inevitably will see her as a potential threat – an older middle-class white woman who has power to make decisions that will significantly affect them. This might be exacerbated for either Tina or Carole if there were other cross-cutting social divisions involved. Sheila also knows that her own power has its limitations, and her actions will be weighed differently by the differing parties to whom she is accountable. As a service user Tina would appear to be particularly vulnerable to the power of Bob and Sheila. Carole's completion of her placement and her course may also be affected.

CARING, DIALOGUE, SOCIAL NETWORKS, HISTORY AND PROCESS

The social networks and systems that influence the lives of the individuals involved are known to Sheila from an agency perspective. This includes her knowledge of whatever information is on file about the service user, the worker or the student. In addition to her own knowledge and experience of them, she can also draw on the knowledge of colleagues, whose histories in the agency may be influential in relation to Bob and Sheila. She will have already been engaged in a process of dialogue with the various people involved, and the reporting of this incident will be set within this continuing discussion. Attending to what colleagues, employees and service users are saying with an empathetic ear is a key aspect of relational feminist ethics, and it relates to key anti-oppressive concepts. Understanding the values and personal identities of those involved requires at least some grasp of their specific personal histories, and current situation. Bob's history of involvement with drugs and his record of service to the agency and any previous incidents might need to be reviewed – as would the histories of others involved, including Sheila's own history of dealing with such issues as a worker and manager. This is a process of continuous assessment which may be deliberately heightened in periods of crisis when allegations such as Carole's are made. Awareness of the impact of formal and informal social systems on people's lives and an ability to 'hear' across the social divisions needs to take account of the historical and contemporary social influences. Armed with this approach, Sheila can attempt to investigate, reaching a position where she has a reasonably good grasp of what has happened and what should be done, but aware of the limitations of her own social position. She cannot assume that she has reached the 'truth' of the situation and necessarily has to reach her own conclusions in the light of her own commitment and character. However, what she has done is to address the personal and social dynamics of the situation in which she finds herself and demonstrate that she is concerned equally with justice, care and difference, considered across a range of personal, organisational and public accountabilities.

The final outcome would depend on the details that were uncovered in the process of investigation, and could not be definitively predicted on the basis of the above narrative sketch.

FEMINIST ETHICS AND ANTI-OPPRESSIVE ETHICS

It is important to qualify the above brief description of key points in feminist ethics. First, it should be obvious that this is a simplified interpretation of a large body of writing by feminist moral, social and political theorists, which attempts to extract some common themes, but does not reflect the richness of their work. Secondly, the above description makes little attempt to distinguish between various feminist positions apart from indicating the historical development of feminist ethics from the ethics of care. It therefore does little justice to the differences between feminist theorists, which we anticipate will continue, as within any 'body' of theoretical literature, as it develops and changes (see Porter, 1999, pp16–18, and McLaughlin, 2003).

The relationship between feminist ethics and anti-oppressive social work ethics is very close as far as we are concerned. We would argue that feminist ethics, whilst drawing on its roots in the second women's movement, has developed to a point where it is able to offer a series of critical insights into ethics which make a lot of sense for many oppressed groups, and can make an important contribution to social work (cf. Clifford, 2002; Orme, 2002; Parton, 2003). However, the idea of a distinctive range of concerns for women remains important: 'while non-feminist philosophers . . . tend to emphasise the diversity of goods . . . feminists draw attention to diversities of social positions, stations or identities constituted by unshared and unequal powers within communities' (Walker, 1998, p27). These diversities and inequalities are clearly pertinent to the whole range of oppressed social groups with variations relating to their specific configurations and histories. We would therefore contend that any anti-oppressive ethics must draw on recent feminist ethical theorists. It does not mean that particular concepts will always be equally applicable. It does not mean that this approach should be regarded as a grand theory of ethics which encompasses all possibilities. It leaves all the issues up for further discussion and development, but it does provide a defensible basis for thinking through anti-oppressive issues in a way that is highly relevant to social work, and to the interpretation and application of international ethical codes and other codes of practice to which social workers are now required to adhere.

AUTHORS' PERSPECTIVES: DIFFERENTIAL POWERS IN THE CASE STUDY

Sheila's case is different from other cases in this book in that it is set in the context of someone who has management as well as case responsibilities. However, the ethical issues involved in 'management' are not totally different from the accountability issues for any social worker in any hierarchical organisation. There are of course formal differences in relation to job descriptions and responsibilities, and equally important differences in relation to the informal social and political expectations of managers, and their relationships with other managers in the hierarchy.

We have both had some limited experience of management roles, but not of its higher echelons. We have found it to be a pressured environment in which gender is a significant variable (cf. Halford and Leonard, 2001). However, ethnicity and class are also key issues in management – whilst other social divisions are often hidden or ignored, given the 'male, middle-class, white, manager' stereotype – a generalisation that has many exceptions, but the continuing existence of the 'glass ceiling' and other related gender issues (particularly harassment and bullying, and inequalities of pay) demonstrates is still a major aspect of contemporary bureaucracies. This means that we would each have to guard against reactions that would lead us to collude with unjustifiable gendered approaches.

Would a male manager be more likely to collude with the male employee, assuming a relaxed attitude to apparent rule-breaking on the utilitarian grounds that no one is harmed and the eventual outcome is likely to be to the benefit of the organisation as a whole given this employee's apparent past good record? Would a male manager be too confident of male understanding of his rationale and of his judgement? Would he empathise sufficiently with the vulnerability of the female service user? Would a female manager feel less sure of her position as manager in a male dominated bureaucracy and need to demonstrate strict adherence to agency policy without considering sufficiently the need to engage in discussion? But would going down a procedural route polarise positions and hence decrease the relational aspects of interpersonal communications which a feminist relational ethics would support? Might she tend to rely too quickly on the rules, given that the female service user is clearly vulnerable, with the potential for undisclosed abuse? We would both need from our different starting positions to think reflexively about our own perspectives, and consider alternative possibilities. It would be important to facilitate discussion with those involved, and a male manager would need to reflect on his ability to listen and 'hear' the service user. It might be an issue that raised agency policies on harassment or abuse, and involve questioning whether the agency had adequate support in place to enable service users to complain. The female manager might have the opposite difficulty – how could she get her senior management to accept her concerns about the vulnerability of a service user to an established worker, and would being a black female manager make this more difficult? How well could she hear the concerns of this male worker, and would he share his concerns with her? How good would her own support networks be – across *both* gender and ethnic lines? For both of us the task of weighing up issues of justice and care, combining them with autonomy and integrity would require thorough investigation of both service-user and employee rights and responsibilities in relation to our own. A feminist reflexive and relational ethic would make us consider carefully and, we think, productively about these issues in relation to our own social locations and identities.

In addition to our different membership of social divisions we would need to consider our location within a professional bureaucracy, and its relative power *vis-à-vis* other professions – as well as towards service users and carers. This would be a complex issue, especially in relation to health professionals in a multi-professional drugs agency, partly depending on their insistence on a 'medical model' that could be a potential source of misunderstanding, and partly depending on the precise way their line managers invoked professional rules of behaviour when dealing with drug users. In addition, our individual membership of social divisions would interact in different ways with those of the particular professionals we met.

On the other hand, our own social work management would be expecting us to process service-user requests efficiently in the light of service policies and priorities. We would feel under some pressure from all directions, and in our thinking we would need to take into account, but go beyond Kantian ethical considerations. We have multiple concerns about ethical choice that a simple universal rule would not easily resolve. The process of reaching an anti-oppressive ethical decision would require us to pay a lot of attention to our own particular social location, the differing kinds and levels of powers involved, including our own personal and agency powers, and their impact on the situation. In the end we would need to make an ethical and a political decision about which powers needed to be positively used, and which reinforced or resisted, in dialogue with the individuals involved, and mindful of the vulnerability of the least powerful both to ourselves and to the system.

CHAPTER SUMMARY

In this chapter we have described the evolution of feminist relational ethics from the ethics of care, and have argued that more recent feminist relational ethics are supportive of an anti-oppressive position. We examined a case study and showed how feminist relational ethics raised questions of great importance from an anti-oppressive perspective.

FURTHER READING

Clifford, D.J. (2002), 'Resolving Uncertainties? The Contribution of Some Recent Feminist Ethical Theory to the Social Professions'. This paper argues that feminist ethics makes an important contribution.

Edwards, R.and Mauthner, M. (2002) 'Ethics and Feminist Research: Theory and Practice'. A study of feminist ethics in relation to research issues.

Held, V. (2006) *The Ethics of Care: Personal, Political and Global*. A recent attempt to summarise the development of feminist ethical theorising in relation to the central concept of care.

McLaughlin, J. (2003) *Feminist Social and Political Theory*, chapter 3. A summary of recent work in feminist ethics.

Orme, J. (2002) 'Social Work: Gender, Care and Justice'. A summary of the contribution of feminist ethics to social work, with special reference to community care.

Parton, N. (2003) 'Rethinking Professional Practice: The Contributions of Social Constructionism and the Feminist "Ethics of Care"'. A paper which argues that feminist ethics of care and post-modern ethics both make a contribution to contemporary social work.

Chapter 9

Anti-Oppressive Ethics and Good Practice

In this chapter we will offer an anti-oppressive approach for reflecting on ethical issues, and practising as ethically as possible. The approach offered is therefore in the spirit of a *framework* (Hugman, 2005) to facilitate reflection and action, rather than a prescriptive set of rules. We aim to offer assistance in both reflecting on and making ethical judgements, and/or decisions in the face of ethical problems, issues and dilemmas (Banks and Williams, 2005). Additionally we intend this approach to assist in the evaluation of social situations where none of these concerns are explicit, in support of competent, proactive and reflective professional practice. We do not think that it is – or ever will be – possible to reach absolutely certain conclusions that will always be applicable. This guidance is not presented as an absolutist approach to ethics, capable of explaining or prescribing everything. Nevertheless, as with any attempt to argue for a particular approach to understanding personal and social values, there are obvious and explicit commitments in the way we have drawn this framework – as already indicated in Chapter 1.

ETHICAL AND POLITICAL AWARENESS IN PROFESSIONAL PRACTICE: AN ANTI-OPPRESSIVE APPROACH

McAuliffe and Chenoweth (2008) suggest that there are three broad approaches to frameworks that guide ethics in professional practice: a rational or process approach usually involving a stepwise model for logical consideration of ethical principles; a cultural model that attempts to provide greater consideration of transcultural issues; and a 'reflection' framework that prioritises the intuitive and reflexive aspects of ethical decision-making. However, their discussion is in the context of helping to make ethical *decisions,* especially where ethical dilemmas are in evidence, when different principles clash. Most commonly guidance for ethics in social work practice (and in many other areas) centres on the process model, and includes a series of steps or a checklist which enables the individual to make an ethical decision, or to reach an ethical judgement about a specific situation, often one that embodies an ethical dilemma. However, we would contend that although this is an important part of providing guidance on ethical issues, there is a prior stage that needs to be addressed before judgements and decisions are considered. We would further argue that guidance should not be limited to those situations where an ethical decision is required, and that 'transcultural' and reflexive issues are always a basic part of the anti-oppressive framework.

Ethical guidance that focuses only on situations where the individual professional is able to decide to intervene does not give enough guidance. It presumes the individualistic model of the rational chooser so beloved of dominant male ethical traditions (Held, 2006). It fails to support the thinking or actions of the professional worker faced with, as McAuliffe and Chenowith (2008) admit, the stress and concerns that arise from moral conflicts between individual and social work values on the one hand and government and organisational values on the other. These are defined as being outside the domain of ethical decision-making. It thus ignores the painful experiences so common amongst social and community workers of 'moral regret' (Banks, 2005, p1005), where intervention is either not possible or when the 'least of two evils' has to be chosen, and where social relationships both engender and continue the processes of moral reflection. Furthermore it also fails to deal with the possibility that unethical institutional forms of discrimination and oppression may operate outside the recognised field of ethical dilemmas – they are not likely to be seen as ethical issues at all, but simply administrative routines, policies or informal customs and practices. Their apparent invisibility does not mean they should be ignored by a framework for ethical guidance, even though they may be (sometimes) intractable to individual intervention.

We would argue that guidance for making decisions is only part of the guidance that is needed and that a (modified) checklist model may have its place, but must be integrated within a broader approach. Consistent with the framework discussed in Chapter 1 we would stress that a reflexive self-critical awareness of the social, cultural, ethical and political dynamics of

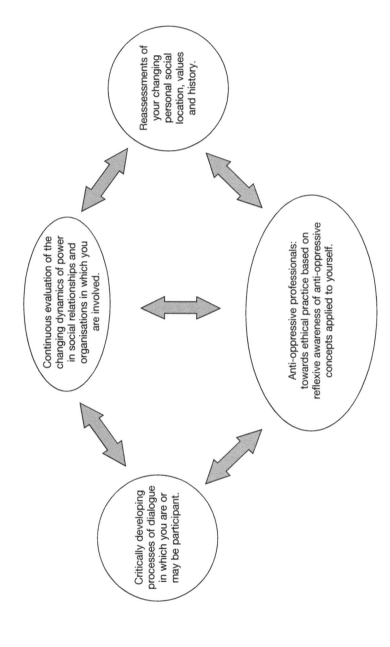

Figure 1 Ethical and political awareness in professional practice

specific situations is not only a prerequisite for judgements and decisions, but constitutes in itself a key component of an anti-oppressive approach to ethics, and is an obligation which should be embraced regardless of any specific decision that may be required or indeed of any specific problem that may arise. There are at least three relevant considerations: (1) Evaluation of the operation of power in social relationships; (2) the reflexive qualities of the actor – their social location, and character; and (3) dialogue that underpins and might enhance ethical awareness (see Figure 1).

I Continuous evaluation of the changing dynamics of power in social relationships

It has already been noted in Chapter 1 that feminist concerns about power are often expressed in terms of the way that dominant powers are both internalised into people's perspectives and into routinised institutional arrangements (Walker, 1998, p218). This means that well before any judgements or decisions are considered, 'reflective analysis' of forms of life and 'critical reflection' is required (Walker, 1998, p9). Feminists argue for awareness of the political arrangements, drawing on the importance of relational and contextual aspects of ethical situations: 'moral values and practices are inseparable from the broader social and political context within which they operate, and ethics is never entirely divorced from power' (Hutchings, 2000, p121). This context always needs to be understood before there is any rush to judgement, and the social context is very much a part of the relational approach to ethics which emphasises that ethical questions arise in the course of human interaction, and especially in relation to the dimensions of diversity and inequality. Judgment itself is only a part of ethics: *trying to understand the social world is a key ethical task in itself*. We regard this as a matter of understanding the different dynamics of power at the varied levels of social interaction, from micro-social to meso- and macro-levels, taking bureaucratic powers, informal group influences and national organisations into account.

The whole social context needs to be considered in order to ascertain the ethical dimensions of power and injustice in social situations which may be obscured because of the dominance of powerful perspectives and routinised assumptions. Such powers are able to exist and be effective without decisions being made, as Lukes (2005) has long argued. Ethical issues may not even be apparent, but may *become* so when the inequalities and differences are analysed and the structuring of social situations is uncovered. An obvious example would be institutionalised racism, which would require no ethical decisions or judgements and would not be apparent unless someone took the trouble to analyse particular organisational policies and practices. Similar considerations apply in all social contexts and to all social divisions. Even when judgements *are* called for, 'Ethical analysis . . . has to go beyond the actions of the perpetrators in isolation, to analysing and deconstructing the background values, practices and institutions which give these actions meaning' (Hutchings, 2000, p129). We would propose that the key concepts we have set out in Chapter 1 are useful criteria for working out social dynamics relevant to differences of power and potential ethical issues, those concepts having been drawn from the social perspectives of dominated social groups themselves. In practice therefore the first ethical guideline is to use anti-oppressive concepts to understand the social world, especially its changing powers, its inequalities and differences. We have provided examples of this kind of analysis throughout this book.

2 Reassessments of changing personal social location

Closely associated with the first major guidance point is to turn this spirit of social enquiry upon oneself: critical reflection in this context means assessing one's own social location in relation to others, and this has been partly described above – especially in the chapter on virtue ethics. The importance of this ethical obligation from an anti-oppressive perspective is partly to foster the development of character – as in virtue ethics. However, it is also important because the actor is herself a participant in the various inequalities and diversities and must analyse her own social location, values and her own particular organisational and other social powers in relation to specific others. Her own ability to communicate with particular other people from different social divisions will be one of the issues, as will their willingness and ability to reciprocate. This is partly a political question about the nature of the relationships involved and partly a matter of the virtue of the actor in recognising her own limitations and powers. It is an issue of how those involved are jointly able to negotiate with each other, overcoming obstacles of difference and power. It is also an issue about accountability and who is responsible for what – an issue where legal and policy guidelines may limit the kind of dialogue that is possible.

This second preliminary guideline for an anti-oppressive approach to ethical practice requires continuing analysis of the actor's own social location and values. This has some relatively stable characteristics – membership of the major social divisions, for example, though even this may change (e.g. in relation to age or disability). However, the significance of this social and cultural heritage can change over time, and will certainly be changing rapidly in the process of specific social interactions, and the personal history of human relationships that constitute the groundwork of ethical practice. The interaction between individuals and groups in specific circumstances will require reassessment of the actor's own position in the light of the changing expectations and perceptions of others. It may even change actors' perceptions of themselves. Therefore awareness of one's own values, and willingness to tolerate other values and ethical differences, and ability to be literate about other ethical and cultural traditions are continuous in ethical life, and precede any particularly marked point at which a decision appears to be required. Indeed it enables the individual to be proactive in their thinking about both unethical and institutionalised practices, and also be more aware of individual relationships where no one is complaining or expressing concern, but where potential ethical issues can be discerned.

The process of self-analysis involved needs to be in principle both a social analysis and a social history of one's self. Understanding the impact of membership of social divisions on the lives of social workers has been an underpinning part of the courses we have taught. The authors have led modules on the sociology of the social divisions in relation to reflexive and biographical issues for a long time. This has consistently led students both to self-reassessment, and to greater awareness of difference – and sometimes similarity – with others. We have also involved service users in the process, sharing the similarities and differences between their experiences of life and those of student social workers. This module has been a significant self-awareness-raising exercise for students, and an extremely useful foundation for a later module on ethics. We would contend that there is never any end to this process, given the changing situations which we all experience, and through which we continue to grow, as conscious ethical actors.

This means that the actor is not a neutral individual objectively assessing the rationality of an action, nor even a subjective individual reacting to the emotions of relationships according to their particular dispositions. The anti-oppressive framework requires a critical self-awareness about the sociological, political and cultural location of the actor, so that relevant ethical issues can be proactively considered. This will involve both reason and evidence about the past and how it has affected the character and social position of the actor in the present, but it will also engage emotions about the meaning of that past life and how current powers, inequalities and diversities in relationships impinge on their lives in the present.

3 Critically developing processes of dialogue

The final *general* element of anti-oppressive guidance would be about self-awareness developing in the context of continuing dialogue – a key feature of the moral landscape. In one sense the feminist relational ethic previously discussed has emphasised the importance of continuing dialogue as a characteristic of the nature of moral life. Caring, justice and empathy are carried out by way of intercommunicative processes – negotiations between individuals and groups. The point has been picked up by other ethical and social theorists who emphasise the importance of communication as a basic and valuable aspect of ethics (e.g. Hugman, 2005; Gray and Lovat, 2007)). However, this dialogue should not be decontextualised: it has to be understood reflexively by the actor using an anti-oppressive framework. The possibility of dialogue has to be assessed in anti-oppressive terms: the degree to which communication is free; the degree to which the actor is able to understand the 'other' the degree to which the 'other' is enabled to understand the actor; and the institutional and other political, physical, cultural and social barriers to dialogue and action. The full range of anti-oppressive concerns with social and cultural difference and inequality is relevant to dialogical issues. The idea of 'experts by experience' when used of individual service users needs to be seen as part of a range of different perspectives that need to be consulted, including those developed by user, campaign and community groups at local and national level, as well as interdisciplinary views. Awareness of and dialogue with a service user's perspective needs to be complemented with a similar openness to communication with relevant social groups, whose advice and insight may either complement or contradict the individual carer or service user. Consumerist and managerial approaches to service users ignore the internalisation of dominant norms, and the politics of representation, and the consequent need for dialogue at different levels with different parties. The existence of differing views does not give the social worker carte blanche to impose their own, but it does make clear the moral obligation to learn from others, and develop a dialogue as well as possible that will take account of those differing views. Yet the social worker is morally responsible for their own end position on the ethical issue at hand, and especially in relation to the service user whose life may be affected.

Guidance from an anti-oppressive perspective for professionals must therefore include continuing assessment of:

1   the multiple power inequalities in the interactions in which they are involved, and the potential, and possibly latent ethical issues which arise from them;
2   their own social location, their own values and emotions and their powers in relation to significant others, and account-taking of their own strengths and weaknesses;
3   dialogue with significant others in the near environment, and engagement where possible in dialogue with more distant individuals and groups whose perspectives are potentially valuable, especially where they express the views of dominated social groups.

What this means in practice has been sketched out in Chapter 1, and has been given more concrete expression in subsequent chapters. Throughout the book there has been an emphasis on the reflexive consideration of the professionals' position. However, there are clearly also situations where ethical judgments have to be put into practice when there are decisions to be made, and this prior anti-oppressive standpoint has to be supported by a logical approach to the evidence and the norms relevant to a specific situation.

RESOLVING PROBLEMS, MAKING DECISIONS: CRITICAL AND REFLEXIVE ISSUES

Many attempts to provide a framework for making judgements about ethical problems and implementing ethical decisions tend to follow a similar logical pattern. Whatever the moral theory which underlies the approach, many authors (cf. Thompson, 1999, p98; Fox and DeMarco, 2001, pp306–7; Goovaerts, 2002 p88; Reamer, 2001, pp73–118; Davis, 1999, pp166–7; Windheuser, 2003, p95) recommend:

- A statement of the ethical problem: what exactly is the issue?
- A statement of the facts relevant to the situation.
- In any professional context, the relevant law and professional codes consulted.

- The different ethical concepts and theories considered.
- Various alternative options examined.
- A decision in favour of the best of the alternatives, as informed by the previous steps.

The authors usually add that this sequence is not unalterable and each step may be returned to. Making any kind of decision in social work requires some kind of practical process (cf. O'Sullivan, 1999, p126). However, in social work decision-making there is usually some additional reference to consultation. For example, Reamer refers to the need to 'consult with colleagues and appropriate experts' (Reamer, 2001, p108). O'Sullivan makes it clear that clients and colleagues all should be involved in the decision-making process throughout, as 'stakeholders working together' (O'Sullivan, 1999, p63). In addition the emphasis in recent social work texts has been upon the circular nature of any guidance, and the importance of it being inclusive in relation to ethical concepts. (Bowles *et al.*, 2006; McAuliffe and Chenoweth, 2008).

These are common assumptions of contemporary social work across the globe, and we are drawing on the common logic of the above, but with some critical differences:

- The use of any checklist or procedure is premised on the prior commitment of the professional to an anti-oppressive reflexive awareness as described above.
- The notion of dialogue and consultation is built into the process in a prominent way, and is problematised rather than sidelined. We have pointed out the significance of feminist ideas about relational issues in ethics. The idea of a specific kind of dialogue which takes account of the power and inequality issues is a primary rather than a secondary ethical issue.
- Anti-oppressive concepts are used systematically to interrogate the meaning and significance of any point in the process. These supply some specific critical questions about the nature of the situation, re-figuring the common practical logic of ethical decision-making, and linking it to the continuous process of ethical reflection and evaluation described above. This helps to rule out certain possible directions, and rule in the most likely areas where an anti-oppressive ethical course of action may be pursued, identifying those 'hotspots' where differentials of power and inequality make ethical considerations really important.

The diagram in the box below summarises the important aspects of ethical decisions which need to be considered to take account of the various claims on professional values, and offers basic guidance for making an ethical decision from an anti-oppressive perspective. Various kinds of obligations – to the law, to service users and employers – are included. There is a consensus in social work that professionals need to 'leave no stone unturned' (McAuliffe and Chenoweth, 2008) and that ethical decisions need to take account of the range of both accountabilities and ethical concepts that can

---

Resolving specific issues and problems, making decisions: a summary

Reflexive ethical and political awareness using anti-oppressive concepts, underpinning consideration of:

1   The Identification of Ethical Issues
(discussed in previous section)
2   The Professional Context
- Legal and policy directives
- Professional codes
3   Consultation and Dialogue
- Individual service users and carers
- Colleagues and other professions
- Advocates: service user and social groups
4   Assessing the Options: Evidence and Perspectives
- Case evidence
- Relevant research evidence
- Evidence from consultation and dialogue
5   Reviewing Relevant Ethics
- Using a broad anti-oppressive approach to ethics
- Critically drawing on the insights of the various ethical theories
- Critically prioritising ethical concerns
6   Resolving problems, making decisions
- Taking responsibility – using and questioning personal values and virtues
- Working in partnerships: critically assessing the implications in the light of the above considerations

Note: The above does *not* represent stages in a linear process. The diagram simplifies elements which may reoccur in various combinations in the continuing process of identifying ethical issues, problems and dilemmas. The first item in the list corresponds to the reflexive process described in the previous section, out of which specific actionable issues may emerge, depending on circumstances.

be drawn from the various ethical traditions. The argument of this book is that this inclusiveness is indeed appropriate, but needs to be understood in the context of a rigorous, reflexive application of anti-oppressive criteria both to the array of obligations and to the range of ethical concepts. This is what binds the various elements together, providing a decisional framework that is informed by an anti-oppressive approach to the ethical values of social work, and facilitating the 'practical reasoning' necessary for social work professionals in uncertain situations (Clark, 2006).

1   Identifying ethical issues

The anti-oppressive practitioner will attempt to be alert to the various ethical possibilities that arise from a systematic consideration of all the dimensions of social life highlighted by anti-oppressive concepts in Chapter 1, and as further discussed in the previous section above, especially power and social difference, applying them reflexively to themselves and their relationships with users and colleagues, in the context of critical dialogue, and legal and organisational demands and possibilities. There is therefore an initial sensitivity to ethical issues even before they may become significant for an individual or organisation. However, there needs to be further clarification of ethical issues, problems and dilemmas when they become explicit, and decisions need to be taken and implemented.

2   The professional context

Chapter 2 above offers further explanation of the ethical issues arising from these considerations. Key areas are:

- National and international law, especially:
  - Legal obligations related to social care
  - Human Rights
  - Equal Opportunities legislation
- National codes of practice
- National and international professional ethics codes
- Agency practice and policy
- Trade union and professional association practice and policy

In relation to all these rules, policies, codes and regulations there are three general issues:

1   To what extent are they compatible with anti-oppressive ethics and can therefore be used with some purpose?
2   To what extent do they appear to be in conflict with anti-oppressive ethics, and need to be resisted, either by insider strategies, or by whistle-blowing or by collective and political means?
3   To what extent are conflicting interests and principles involved?

In the latter case there are both political and ethical decisions to be made about whose interests and which principles should have priority. Section 5 below on reviewing ethics offers some help in terms of prioritising ethical principles. However, prioritising ethics also has to be placed in the context of anti-oppressive concepts to ensure that it is checked against basic ethical concerns arising from oppression. There is no easy solution to such dilemmas, but we would argue that the anti-oppressive concepts provide some assistance in raising key issues of ethical relevance. National and international legislation against discrimination and in favour of human rights offers significant opportunities for social workers to develop policies and practice which are ethical in their regard and respect for those subject to discrimination.

However, managerialism in social services organisations can be seen as having 'totalitarian tendencies' (Nellis, 2000), in that the demands of efficiency and output very quickly take precedence over other considerations, including ethical concerns. The legal and policy mandates are critical both in directing and legitimising the work of the professional, setting a context of values and an organisational agenda which requires systematic and continual questioning and review. The law itself or an organisation's application of it, may need to be opposed, and this can provide moral dilemmas and difficulties for practitioners (cf. Humphries, 2004).

Other organisations such as trade unions and professional associations also have a role to play in relation to professional workers' service conditions in bureaucratic organisations and helping to ensure the delivery of good services. Particularly relevant are trade union and professional commitments to ethical positions which they themselves develop. However trade unions and professional bodies also have specific vested interests and may be subjected to similar anti-oppressive ethical critiques as employing agencies. Practical reasoning includes reference to what the social worker is able to understand as professionally relevant in the specific circumstances in the light of anti-oppressive ethical values and concepts.

3 Consultation and dialogue

The service users' and carers' perspectives and their involvement in the assessment of their own situation, and the decisions that then need to be made, cannot be assumed to be simply a matter of consumer choice, but need to be a matter for continuing negotiation and dialogue. There are a series of issues about the relative powers of users and carers, as well as professional colleagues, and the people they affect which need to be analysed, including the extent to which dialogue is itself a feasible option in the given circumstances, as already discussed above. The circumstances relating to working in partnership will vary widely with the setting, and the relevant legislation, but for the worker 'hearing' across the social divisions is always difficult (see Chapter 8) – as it is indeed for the service user or carer.

A worker's statutory role designed to protect the vulnerable may make dialogue even more difficult. They have to make ethical choices about the degree to which they are able to make a 'relationship' of apparent equality, and use that access to hear and listen to hostile perspectives, with the possibility that testimony may later be required before a court of law. On the other side of the balance there is the legitimate use of authority to protect vulnerable individuals of all kinds, which may involve conflicting ethical considerations, including non-disclosure of information, and difficult decisions about exactly with who, how and how much to participate at any given point in the process, as in the example in Chapter 4.

In the event of dialogue becoming difficult or impossible for whatever reason, there is still no excuse for workers to ignore the potential arguments which could be put on behalf of or by users and carers. The involvement of advocates and the examination of the perspectives of user and carer groups, relevant campaign groups and advocates for subordinate social groups needs to be a continuing live option for workers and teams. This will be relevant whether there is an easy partnership with particular service users or not. The worker needs to be aware of other perspectives and forms of 'expertise' than those officially accredited. It is important to consider, for example, the views of a local minority ethnic community in relation to the treatment of one of its members as a service user, as for example in Chapter 6. Such a community and its representatives will be the holders of different knowledges and perspectives, which are invaluable resources – yet cannot be uncritically accepted. Equally, the organisers of women's refuges, and mental health survivors' organisations and professional advocacy services (e.g. Dalrymple,

2004) will have critically important perspectives relevant to many service users' situations. Service users and carers may not *themselves* be aware of different but related perspectives to their own, such as user movements and community organisations. Social workers need to know, and be prepared to connect, the users, carers, advocates and other organisations whenever possible. However, this dimension and this kind of intervention also requires ethical reflection: who to involve in the dialogue is itself an ethical issue. It also involves practical issues concerning available time and resources that necessitate ethical reflection on possible outcomes.

Similar considerations apply to dialogue with inter-professional colleagues and members of the public, where there are likely to be all kinds of social and cultural differences which engender differing perspectives on a specific case. There will be opportunities to learn from, understand, and sometimes contest the differing perspectives. There should be the opportunity to collect and collate significant bits of information which will need to be analysed and assessed, and integrated into the narrative being constructed by the social worker attempting to make sense of the case. Lack of space and opportunity to engage in dialogue and reflect is ethically significant.

4   Assessing the options: evidence and perspectives

Examining the different options available will depend very much on the comprehensive assessment of the case that the social worker makes, and the 'factual' information and differing perspectives that have emerged from the negotiations having occurred. Guidelines for working in partnership with service users, and working together with other professionals may help to produce a comprehensive assessment of a situation informed by a variety of perspectives emerging from a dialogue between the participants. To a degree the outcomes will be predetermined by the 'value-slope' that has been engendered by the process of investigation and dialogue. That is to say that the availability and interpretation of the evidence will have already narrowed down the possible ethical 'solutions'. However, this does not offer guidance about how to choose ethically between the various perspectives still on offer: consensus is hardly likely in sensitive situations unless some voices are unintentionally or deliberately muted.

An anti-oppressive perspective assists the worker in alerting her to the distribution of powers between the various perspectives, and the need for muted and dominated views and values to be taken into account. It also offers a critique of evidence-based practice, whilst still requiring a rigorous (indeed more rigorous) assessment of the available case and research evidence. Identifying the powers and interests involved in a given perspective (whether that of a service user, carer or professional colleagues) does not necessarily invalidate the opinion expressed, but it helps to raise question marks against the evidence being used to support a given case, and suggests where different evidence might be sought (e.g. from a source untainted by a particular set of interests). It raises the issue of the depth and accuracy of knowledge claimed by all participants, and respects the knowledge of both professional colleagues and service users (and others) but without assuming that their knowledge can be uncritically accepted because of their status (whether high or low). The mere presentation of evidence is not enough – the clarity of perspective involved and the account taken of evidence (especially alternative evidence from disempowered sources) is a key test of significant information.

It is clearly important for workers to be generally aware of the oppositional perspectives provided by the various social movements, as well as the differing views provided by service users, carers and colleagues. This is not only an 'ethical' policy but is an important aspect of social science research methodology – testing hypotheses against alternative evidence, and alternative perspectives. Given the premises of an anti-oppressive ethic, the search for alternative explanations and disconfirming evidence can hardly be undertaken in a more useful area than with social movements struggling for social justice, their local organisations and advocates, and the wider literature associated with them. They will often understandably aim to provide alternative accounts to those dominant in our society.

The social worker's detailed participatory knowledge of a social situation can itself be seen as constituting a form of ethnographic research (cf. Clifford, 1998), and is an important contribution not only to good assessment, but simultaneously to good ethical judgement. Anti-oppressive ethics needs to draw on such a context in order to understand the variety of factors that are often involved in complex situations. However, it is also a potential source of difficulty in cases where there is *not* much available evidence, no time to collect it, or the sources of further evidence may be themselves too vulnerable or too unwilling to cooperate in order to collect the data required. There is therefore an inherent tension between the need to collect information that will support ethical assessment, and the need to make ethical judgements about the appropriateness of further investigation. The dangers include possibly counterproductive damage or unjustifiable pressure on vulnerable individuals, or unethical intrusion into people's private and family lives. This is the kind of situation that arises often in social work, and requires the use of ethical judgement in situations of inherent uncertainty. In such cases, the importance of the character of the worker is very apparent, as in Chapter 5, and the need to make an existential moral choice, as in Chapter 7. The application of principles will not be conclusive when the situation contains probabilities, subtleties and unknown or contested facts that cannot easily be reduced to clear logical or measurable terms.

The need to consider also the wider parameters of social situations arises because of the unavoidable connections between individual and family circumstances and the systemic and historical factors which have conditioned the current interactions, and continue to do so. The kind of evidence that can be relevant here will include specific pieces of research evidence related to the kind of case being dealt with. For example, this might conclude evidence about the risk involved to children in circumstances of various kinds of neglect. This kind of evidence is available these days through a number of sources including the internet, and workers have a moral responsibility for keeping as abreast as they are able with relevant research evidence of this kind. Their employing organisations equally have a responsibility to assist their workers in accessing research evidence. The issue of judgement is simultaneously empirical and ethical as the worker has to question both how far the evidence applies to a particular case, and the validity and provenance of the original research.

In addition to the evidence of research about this particular type of situation, there is also the wider body of evidence within the social science disciplines about how the social system works, and what factors need to be attended to in order to reach an informed view. The general education of social workers, and their continued post-qualifying training, is obviously of relevance here. The worker's responsibilities will include an understanding of the way in which anti-oppressive interpretation involves key methodological concepts for understanding social circumstances, drawn from a long history of continuing debate about understanding social life. It should also include an appreciation of the way that social values and social science methods are interconnected.

5   Reviewing relevant ethics

Using a broad anti-oppressive ethical framework

Although a social worker's personal values may inform her understanding of the social work task, she needs to follow the broader framework provided by anti-oppressive social work ethics. This means that whatever kind of religious or secular view she has, she has refrained from imposing her judgements on service users. The framework provided here allows for social workers themselves to have differing personal values, yet it challenges the worker to place them within the wider framework where accountabilities to others require them to refrain from imposing their views, and question their own values. This kind of 'bilateral view' is necessary for competence in social work ethics, but the connection between 'local' and 'universal' values, is complex, and cannot rest on assumptions about uncontestable universal human values (Hugman, 2007; see also Chapter 2 above). An anti-oppressive approach to ethics must be pluralist in its approach, avoiding a focus on a specific religious or secular interpretation of what is morally good. Both the uncertainty of the social world, and the responsibility of equal services to all groups in a universalistic policy environment also necessitate such an approach (Hugman, 2005).

Drawing on the insights of the various ethical theories

The whole range of ethical concepts needs to be considered, since it is clear that there are various aspects to ethics which may all be relevant. Codes of Practice typically enjoin consideration for various ethical principles, and as we saw previously, feminist and anti-oppressive ethics require the re-figuring of the range of ethical concepts. It is important to be aware of the different contributions made by the various ethical perspectives in relation to any particular set of circumstances. For further information about the concepts involved the reader is referred back to the relevant chapters of this book.

However, not only do they need to be reconsidered in the light of an anti-oppressive critique, but they also need to be examined in relation to each other. This is especially important when, as sometimes happens they are in conflict. When this happens there has to be some prioritising of values in relation to the details of a specific situation. Some general, though not binding, suggestions have been made about the possibility of using an 'ethics screen' to help workers think through priorities when ethical concepts do not fit neatly together. The following section discusses different ethical concepts in the light of this suggestion, and at the same time brings anti-oppressive concepts to bear on the discussion.

Prioritising: critically using an ethics screen?

A problem that often arises is conflict between ethical ideas that apply simultaneously. In order to assist with this situation two American theorists (Loewenberg and Dolgoff, 1996) have presented an 'ethics screen' which prioritises the ethical rules, making it easier to decide between competing concepts. It does not in fact resolve all the dilemmas, but offers some assistance in thinking the issues through. The rules are listed in order of importance, and normally one would choose a higher-order rule over one that is lower in the list. We do not think this screening method should be followed uncritically, and it does not absolve the worker from serious ethical reflection; however, it will help to reflect on those issues if used from an anti-oppressive perspective, as suggested here.

1   The protection of life

This is clearly a paramount consideration, on almost any ethical basis. The difficulty often arises of not being able to predict exactly what factors are actually life-threatening, or life-preserving, although some are more obvious than others. An anti-oppressive approach to ethics highlights multiple perspectives on the key issues of power and vulnerability, helping to assess risk in complex cases.

2   The equality and inequality of power

This is not so immediately obvious but is a high priority practice principle, consistent with anti-oppressive values. It means that persons of equal status or power 'have the right to be treated equally', whereas those of unequal status or power 'have the right to be treated differently if the inequality is relevant to the issue in question' (Loewenberg and Dolgoff, 1996, p63). The relative power of social workers means that they should not exploit people with whom they work by neglecting to meet their need for protection from those more powerful – including the social workers themselves and their agencies. The social worker also has to assess the differences in powers between others, in order to have a clear idea of who is most vulnerable and who has the most ability to exercise power. Identification of the distribution of powers, as in the anti-oppressive ethical framework, is an important part of this ethics screen, and a useful contribution to ethical practice.

3 Autonomy and freedom

The aim to 'foster a person's autonomy, independence, and freedom' (Loewenberg and Dolgoff, 1996, p64), is clearly related to the continuing significance of the Kantian ideal of respect for persons. However, as we have seen in Chapters 3 and 8, this needs to be interpreted in the light of the feminist and anti-oppressive commitment to a relational form of autonomy in which the interdependence of persons is equally recognised at the same time as their right to respect as individuals.

4 Least harm

Choosing the option that will cause 'the least harm, the least permanent harm, and/or the most easily reversible harm' (Loewenberg and Dolgoff, 1996, p64) is a negative form of utilitarianism, clearly focusing on the likely outcomes of intervention. It appropriately comes before the more positive utilitarian idea in the next principle – the quality of life (below) – because the negative aim preserves the minimum best possible outcome. After that has been ensured, then a more positive end can be pursued. The anti-oppressive ethical framework presented above usefully problematises the idea by questioning *whose* interpretation is relied on to select the 'facts' and assess the potential risk, and by paying critical attention to the knowledge claims of both 'experts' and the relatively powerless.

5 Quality of life

This is to promote 'a better quality of life for all people, for the individual as well as for the community' (Loewenberg and Dolgoff, 1996, p64). It is a positive form of utilitarianism, emphasising the importance of good outcomes for individuals and groups, and is also reflected in the altruistic characteristics of virtue ethics, with its concern for the self-realisation of the potential for good in people. However, it is also open to question from an anti-oppressive perspective in that the issue of who has the power to define the quality of life is obviously crucial, and the voices of service users and carers are clearly relevant but often marginalised. At the same time, the anti-oppressive ethic also problematises the notion of community, and whose needs are being met in the assessment of the quality of life in specific communities such as minority ethnic communities, as well as in the community as a whole.

6 *Privacy and confidentiality*

The idea that a social worker should 'practice decisions that strengthen every person's right to privacy' (Loewenberg and Dolgoff, 1996, p62) is a commonplace of social work ethics, inspired mainly by Kantian ethics, but here is given a low priority. This is consistent with the realities of practice, but does not excuse either the obligation to consider its importance in specific situations, and who will be vulnerable if it is not properly regarded. Nor does it excuse the need to question, from an anti-oppressive perspective, exactly whose interests are being protected by confidentiality and privacy, and who will benefit by secrecy. The need for negotiation on this issue with service users and carers is important (cf. Evans and Harris, 2004). Differences between cultures in prioritising this value might also need to be taken into account.

7 *Truthfulness and full disclosure*

Social workers should be honest and 'disclose all relevant information to clients and, where applicable, to others as well' (Loewenberg and Dolgoff, 1996, p 64). However, truth is often a casualty of conflict situations, and social work often involves conflicting interests. It is not always possible to disclose everything, so this aim comes low down the list. This classical moral aim of integrity and truthfulness, often linked with virtue ethics or Kantian and religious ideals, is usefully guided by anti-oppressive ethical attention to differences in powers and outcomes, as well as critical questions about whose truth is being promoted to whose benefit. Who is to say what is relevant? Yet truth may be vital to those who are vulnerable.

6 Resolving problems, making decisions

Making an ethical decision or resolving a moral problem involves issues relating to the worker's perception of herself and her relationships with a range of other people. The social worker will be influenced by her understanding of her role in an agency, the values of her profession, and certainly by her conception of her own character and integrity within these various contexts. Two previous chapters have examined the ethical issues which arise at this point. Chapter 5 examined virtue theory, and the importance of developing qualities which will maximise the good in professional practice.

Chapter 7 discussed the importance of accountability and responsibility in uncertain decision-making. No one should be taking for granted the ethical response which is required. The worker has to use practical reasoning about the situation, making an existential decision for which she is responsible, as an employee, member of the society in which she lives, and the profession in which she works, but ultimately and simply as a human being in a 'postmodern' age of diversity and change.

However, whilst the issue of individual responsibility – or being a 'morally active practitioner' (Husband, 1995) and of good character – is particularly relevant at this point, it is important to recall that the model of ethics as an activity primarily about individual decision-making is inadequate from an anti-oppressive perspective. The ethical issues will have already been influenced by resource issues, and negotiated in the process of assessment, where language will have been manoeuvred into action with various connotations of blame and praise, describing past actions and events in terms of the needs and strengths of the people involved. The 'decision' will have already meaningfully emerged from a dialogical process in which service users, carers and professional colleagues will have all contributed, and they in their turn will have been influenced by the rules and policies of their own agencies. Feminist ethics (see previous chapter) are particularly helpful in emphasising the importance and complexity of dialogue – and the different powers and perspectives which must be critically understood when engaging in, and assessing, the outcomes of dialogue. The decision becomes one which is the outcome of dialogue and (differentially) owned by participants. Nevertheless the social worker has to take their share of responsibility for themselves.

Even in the unlikely event of dialogue between various parties reaching complete agreement, the worker's ethical position is still something which requires commitment and responsibility: the consensus may be mistaken, or it may be subject to criticism from a position which has been silenced or not represented in the discussion so far. The democratic and/or bureaucratic consensus cannot be assumed to be ethically acceptable: the worker has an ethical responsibility for her own actions and decisions. Notoriously, the decision may well be subject to ethical criticism at a later date. There is no avoiding the worker's responsibility for reviewing and making a decision to proceed in one direction rather than another, in the light of an anti-oppressive ethical view about the nature of the dialogue that has taken place. But neither is there any excuse for workers failing to socially locate themselves, and reflect on their final decisions in the light of anti-oppressive ethical questions about their own powers, and the personal and social histories which mould their character, personality and current situation.

A social worker can be confident that having used an anti-oppressive framework, they will have thought through the key ethical issues in a way that takes account of all the elements required of a professional social worker. This will include the obligation to work in a way that demonstrates not only knowledge of relevant ethical concepts and local laws, but also a broader awareness of how ethical values are related to social inequalities and diversities. They will need to take up a nuanced position consistent with a respect for their own values, but also alive to the wider context, and the anti-oppressive values of the profession. In so doing they will be oriented towards a position which may realistically protect, nurture and promote the vulnerable, without imposing their values on people, and with a questioning approach to their own assumptions about what is possible and ethical.

CHAPTER SUMMARY

This chapter sets out an anti-oppressive framework for good practice in ethics, drawing on a number of sources in a critical way, and relating the different aspects of the process to anti-oppressive concepts, beginning with the priority of understanding the self as socially located and reflexive, involved in continuing dialogue with others.

FURTHER READING

Clifford, D.J. and Burke, B. (2007) 'Competence in Social Work Ethics'. An application of our own framework to English social work training requirements.

Note: the following references do not succeed in taking fully into account the anti-oppressive considerations which we have argued above are an essential part of ethical thinking in social work. However, they provide a more detailed account of some of the points made in this chapter.

Banks, S. (2006) *Ethics and Values in Social Work*, 3rd edn, chapter 8, pp160–85. A discussion of practice dilemmas and decision-making which emphasises 'critical reflection'.

Bowles, W. *et al.* (2006) *Ethical Practice in Social Work: An Applied Approach*. A related Australian text.

Cournoyer, B. (2000) *The Social Work Skills Workbook,* 3rd edn, Chapter 3, pp67–92. This American textbook outlines the ethical screen in the context of traditional ethics.

Loewenberg, F. M. and Dolgoff, R. (1996) *Ethical Decisions For Social Work Practice.* Includes discussion of their ethical screen.

O'Sullivan, T. (1999) *Decision-Making in Social Work,* Chapter 6, pp103–26. A general discussion of decision-making, in which social work values play an important part.

Conclusion: Ethics and Organisations

INTRODUCTION

In this final chapter we want to review some of the key arguments in the book, but to do so with some consideration of the settings within which professionals work. Throughout this book we have been at pains to emphasise that although individuals have to be responsible for their own values and actions, ethics is not something that can or should be solely restricted to situations of individual moral choice. In most of the case scenarios there have been issues about the relationships between the protagonists and all the surrounding formal and informal social networks, including the organisations within which they work. We have also emphasised the importance of engaging reflexively with the ethical issues that do not immediately or obviously present themselves as moral dilemmas requiring individual decisions. In organisations ethical issues may arise in interpersonal contexts, and in equal opportunities or management, trade union and interprofessional contexts – often in both at the same time, as well as being inherently a part of the professional development of services to users and carers. We will deal with organisational ethics that affect individuals collectively within organisations, with a particular focus on 'equal opportunities', interpreted very broadly to include issues of ethical importance across the range of services and functions, not just as a personnel or employment matter.

We do not expect ethics and values alone to necessarily make significant differences to social, and political systems, including organisations. We agree that social work values 'cannot of themselves bring about the changes necessary to eradicate structural inequalities' (Dominelli, 2004, p62). Similarly, there is little evidence that ethical aims pursued by means of equal opportunity policies by themselves make a great deal of difference (Aitkenhead and Liff, 1991). However, neither do we think that individuals are merely 'puppets' of the various macro-social systems. Individual actions combined with collective actions and policies do make some differences to some people, and occasionally can initiate or complement wider organisational or social change. But this is only likely to be the case if practitioners individually and collectively ask themselves the difficult anti-oppressive questions in the above framework, discussing them and working together to make a difference. These questions continually query the way organisations impinge on and construct the issues, patterning the flows of power and influence between different levels, and between different social divisions. The culture of an organisation is something to which individuals and groups, internal and external, may contribute knowingly or not. The broader economic and social systems remain as targets for individual and collective intervention outside the organisation at the same time as some of their effects can be resisted – or appropriated – within it.

INDIVIDUAL AND COLLECTIVE ETHICAL COMMITMENTS AND POLITICAL CHOICES

Individuals can use their relative power and influence to cooperate with, or to resist, organisational procedures, customs, cultures and office-holders. The end result should aim for, but may or may not produce a conducive context for ethical action – a 'competent organisation' which helps to empower reflective ethical action on the part of individuals' (Braye and Preston-Shoot, 1995, pp69–70). Given the dialogical nature of anti-oppressive ethics, the umbrella of a healthy organisation that takes its equality and diversity issues seriously provides a much more facilitative environment for ethical practice. The structure of organisations can sometimes be changed and their services altered to meet the needs of service users. Sometimes individuals simply have to act responsibly with or without organisational support. However, wider economic and political systems set financial, legal and other parameters with which organisations have to contend. Globalisation is often cited as one of the major obstacles to organisational ethical practice, but its impact is not uniform or monolithic. The potential for, and significance of, change is bound to vary. The global social systems themselves can change and be influenced by individual and collective actions. Indeed it has been argued that feminist relational ethics, on which we have drawn, offers a better guide for international relations and global politics than traditional human rights arguments because of its capacity to deal with 'the realities . . . of unequal power and unchosen relations', in 'our ties to various social groups and our historical embeddedness', thus offering 'resources to understand group and cultural ties, and relations between groups sharing histories or colonial domination' (Held, 2006, pp156–7).

In the more local context of organisations employing social workers the worker has to be aware of the unequal distribution of power and legitimacy in hierarchical systems requiring an 'understanding of the political nature of oppression' even in supposedly caring organisations (McLeod and Sherwin, 2000, p276), and to make strategic decisions about how to advocate, negotiate, and intervene in organisational structures. It involves developing strategies and policies for change, including informal and formal avenues within the organisation, such as lobbying of managers and trade unions and networking with colleagues, carers, patients and service-user organisations, in addition to political options outside the remit of the social worker as employee (Dominelli, 2002a, chap 6). It would imply an obligation to record and complain ('whistle-blow') about failure to support service users' autonomy or meeting of need. In the end it requires the worker to consider whether to continue working for an organisation that repeatedly ignores a service user's need for autonomy, or a worker's need for integrity. These are simultaneously ethical and political decisions (see Chapter 5 above). Equally the worker may feel so alienated by the organisation's limited mandate and effectiveness that it may seem more ethical to work on the same range of issues, but from outside the organisation rather than within it (cf. Ferguson and Lavalette, 2004). Working 'in and against' an organisation or leaving it completely in order to attack its performance from outside, or simply to develop critical alternative services, are all options involving political and ethical choices.

The monitoring and assessment of organisational performance, and the reflexive consideration of the individual's position within that setting are ethical issues. When the organisation functions only poorly in relation to its supposed objectives in meeting service users' needs, and when the character of the worker is diminished by their allegiance to it, then an ethical decision is when to resign or move on. Even this situation is complicated by obligations a worker may have to their own family, to service users or colleagues not to withdraw precipitately from employment. The moral dilemma posed by situations such as these cannot be judged outside a particular context, and workers have to make their own ethical decisions. The following discussion of organisational issues and ethical practice attempts to summarise the argument of this book and apply it to the pressing issue of the social worker's relations with their own and others' organisations. Using our own guidelines for reviewing critical and reflexive issues in anti-oppressive ethical practice, we would identify a range of issues in contemporary organisations employing social workers, including those that employ social work educators (cf. Clifford and Royce, 2008). These issues relate to the anti-oppressive concepts discussed in Chapter 1 including consideration of the range of social differences, the operations of multiple kinds of powers within organisations, and the changing interactions within and between organisations and their political and legal environments. Reflexive awareness begins with the worker's self-awareness of their own biography and social location both within and outside the organisation, and with a similar understanding of the context. This includes the changing law and policy in relation to agency functions and to equal opportunities in organisations, subsequently reframed in the UK as issues relating to equality and diversity. The latter are key issues in anti-oppressive ethical practice, and the particular focus of this concluding review.

HISTORICAL AND LEGAL ASPECTS OF ETHICAL PRACTICE IN ORGANISATIONS

The development of equal opportunities in the Western world generally, especially the USA, was in decline in the last couple of decades of the last century. The dominant power groups and their representatives in the media made a sustained attack against equal opportunity initiatives. Steps made in the USA towards affirmative action for black people had been rolled back (Bonnett, 2000, p254). In the UK the Thatcher Government ensured that local government initiatives in relation to equal opportunities were demonised and abolished, or reversed. Attacks on social work's commitment to anti-racism was part of this offensive, and helped to induce the very uneven development of initiatives in equal opportunities within social services and other organisations (Tomlinson, 2001; Dominelli, 2004).

However, the UK turned away from Thatcherism in the 1990s and several subsequent legal developments had major consequences for equal opportunities in large organisations, some of which have been mirrored or exceeded in other countries. The passing of the Disability Discrimination Act in 1995 and the Race Relations Amendment Act in 2001 both had serious implications for employers and employees. No longer was it sufficient simply to have policies in place, but organisations had to proactively develop and monitor policy and practice towards justice in organisations for disabled, black and minority ethnic people. This new approach to legislation was significantly influenced by the disputed but gradual acceptance of the phenomenon of institutional forms of oppression. The Macpherson Report (1999) supported the idea of institutionalised racism, and the concept of organisational culture was placed on the policy agenda (Penketh, 2000). Other 'equal opportunity' initiatives have followed, including on age and religious discrimination, but most notably in relation to gay and lesbian rights. For example, the Employment Equality (Sexual Orientation) Regulations ban discrimination on the grounds of sexual orientation in employment and came into force in December 2003. The new legislation bans direct and indirect discrimination, harassment and victimisation because of sexual orientation. Other equal opportunities legislation has since followed.

In other countries some similar legislation has occurred, but there does not appear to be a consistent pattern across the globe: the struggles of various groups have met with resistance from powerful forces aligned to renewed nationalist and religious groups, as well as multinational corporations. The European Union has committed itself to Equal Opportunities legislation, and some European countries have made significant steps forward in requiring equal representation of women. There is thus in the UK, and to varying degrees elsewhere, an array of equal opportunities legislation which organisations can ill afford to completely ignore, and this opens up the possibility that individuals can work together for rights and social justice objectives within and between organisations. In addition the development of new social movements, including service-user organisations, offers social workers opportunities for considering the ethics of procedures and practices within their organisations, and for networking constructively with relevant groups of people within and outside their agencies. Reflecting on the organisational and legal history of the recent past is an important part of the work of understanding the context for ethical practice in organisations – especially in assessing how the specific agency concerned has reacted to social and legal change.

RE-FRAMING 'EQUAL OPPORTUNITIES': EQUALITY, DIVERSITY AND REFLEXIVITY

Contemporary feminist and post-modern theory has developed well-known critiques of assumptions associated with equal opportunities, as discussed in previous chapters, and it now needs to be re-framed. There is opposition to the 'binary' thinking implicit in the concepts conventionally associated with equal opportunities such as anti-racism and anti-sexism. This divides the world up too neatly, so that someone is *either* a racist *or* an anti-racist, either 'black' or 'white'. Social situations in organisational settings are much more complex, with changing rather than fixed social categories. There is also opposition to any narrow concept of power as merely top-down and oppressive, as discussed previously in this book. On the other hand, the 'instructionalist' ethos of current bureaucracies has been condemned as exemplifying 'totalitarian tendencies and mentalities', leaving little room for autonomy (Nellis, 2000, p40). We regard an anti-oppressive ethic as drawing attention to inequalities of power of all kinds within organisations, including that of workers, management and service users. The post-modern critiques of power and social difference have already been discussed (Chapters 3 and 7 above), and therefore the 're-framing' of equal opportunity issues itself needs to be critically examined, particularly in view of the strongly hierarchical nature of organisational arrangements favoured by (usually male) business managers.

'Equal opportunity' issues such as discrimination, harassment and equal access are fundamentally about respect for individuals and groups with socially diverse backgrounds. We are interested in the whole range of issues relating to equality and diversity, seeing them simultaneously as matters of policy, *and* also as matters of ethics in which staff have unavoidable responsibility. They demand an ethical response from individuals in the sense that they require a personal commitment to ethical action as well as a simultaneous, coordinated organisational response – a reflexive awareness of the individual's social relations within the agency, and with its environment, consistent with an anti-oppressive ethic.

The reframing of ethical issues in organisations coincides with a European-wide move towards 'mainstreaming' equal opportunities matters within organisations, begun in the context of Swedish gender politics according to Teresa Rees (Rees, 1999). Describing it as 'rooted in the post-modern approach of valuing diversity and difference' (Rees, 1999, p173), she characterises mainstreaming as a 'long-term strategic approach to fostering equal opportunities', which was influential throughout Europe, and adopted by the Equal Opportunities Commission in the UK in the mid 1990s (Rees, 1999, p175). Its particular stress on participation, continual awareness-raising and envisioning of different ways of achieving strategic cultural changes within an organisation, places responsibility on both senior management and *all* members of staff. The implications of this approach are that social workers need to be proactive within their own organisations on ethical issues involving equality and diversity. However, we are also mindful of the *probability* that ethical policies – and even apparently ethical practices – can be used for highly unethical ends. Organisations commonly defend their practices with reference to ethical policies, when it is simultaneously the case that there are hidden agendas. The policy of mainstreaming itself can be used to throw responsibility onto workers, allowing senior management off the hook. We are also mindful of the fact that ethics and values alone are a weak weapon to effect significant change in organisations, and examples of the unethical exercise of power, not least by managers, are not hard to find in most large organisations.

The legal and organisational context of social work offers an ambiguous moral and political environment requiring careful and reflexive consideration of the ethical possibilities. A re-framed concept of 'equal opportunities' thus needs to take account of the *complexities* of diversity and of inequality, requiring action against the various forms of subordination and exclusion. It thus feeds directly into anti-oppressive ethical concerns. It will be concerned with not only traditional recruitment and retention issues, but also the whole spectrum of organisational practices, policies and procedures which formally and informally impinge differentially upon diverse and unequal workers, managers, colleagues and service users. It requires the worker to take responsibility for their own ethical reflection and action, but in a context where negotiation and networking are vital. The worker has obligations to employers, the law, professional codes, the wider community and the service user. These have to be enacted within the limits set by organisational functions, and if the ethics do not coincide, then difficult decisions may be necessary. Some possible questions are listed in the following:

■ What individual or collective feasible strategies would be likely to make a difference to the organisation in which you work or study, to make it an ethically healthy organisation and more environmentally friendly to ethical practice?
■ How far does the organisation have a managerialist culture facilitating or hindering anti-oppressive ethics? How has it reacted to existing legislation?
■ What are its current policies and practices like when viewed from an anti-oppressive ethical perspective?
■ Who is best placed to initiate some changes?
■ What responsibility have you or your colleagues taken in the past?

▨ What arenas and structures are currently available for the monitoring and development of policy and practice, and how well are they being used?

▨ How does the organisation *really* cope with equality and difference, as compared with what it claims to be doing?

▨ How does your own position enable you to influence change, and who may be affected by your relative powers?

In addition to using anti-oppressive concepts to think reflexively through the legal and organisational environment, and taking personal responsibility for being aware of ethical issues, powers and possibilities, the social worker also has to think through the relevant ethical concepts. The next section considers some of the issues that need to be considered, using an anti-oppressive approach to ethical concepts as they may applied to organisations.

THINKING THROUGH ETHICAL POSITIONS IN AGENCIES

This final section is intended to simultaneously summarise some of the key ethical issues raised throughout the book, and at the same time assist reflection on a worker's position within an organisation. We will briefly review all the ethical theories presented above in relation to the issue of ethical orientation of the worker towards equality and diversity issues in organisations. We do not claim these are at all exhaustive or comprehensive as a list of suggested ideas that arise from these theories. We will be using our own guidelines (above) to suggest questions that need to be answered: readers may think of others. However in each case it is important to recall that *each* theory: (1) has something important to offer in terms of ethical ideas; and (2) presents an 'ideal' not as an impossible utopia, but rather as a standard of excellence towards which one should aim. Failure to consider these idea(l)s constitutes a failure to respect the requirements for good practice – which at its worst constitutes neglect of the duty of care owed by professional social workers towards service users.

The **Kantian ethics** discussed in Chapter 3 entails the notion of respect for individuals' rights under the law. The hypothetical contract view of society suggested by Rawls, and influenced by Kant (see above Chapter 6), is based on individuals having respect for their agreement to abide by fair rules to which they have consented. One of the aims of ethical action therefore must be to ensure that agreed laws and policies are adhered to in agencies. This is potentially conservative, in so far as policy and law are not necessarily designed to meet service-user need but to protect the interests of the powerful. However, some of the laws framing the work of social services could hardly be challenged – especially those forbidding violence against the person, for instance. There are many laws which are clearly consistent in their intent with anti-oppressive ethics, but they need to be monitored and put into practice effectively – laws against discrimination, for example. Nevertheless, there are also laws and policies that are neither universally agreed, nor acceptable (see, for example, Humphries, 2004). All laws have to be interpreted and applied to cases with care. The worker therefore needs to take responsibility for their own ethical stance on relevant law and policy and how it is to be interpreted and applied in their agency.

Kantian arguments about respect and autonomy also have other organisational implications for both workers and service users, including colleagues. The importance of the traditional concerns about consent, confidentiality and respect for persons needs to be thoughtfully examined from an anti-oppressive ethical perspective (see Chapter 3). In addition, it is important to avoid taking for granted the 'individualistic' stereotype of 'Kantian' ethics (cf. O'Neill, 1993) which should not deter workers from considering carefully the potentially radical implications for the way all individuals are treated by bureaucratic organisations. Workers need to continually review this issue for themselves as well as for service users, and consider what tactics can usefully be pursued.

The **utilitarian** implications for organisational behaviour depends whether act or rule utilitarianism is being discussed. We will discuss the latter here, because the whole organisational rationale is so dependent on the existence of rules (but readers can also consider what difference it would make if act utilitarianism were the basis for reflection). In Chapter 3 some organisational issues impinged on the particular issue of confidentiality, but more generally, empirical utilitarian calculations about the best value and good outcomes are a very significant part of current practice. There are numerous aspects to the mobilisation of this idea at an organisational level. The worker needs to think about the appeal of managers to maximise the effectiveness and success of the organisation in achieving its objectives. The vogue for 'mission statements' plays upon this utilitarian impulse, but there will always be issues about whether the agency's objectives are appropriate; are they the *real* objectives; and are they actually implemented at all in daily practice. Clearly managers have vested interests – and so do workers and service users, but some have more power than others to define 'good outcomes'. In addition the use of evidence in relation to social work cases raises issues about the accessibility of evidence, and about who researched this evidence, when and where, the methodology on which it was based, and the way it is being used. Again, the stereotypically number-crunching Dickensian view of utilitarianism should not deter workers from using utilitarian arguments in a critical way to defend outcomes which can be shown to be positive for oppressed groups and individuals, especially when service users also participate in the evaluation of those outcomes. It is too important an ethical idea to be jettisoned simply because of its insensitive or politically expedient use by some.

When **virtue ethics** is considered, the discussion of Chapter 5 has already dealt with many of the issues arising in connection with working in an organisation. Virtue ethics relies on the dialogical development of ethical traditions and practices within a culture, therefore besides the good character of the worker there certainly needs to be an ethically healthy and competent organisation in which she can flourish. However, the tendency to see virtue ethics simply in idealistic terms should be resisted if good practice and standards of excellence in human relationships are really to be valued, since 'vices' can sometimes be effectively used to critically assess and resist what are conventionally passed off as 'virtues', especially when an organisation may be promoting as 'virtuous' policies used to depress marginalised groups. The worker needs to consider *which* of the virtues are most realisable and valuable from the perspective of oppressed groups and the service users of her particular agency, and how far the agency is able to include the participation of individuals – service users and professional workers – in respectful dialogue.

From our contact with service users about what to teach about ethics, the integrity of virtue ethics is certainly something *they* value. They were adamant that social work is not 'just a job' – the virtues of being a good social worker needed to be part of their character (Voices in Partnership, 2003). We would suggest that in a healthy organisation workers will also value 'virtue' in human relationships, as they get satisfaction and self-respect from doing a difficult job well, and knowing that service users and managers might also respect them and their work. We realise that really healthy organisations are hard to find in societies that tends to overvalue money, leadership and power. However, we are talking about a continuum of organisational practices, in which a worker participates, and may be able to influence, depending on the particular organisational setting.

Radical ethics is a broad term which we used in Chapter 6 to describe structural and human rights approaches, focusing on Marxist and Rawlsian social democratic perspectives. We saw there could be differing interpretations of radical positions, but that some similar issues would arise about any organisation that is set up to deal with social issues in a society based on exclusion, hierarchy and oppression. These approaches to ethical issues are sometimes distinguished by a critical view or rejection of ethics in favour of a political commitment – which is nevertheless ethical in itself. As with other ethics presented here, it is too easy to create a straw target and focus on the stereotypical and utopian emancipatory ideals implied by these commitments. However, these views require serious consideration if workers are not to conform mindlessly to expectations which ignore the impact of macrolevel social divisions on the activities of individuals and organisations. Whatever strategy may be favoured by differing radical approaches the arguments begin with the need for a thorough critique of the services offered by an organisation grounded in oppression, and only able to deliver stigmatising and exclusionary services. What may be viewed as ironic about this is not the unrealisable emancipatory ideal, so much as the relative neglect of ethics by a politically focused activist. What could be more of a moral dilemma than working for such an agency?

From an anti-oppressive ethical perspective the power of the social divisions to create social problems and to constrain the so-called solutions to them is a basic factor for workers to take into account at both personal and organisational levels. On this argument service users as citizens will have little influence on the national and global decision-making of politicians and financiers, and limited influence on organisations. Therefore how, and how far, should the worker attempt to adapt their own actions to the demands of a radical perspective which is so critical of the agency they are working for? Chapter 6 suggested some possible ways forward in relation to a particular case, but the answer has to be generalised to include the worker's attitude to the agency and especially towards its managers, professional and trade unions. Our aim is not to provide the 'solution', but to insist that workers do not ignore the scope of the ethical dilemmas they are faced with in organisations, and the possibility of changes, at the same time as they (rightly) acknowledge the economic and political constraints.

Post-modern perspectives on ethics are sometimes criticised for their lack of clear application to the real world – as with the stereotypical assumptions made about other ethical theories. However, in Chapter 7 we examined the complexity and uncertainty surrounding a typical social work decision, and saw how a post-modern ethic could have considerable attraction for an intelligent worker trying to come to terms with complex situations. In relation to the organisation that employs the worker, there would need to be an environment in which radical criticism and diversity of values was acceptable in both service-user language, and in worker discourses. An organisation which inflexibly required workers to follow a rulebook without allowing for professional ethical judgements to digress from convention would be an ethically unhealthy place in which to work. Similarly the organisation which was not able to offer services that could adjust to a wide range of differing service-user values and cultures would be unacceptable. At what point the worker would feel obliged to whistle-blow or resign would be an existential decision for them to make – and a serious one from an anti-oppressive ethical perspective to consider. It is a critical issue for postmodern ethics that workers do not avoid the ethical issues that face them by passing responsibility off onto the senior management or the organisation itself.

Feminist relational ethics suggests that the impact of unequal social divisions has to be thoroughly understood in organisations, and not only in respect of the gender divide. These ideas are reflected in feminist analyses of organisations. One such study of gender and organisations (Halford *et al.*, 1997, pp13–28) argues that gender is 'embedded' in organisations, meaning that gender issues are not simply carried into organisations by the individuals who staff them: the organisational process is not itself neutral. Conventional organisational designs and processes fit the needs and culture of men's lives rather than women (cf. Billington, *et al.*, 1998, pp153–6). Sexual harassment, for example, fits smoothly into a system which itself provides for women to be kept in subordinate positions, and therefore is likely to be an integral aspect of the social interactions which take place:

> Men are invariably in positions of seniority at work, but quite independently of work men have power because of their position in society. Most of the time sexual harassment occurs when men abuse the power they have over women.
>
> (Collier, 1995, p27)

The various forms of power and oppression will overlap and interconnect: 'Racisms are forms of subordination and exclusion *and work in tandem with* class-related and gender-related forms of subordination and exclusion' (Anthias, 1999, 7.1). They also work in tandem with other forms of discrimination such as those related to disability, sexuality and age. Feminist relational ethics points to the interconnectedness of unequal powers in organisations, and at the same time the importance of working out strategies for developing respect and nurturing care across these divides, taking individual and collective responsibility for ethical practice. This approach requires sensitivity to both the politics and ethics of specific situations, with special reference to the most vulnerable, including service users and carers.

Given the position of an organisation as a mezzo-level social system it will continue to be subject to the stresses of social and political change, including the developing patterns of various forms of social oppression. The dimension of time means that organisational arrangements which appear appropriate at one point may not be later. Agencies can achieve little, or sometimes get worse in relation to diversity and equality issues. There is therefore a need for continuing ethical review of practices and policies, with assessment of the organisational culture and its impact on workers and users. Individual ethical responses of workers will be more likely if the context of work facilitates rather than hinders their deliberations. But effective review and monitoring is much more likely where an anti-oppressive approach to ethics is used individually and collectively to influence the course of change.

In comparison with the discussion of case studies in previous chapters, there is a significant point to be made about the use of case and research evidence in ethical practice in organisations. In many large organisations information is sometimes not easy to access or assess, due to the secretive nature of bureaucracies, where managements control the flow of information. This makes it even more important to develop networks that can provide alternative sources of information – especially where service users and carers are involved with organisations. Consultation and negotiation with a range of colleagues within and outside the organisation is part of the usual procedure of professional practice, but from an anti-oppressive perspective it has another function – one of assisting the worker in understanding different perspectives and differential access to information. This will include interprofessional colleagues as well as service users and carers, and perhaps especially advocates, whose given role is to take up adversarial positions against organisations on behalf of their clients.

The model for anti-oppressive ethical practice described in Chapter 9 applies in more general ways to issues in organisations, but it certainly applies. In particular, it implies the importance of awareness and knowledge of the social world of the organisation, and reflection on its patterns of inequality. The framework enables the worker to think proactively, with or without the aid of a live ethical issue, problem or dilemma to consider, so that forms of institutionalised racism or other kinds of systemic discrimination are recognised. This takes us back to where we started in this chapter – the ethical health of organisations, facilitating or limiting workers in being 'morally active practitioners' (Husband, 1995).

CHAPTER SUMMARY

Our aim in this Conclusion has been to review an anti-oppressive approach to ethical practice whilst applying it to the organisational settings in which social workers pursue their professional aims. It is not intended as an exhaustive explanation of possibilities, but rather as a discursive approach to using the anti-oppressive ideas outlined in Chapter 1 and elaborated in the rest of the book. It discusses the way the historical and legal background provides the basis for reflection, and the necessity of understanding one's personal position in relation to the unequal powers of the various social divisions and the intervening hierarchies and systems of contemporary organisations. It emphasises the importance of reviewing the range of ethical concepts, and the links with various networks, including service users and carers, translating individual ethics into organisational and collective action.

References

Adams, R. (2002) *Social Policy for Social Work*, Basingstoke: Palgrave Macmillan.

Adams, R. Dominelli, L. and Payne, M. (eds) *Critical Practice in Social Work*, Basingstoke: Palgrave.

Ahmed, S. (1998) *Differences that Matter: Feminist Theory and Postmodernism*, Cambridge: Cambridge University Press.

Aitkenhead, M. and Liff, S. (1991) 'The effectiveness of equal opportunity policies', in Firth-Cozens, J. and West, M. (eds) *Women at Work: Psychological and Organisational Perspectives*, Milton Keynes: Open University Press.

Anderson, K. and Jack, D.C. (1991) 'Learning to listen: interview techniques and analyses', in Gluck, S.B. and Patai, D. (eds) *Women's Words, The Feminist Practice of Oral History*, London: Routledge.

Anthias, F. (1999) 'Institutional racism, power and accountability', in: *Sociological Research Online*, 4: 1. <http://www.socresonline.org.uk/4/lawrence//anthias.html>.

Australian Association of Social Workers (AASW) (1999; 2nd edn, 2001) *Code of Ethics*, Canberra: AASW.

Ayer, A.J. (2002) 'Language, truth and logic' (selections), in Cahn, S.M. and Markie, P. (eds) *Ethics: History, Theory and Contemporary Issues*, Oxford: Oxford University Press.

Baistow, K. (1994/5) 'Liberation and regulation? Some paradoxes of empowerment', *Critical Social Policy*, issue 42.

Banks, S. (1995; 2nd edn, 2001; 3rd edn, 2006) *Ethics and Values in Social Work*, London: Macmillan.

Banks, S. and Nohr, K. (eds) (2003) *Teaching Practical Ethics for the Social Professions*, <wwwfeset.dk: European Social Ethics Project>.

Banks, S. (2004) *Ethics, Accountability and the Social Professions*, Basingstoke: Palgrave Macmillan.

Banks, S. and Williams, R. (2005) 'Accounting for ethical difficulties in social welfare work: issues, problems and dilemmas, *British Journal of Social Work*, 35:7, pp1005–22.

Barnes, M. (2006) *Caring and Social Justice*, Basingstoke: Palgrave Macmillan.

Baumann, Z. (1989) *Modernity and the Holocaust*, Oxford: Blackwell.

Baumann, Z. (1992) *Postmodern Ethics*, Oxford: Blackwell,

Baumann, Z. (1998) 'What prospects of morality in times of uncertainty?', *Theory, Culture and Society*, 15:1, pp11–22.

Baumann, Z. (2000) 'Am I my brother's keeper?', *European Journal of Social Work*, 3:1, pp5–12.

Beauchamp, T. L., and Childress, J.F. (2001) *Principles of Biomedical Ethics*, 5th edn, New York: Oxford University Press.

Beckett, C. (2007) 'The reality principle: realism as an ethical obligation', *Ethics and Social Welfare*, 1:3, pp269–81.

Begley, A.M. (2005) 'Practising virtue: a challenge to the view that a virtue centred approach to ethics lacks practical content', *Nursing Ethics*, 12:6, pp622–37.

Benhabib, S. (1992) *Situating the Self, Gender, Community and Postmodernism in Contemporary Ethics*, New York: Routledge.

Beresford, P. and Croft, S. (2004) 'Service users and practitioners reunited: the key component for social work reform', *British Journal of Social Work*, 34:1, pp53–68.

Biestek, F. (1961) *The Casework Relationship*, London: Allen and Unwin.

Billington, R., Hockey, J., Strawbridge, S. *et al.* (1998) *Exploring Self and Society*, London: Macmillan.

Bisman, C. (2004) 'Social work values: the moral core of the profession', *British Journal of Social Work*, 34:1, pp109–23.

Black, P.N. *et al.* (2002) *Teaching Social Work Values and Ethics: A Curriculum Resource*, Alexandria, V.A.: Council on Social Work Education.

Bonnett, A. (2000) *Anti-Racism*, London: Routledge.

Bowden, P. (1997) *Caring: An Investigation in Gender-Sensitive Ethics*, London: Routledge.

Bowles, W., Collingridge, M., Curry, S. and Valentine, B. (2006) *Ethical Practice in Social Work: An Applied Approach*, Maidenhead: Open University Press.

Bradley, H. (1996) *Fractured Identities*, London: Polity Press.

Braye, S. and Preston-Shoot, M. (1992; 2nd edn, 1997), *Practising Social Work Law*, Basingstoke: Macmillan.

Braye, S. and Preston-Shoot, M. (1995) *Empowering Practice in Social Care*, Buckingham: Open University Press.

Brayne, H. and Martin, G. (1990) *Law for Social Workers*, London: Blackstone Press.

Briskman, L. and Noble, C. (1999) 'Social work ethics: embracing diversity', in Pease, B. and Fook, (eds) *Transforming Social Work Practice*, St Leonard's, NSW: Allen and Unwin, pp57–69.

Brown, H.C. and Kershaw, S. (2008) 'The legal context for lesbians and gay men in the UK: updating the educational context', *Social Work Education*, 27:2, pp122–30.

British Association of Social Workers (BASW) (2002) *Code of Ethics for Social Work*, Birmingham: BASW.

Butler, I. (2002) 'A code of ethics for social work and social care research', *British Journal of Social Work*, 32:2, pp239–48.

Cahn, S.M. (2002) 'Two concepts of affirmative action', in Cahn, S.M. and Markie, P. (eds) *Ethics: History, Theory, and Contemporary Issues*, Oxford: Oxford University Press.

Cahn, S.M. and Markie, P. (eds) (2002) *Ethics: History, Theory and Contemporary Issues*, Oxford: Oxford University Press.

Calhoun, C. (2004) 'Introduction', in Calhoun, C. (ed.) *Setting the Moral Compass: Essays by Women Philosophers*, Oxford: Oxford University Press.

Calhoun, C. (ed.) (2004) *Setting the Moral Compass: Essays by Women Philosophers*, Oxford: Oxford University Press.

Canda, E. and Furman, L. (1999) *Spiritual Diversity in Social Work Practice: The Heart of Helping*, New York: The Howarth Press.

Charles, M. and Butler, S. (2004) 'Social workers' management of organisational change', in Lymbery, M. and Butler, S. (eds) *Social Work Ideals and Practice Realities*, Basingstoke: Palgrave Macmillan.

Charlton, L., Crank, M., Kansara, K. and Oliver, C. (1998) *Still Screaming: Birth Parents Compulsorily Separated from Their Children*, Manchester: After Adoption.

Clark, C. (2000) *Social Work Ethics: Politics, Principles and Practice*, Basingstoke: Macmillan.

Clark, C. (2006) 'Moral character in social work', *British Journal of Social Work*, 36:1, pp75–89.

Clark, C. (2007) 'Professional responsibility, misconduct and practical reason', *Ethics and Social Welfare*, 1:1, pp42–55.

Clayton, M. and Williams, A. (eds) (2002) *The Ideal of Equality*, Basingstoke: Palgrave Macmillan.

Clifford, D.J. (1998) *Social Assessment Theory and Practice: A Multi-Disciplinary Framework*, Aldershot: Ashgate.

Clifford, D.J. and Burke, B. (2001) 'What practical difference does it make? Anti-oppressive ethics and informed consent', *Practice* (Journal of the British Association of Social Workers), 13:1, pp17–28.

Clifford, D.J. (2002) 'Resolving uncertainties? The contribution of some recent feminist ethical theory to the social professions', *European Journal of Social Work*, 5:1, pp31–41.

Clifford, D.J. and Burke, B. (2004), 'Moral and professional dilemmas in long-term assessment of children and families', *Journal of Social Work*, 4:3, pp305–21.

Clifford, D.J. and Burke, B. (2005) 'Developing anti-oppressive ethics in the new curriculum', *Social Work Education*, 24:6, pp677–92.

Clifford, D.J. and Burke, B. (2007) 'Competence in social work ethics', in O'Hagan, K. (ed.) *Competence in Social Work Practice*, 2nd edn, London: Jessica Kingsley.

Clifford, D.J. and Royce, M. (2008) 'Equality, diversity, ethics and management in social work education', *Social Work Education*, 27:1, pp3–18.

Code, L. (2000) 'The perversion of autonomy and the subjection of women: discourses of social advocacy at the century's end', in Mackenzie, C. and Stoljar, N. (eds) *Relational Autonomy: Feminist Perspectives on Autonomy, Agency and the Social Self*, Oxford: University Press.

Collier, R. (1995) *Combatting Sexual Harassment in the Workplace*, Milton Keynes: Open University Press.

Collins, P. (1990) *Black Feminist Thought*, London: Hyman.

Congress, E. and McAuliffe, D. (2006) 'Social work ethics: professional codes in Australia and the United States, *International Social Work*, 49:2, pp151–64.

Cournoyer, B. (2000) *The Social Work Skills Workbook*, 3rd edn, Belmont, Ca.: Wadsworth.

Cowden, S. and Singh, G. (2007) 'The "user": friend, foe or fetish?: A critical exploration of user involvement in health and social care', *Critical Social Policy*, 27:1, pp5–23.

Cull, L.-A. and Roche, J. (2001) *The Law and Social Work: Contemporary Issues for Practice*, Basingstoke: Palgrave.

Dalrymple, J. and Burke, B. (1995; 2nd edn, 2006) *Anti-Oppressive Practice Social Care and the Law*, Maidenhead: Open University Press.

Dalrymple, J. (2004) 'Professional advocacy as a force for resistance in child welfare', *British Journal of Social Work*, 33:8, pp1043–62.

D'Cruz, H., Gillingham, P. and Melendez, S. (2007) 'Reflexivity, its meanings and relevance for social work: a critical review of the literature: different meanings of "reflexivity"' *British Journal of Social Work*, 37, 1:pp73–90.

Department of Health (1995) *Child Protection: Messages from Research*, London: HMSO.

Department of Health (2001) *Seeking Consent: Working with Older People*, London: HMSO.

De Silva, P. (1993) 'Buddhist ethics', in Singer, P. (ed.) *A Companion to Ethics*, Oxford: Blackwell.

Dominelli, L. (2002a) *Anti-Oppressive Social Work Theory and Practice*, Basingstoke: Palgrave Macmillan.

Dominelli, L. (2002b) *Feminist Social Work Theory and Practice*, Basingstoke: Palgrave Macmillan.

Dominelli, L. (2002c) 'Values in social work', in Adams, R. Dominelli, L. and Payne, M. (eds) *Critical Practice in Social Work*, Basingstoke: Palgrave Macmillan.

Dominelli, L. (2004) *Social Work: Theory and Practice for a Changing Profession*, Cambridge: Polity Press.

Davis, M. (1999) *Ethics and the University*, London: Routledge.

Erion, G.J. (2005) 'Engaging student relativism', *Discourse: Learning and Teaching in Philosophical and Religious Studies*, 5:1, pp120–33.

Edwards, R. and Mauthner, M. (2002) 'Ethics and feminist research: theory and practice', in Mauthner, M., Birch, M., Jessop, J. and Miller, T. (eds) *Ethics in Qualitative Research*, London: Sage.

Evans, T. and Harris, J. (2004) 'Citizenship and social inclusion and confidentiality', *British Journal of Social Work*, 34:1, pp69–91.

Feary, V. (2003) 'Virtue-based feminist philosophical counselling', *Practical Philosophy*, 6:1, spring, pp7–26 <http://www.practicalphilosophy.org.uk/Volume6Articles/Virtue.htm>.

Ferguson, H. (2003) 'Outline of a critical best practice perspective on social work and social care', *British Journal of Social Work*, 33:8, pp1005–24.

Ferguson, H. and Lavalette, M. (2004) 'Beyond power discourse: alienation and social work', *British Journal of Social Work*, 34:3, pp297–312.

Fook J. (2002) *Social Work: Critical Theory and Practice*, London: Sage.

Fox Harding, L. (1997) *Perspectives in Child Care Policy*, 2nd edn, Harlow: Addison-Wesley/Longman.

Fox, R.M. and DeMarco, J.P. (2001) *Moral Reasoning: A Philosophical Approach to Applied Ethics*, Fort Worth, Tex: Harcourt College Publishers.

Fricker, M. (2000) 'Feminism in epistemology: pluralism without postmodernism', in Fricker, M. and Hornsby, J. (eds) *The Cambridge Companion to Feminism in Philosophy*, Cambridge: Cambridge University Press.

Frost, M. (2003) *Constituting Human Rights: Global Civil Society and the Society of Democratic States*, New York: Routledge.

Gallagher, A. (2004) 'Do virtues have a role in the practice of counselling?', in Martin, R., Barrett, S., Komaromy, C. and Rogers, D. (eds) *Communication, Relationships and Care: A Reader*, London: Routledge.

Gant, V. (2008) 'The needs of older carers of adults with learning disabilities', unpublished PhD thesis, Liverpool John Moores University.

General Social Care Council (GSCC) (2002) *Codes of Practice for Social Care Workers and Employers*, London: GSCC.

Gilligan, C. (1982) *In a Different Voice, Psychological Theory and Women's Development*, Cambridge, Mass.: Harvard University Press.

Gluck, S.B. and Patai, D. (eds) (1991) *Women's Words, the Feminist Practice of Oral History*, London: Routledge.

Goodin, R.E. (1991) 'Utility and the good', in Singer, P. (ed.) *A Companion to Ethics*, Oxford: Blackwell, pp241–8.

Goovaerts, H. (2002) 'Working with a staged plan', in Banks, S. and Nohr, K. (eds) *Teaching Practical Ethics for the Social Professions*, <wwwfeset.dk>: European Social Ethics Project, pp83–94.

Graham, M. (2002) *Social Work and African-Centred Worldviews*, Birmingham: Venture Press.

Graham, M. (2007) 'The ethics of care, black women and the social professions: implications of a new analysis', *Ethics and Social Welfare*, 1:2, pp209–15.

Gray, M. and Lovat, T. (2007) 'Horse and carriage: why Habermas's discourse ethics gives virtue a *praxis* in social work', *Ethics and Social Welfare*, 1:3, pp310–28.

Gray, M. (2008) Viewing spirituality in social work through the lens of contemporary social theory', *British Journal of Social Work*, 38:1, pp175–96.

Habermas, J. (1990) *Moral Consciousness and Communicative Action*, Cambridge: Polity Press.

Halford, S., Savage, M. and Witz, A. (1997) *Gender, Careers and Organisations: Current Developments in Banking Nursing and Local Government*, London: Macmillan.

Halford, S. and Leonard, P. (2001) *Gender, Power and Organisations*, Basingstoke: Palgrave Macmillan.

Healey, K. (2000) *Social Work Practices*, London: Sage.

Healey, K. (2005) *Social Work Theories in Context: Creating Frameworks for Practice*, Basingstoke: Palgrave Macmillan.

Healey, K. and Meagher, G. (2004) 'The re-professionalization of social work: collaborative approaches for achieving professional recognition', *British Journal of Social Work*, 34:2, pp243–60.

Healy, L. (2007) 'Universalism and cultural relativism in social work ethics', in *International Social Work*, 50:1, pp11–26.

Hekman, S. (1995) *Moral Voices, Moral Selves: Carole Gilligan and Feminist Moral Theory*, London: Polity Press.

Hekmans, R. Arend, van der A. *et al.* (2007) 'Dutch nurses' views on codes of ethics', *Nursing Ethics*, 14:2, pp156–70.

Held, V. (2006) *The Ethics of Care: Personal, Political and Global*, Oxford and New York: Oxford University Press.

Holland, S. (2000) 'The assessment relationship: interactions between social workers and parents in child protection assessments', *British Journal of Social Work*, 30:2, pp149–63.

Holland, T.P. and Kilpatrick, A.C. (1991) 'Ethical issues in social work: toward a grounded theory of professional ethics', *Social Work*, 36:2, pp138–44.

Holloway, M. (2007) 'Spiritual Need and the Core Business of Social Work', *British Journal of Social Work* 37:2, pp265–80.

hooks, b. (1982) *Ain't I a Woman?, Black Women and Feminism*, London: Pluto Press.

Homiack, M.L. (1999) 'Feminism and Aristotle's rational ideal', in Sherman, N. (ed.) *Aristotle's Ethics: Critical Essays*, Lanham, Md.: Rowman and Littlefield, pp301–24.

Hooker, B. (2002) 'Rule-utilitarianism and euthanasia', in LaFollette, H. (ed.) *Ethics in Practice: An Anthology*, 2nd edn, Oxford: Blackwell Publishers, pp22–31.

Houston, S. (2003) 'Establishing virtue in social work: a response to McBeath and Webb', *British Journal of Social Work*, 33:6, pp819–24.

Hugman, R. and Smith, D. (eds) (1995) *Ethical Issues in Social Work*, London: Routledge.

Hugman, R. and Smith, D. (1995) 'Ethical issues in social work: an overview', in Hugman, R. and Smith, D. (eds) *Ethical Issues in Social Work*, London: Routledge, pp1–15.

Hugman R. (2003) 'Professional values and ethics in social work: reconsidering post-modernism?', *British Journal of Social Work*, 33:8, pp1025–41.

Hugman, R. (2005) 'Exploring the paradox of teaching ethics for social work practice', *Social Work Education*, 24:5, pp535–45.

Hugman, R. (2008) 'Ethics in a world of difference', *Ethics and Social Welfare*, 2:2.

Humphries, B. (ed.) (1996) *Critical Perspectives on Empowerment*, Birmingham: Venture Press.

Humphries, B. (1997) 'Reading social work: competing discourses in the "Rules and Requirements for the Diploma in Social Work"', *British Journal of Social Work*, 27:5, pp641–58.

Humphries, B. (2004) 'An unacceptable role for social work: implementing immigration policy', *British Journal of Social Work*, 34:1, pp93–107.

Hursthouse, R. (1997) 'Virtue theory and abortion', in Crisp, R. and Slote, M. (eds) *Virtue Ethics*, Oxford: Oxford University Press.

Husband, C. (1995), 'The morally active practitioner, and the ethics of anti-racist social work', in Hugman, R. and Smith, D. (eds) *Ethical Issues in Social Work*, London: Routledge.

Hutchings, K. (2000) 'Towards a feminist international ethics', *Review of International Studies*, 26:1, pp111–30.

Ife, J. (2001) *Human Rights and Social Work: Towards a Rights-Based Practice*, Cambridge: Cambridge University Press.

Ifekwunigwe, J. (1997) 'Diaspora's daughters, Africa's orphans? On lineage, authenticity and "mixed race" identity', in Mirza, H.S. (ed.) *Black British Feminism*, London, Routledge, pp127–52.

International Federation of Social Workers (IFSW) and International Association of Schools of Social Work (IASSW) (2004) *Ethics in Social Work, Statement of Principles*, Berne, Switzerland: IFSW/IASSW.

Jaggar, A.M. (2000) 'Feminism in ethics: moral justification', in Fricker, M. and Hornsby, J. (eds) *The Cambridge Companion to Feminism in Philosophy*, Cambridge: Cambridge University Press.

Jaggar, A.M. (2004) 'Globalizing feminist ethics', in Calhoun, C. (ed.), *Setting the Moral Compass: Essays by Women Philosophers*, Oxford: Oxford University Press.

Jawad, R. (2007) 'Human ethics and welfare particularism: an exploration of the social welfare regime in Lebanon', *Ethics and Social Welfare*, 1:2, pp123–46.

Jenkins, K. (1995) *On 'What is History': From Carr and Elton to Rorty and White*, London: Routledge.

Jewson, N. and Mason, D. (1992) 'The theory and practice of equal opportunities policies: liberal and radical approaches', in Braham, P., Rattansi, A. and

Skellington, R. (eds) *Racism and Anti-Racism: Inequalities, Opportunities and Policies*, London: Sage.

Jones, C. (2002) 'Social work and society', in Adams, R., Dominelli, L. and Payne, M. (eds) *Social Work: Themes, Issues and Critical Debates*, 2nd edn, Basingstoke: Palgrave Macmillan.

Jones, K., Cooper, B. *et al.* (eds) (2008) *Best practice in Social Work: Critical Perspectives*, Basingstoke: Palgrave Macmillan.

Jordan, B. (1979) *Helping in Social Work*, London: Routledge and Kegan Paul.

Jordan, B. (2004) 'Emancipatory social work: opportunity or oxymoron? *British Journal of Social Work*, 34:1, pp5–19.

Kallen, E (2003) *Social Inequality and Social Injustice*, London: Palgrave.

Kant, I. (1993) 'Fundamental principles of the metaphysics of morals', in Singer, P. (ed.) *A Companion to Ethics*, Oxford: Blackwell.

Kennedy, H. (1993) *Eve Was Framed: Women and British Justice*, London: Vintage Books.

Kennedy, H. (2004) *Just Law: The Changing Face of Justice, and Why It Matters to Us All*, London: Chatto and Windus.

Keown, D. (2001) *The Nature of Buddhist Ethics*, Basingstoke: Palgrave Macmillan.

King, M. and Trowell, J. (1992) *Children's Welfare in the Law: The Limits of Legal Intervention*, London: Sage.

Klug, F. (2002) *Values for a Godless Age: The Story of the United Kingdom's New Bill of Rights*, Harmondsworth: Penguin.

Koehn, D. (1998) *Rethinking Feminist Ethics: Care, Trust and Empathy*, London: Routledge.

Lafollette, H. (ed.) (2002, 2nd edn) *Ethics in Practice: An Anthology*, Malden, Mass.: Blackwell Publishing Ltd.

Lloyd, G. (2000) 'Individuals, responsibility and the philosophical imagination', in Mackenzie, C. and Stoljar, N. (eds) *Relational Autonomy: Feminist perspectives on Autonomy, Agency and the Social Self*, Oxford: Oxford University Press.

Lloyd, L. (2006) 'A caring profession? The ethics of care and social work with older people', *British Journal of Social Work*, 36:7, pp1171–85.

Lloyd, M. (1997) 'Foucault's ethics and politics: a strategy for feminism?', in Lloyd, M. and Thacker A. (eds) *The Impact of Foucault on the Social Sciences and Humanities*, London: Macmillan, pp78–101.

Loewenberg, F.M. and Dolgoff, R. (1996) *Ethical Decisions for Social Work Practice*, Itasca, Ill.: F. E. Peacock.

Louden, R. B. (1984) 'On some vices of virtue ethics', in Crisp, R. and Slote, M. (eds) *Virtue Ethics*, Oxford: Oxford University Press.

Lukes, S. (2005) *Power: A Radical View*, 2nd edn, Basingstoke: Palgrave Macmillan.

Lymbery, M. (2004) 'Responding to crisis: the changing nature of welfare organizations', in Lymbery, M. and Butler, S. (eds) *Social Work Ideals and Practice Realities*, Basingstoke: Palgrave Macmillan.

Lymbery, M. and Butler, S. (eds) (2004) *Social Work Ideals and Practice Realities*, Basingstoke: Palgrave Macmillan.

Lynn, E. (1999) 'Value bases in social work education', *British Journal of Social Work*, 29:6, pp939–53.

MacIntyre, A. (1981) *After Virtue*, Indiana: University of Notre Dame Press.

MacIntyre, A. (2002) 'After virtue' (extract), in Cahn, S.M. and Markie, P. (eds) (2002) *Ethics: History, Theory and Contemporary Issues*, Oxford: Oxford University Press.

Mackenzie, C. and Stoljar, N. (eds) (2000) *Relational Autonomy: Feminist Perspectives on Autonomy, Agency and the Social Self*, Oxford: Oxford University Press.

Macpherson Report (1999) *The Stephen Lawrence Murder Inquiry*, London: HMSO. <http://www.official-documents.co.uk/document/cm42/4262/4262.htm>.

Mauthner, M., Birch, M., Jessop, J. and Miller, T. (eds) (2002) *Ethics in Qualitative Research*, London: Sage.

McAuliffe, D. and Chenoweth, L. (2008) 'Leave no stone unturned: the inclusive model of ethical decision-making', *Ethics and Social Welfare*, 2:1, pp38–49.

McBeath, G. and Webb, S. (2002) 'Virtue ethics and social work: being lucky, realistic, and not doing one's duty', *British Journal of Social Work*, 32:8, pp1015–36.

McLaughlin, J. (2003) *Feminist Social and Political Theory: Contemporary Debates and Dialogues*, Basingstoke: Palgrave Macmillan.

McDonald, G. and McDonald, K. (1995) 'Ethical issues in social work research', in Hugman, R. and Smith, D. (eds) *Ethical Issues in Social Work*, London: Routledge.

McLeod, C. and Sherwin, S. (2000) 'Relational autonomy, self-care and health care for patients who are oppressed', in Mackenzie, C. and Stoljar, N. (eds) *Relational Autonomy: Feminist Perspectives on Autonomy, Agency and the Social Self*, Oxford: Oxford University Press.

Meyer, J. and Timms, N. (1970) *The Client Speaks*, London: Routledge.

Millar, M. (2008) ' "Anti-oppressiveness": critical comments on a discourse and its context', *British Journal of Social Work*, 38:2, pp362–75.

Mirza, H.S. (ed.) (1997) *Black British Feminism*, London: Routledge.

Morrison, T. (2007) 'Emotional intelligence, emotion and social work: context, characteristics, complications and contribution', *British Journal of Social Work*, 37:2, pp245–63.

Moss, B. (2005), *Religion and Spirituality*, Lyme Regis, Dorset: Russell House Publishing.

Nanji, A. (1993) 'Islamic ethics', in Singer, P. (ed.) *A Companion to Ethics*, Oxford: Blackwell.

Nellis, M. (2000) 'Taking oppression seriously: a critique of managerialism in social work/probation', in Paylor, I., Froggett, M. and Harris, D. (eds) *Reclaiming Social Work: The Southport Papers*, Vol. 2, Birmingham: Venture Press.

Noddings, N. (1984) *Caring: A Feminine Approach to Ethics*, Berkeley: University of California Press.

Norman, R. (1998) *The Moral Philosophers: An Introduction to Ethics*, 2nd edn, Oxford: Oxford University Press.

Nursing and Midwifery Council (2002) *Code of Professional Conduct*, London: Nursing and Midwifery Council.

Nussbaum, M. (2000) *Women and Human Development*, Cambridge: Cambridge University Press.

Nussbaum, M. (2005) 'The cognitive structure of compassion', in Williams, C. (ed.) *Personal Virtues*, Basingstoke: Palgrave Macmillan.

O'Neill, O. (1993) 'Kantian ethics', in Singer, P. (ed.) *A Companion to Ethics*, Oxford: Blackwell.

Orme, J. (2002) 'Social work: gender, care and justice', *British Journal of Social Work*, 32:6, pp799–814.

O'Sullivan, T. (1999) *Decision-making in Social Work*, Basingstoke: Palgrave Macmillan.

Outhwaite, W. (1999) 'The myth of modernist method', *Journal of European Social Theory*, 2:1, pp34–47.

Parton, N. (2003) 'Rethinking professional practice: the contributions of social constructionism and the feminist "ethics of care"', *British Journal of Social Work*, 33:1, pp1–16.

Pattinson, S. (2001) 'Are nursing codes of practice ethical?', *Nursing Ethics,* 8:1, pp5–17.

Payne, G. (ed.) (2006) *Social Divisions*, 2nd edn, Basingstoke: Palgrave Macmillan.

Pence, G. (1993) 'Virtue theory', in Singer, P. (ed.) *A Companion to Ethics*, Oxford: Blackwell.

Penketh, L. (2000) *Tackling Institutional Racism: Anti-Racist Policies and Social Work Education and Training*, London: Policy Press.

Pettit, P. (1993) 'Consequentialism', in Singer, P. (ed.) *A Companion to Ethics*, Oxford: Blackwell, pp. 230–40.

Phillipson, J. (1992) *Practising Equality: Men, Women and Social Work*, London: Central Council for Education and Training in Social Work.

Porter, E. (1999) *Feminist Perspectives on Ethics*, London and New York: Longman.

Preston, R. (1993) 'Christian ethics', in Singer, P. (ed.) *A Companion to Ethics*, Oxford: Blackwell.

Preston-Shoot, M. (2001) 'Evaluating self-determination: an adult protection case study', *Journal of Adult Protection*, 3:1, pp23–48.

Preston-Shoot, M. (2003) 'Teaching and assessing social work law: reflections from a post-qualifying progamme', *Social Work Education*, 22:5, pp461–78.

Preston-Shoot, M., Roberts, G. and Vernon, S. (1998) 'Social work law: from interaction to integration', *Journal of Social Welfare and Family Law*, 20:1, pp45–87.

Preston-Shoot, M., Roberts, G. and Vernon, S. (2001) 'Values in social work law: strained relations or sustaining relationships?', *Journal of Social Welfare and Family Law*, 23:1, pp1–22.

Rachels, J. (2002) 'The ethics of virtue', in Cahn, S.M. and Markie, P. (eds) *Ethics: History, Theory and Contemporary Issues*, Oxford: Oxford University Press.

Ramazanoglou, C.F. with Holland, J. (2002) *Feminist Methodology: Challenges and Choices*, London: Sage Publications.

Rawls, J. (2002) 'A theory of justice', in LaFollette, H. (ed.) *Ethics in Practice: An Anthology*, 2nd edn, Oxford: Blackwell, pp514–26.

Reamer, F.G. (2001) *Ethics Education in Social Work*, Alexandria, VA: Council on Social Work Education.

Rees T. (1999) 'Mainstreaming equality', in Watson, S. and Doyal, L. (eds) *Engendering Social Policy*, Open University Press, Buckingham.

Roche, J. (2002) 'Social work values and the law', in Cull, L.-A. and Roche, J. *The Law and Social Work: Contemporary Issues for Practice*, Basingstoke: Palgrave Macmillan.

Rogers, C.R. (1957) 'The necessary and sufficient conditions of therapeutic personality change', in Martin, R., Barrett, S., Komaromy, C. and Rogers, D. (eds) *Communication, Relationships and Care: A Reader,* London: Routledge.

Sakamoto, I and Pitner, R. (2005) 'Use of critical consciousness in anti-oppressive social work practice: disentangling power dynamics at personal and structural levels', *British Journal of Social Work*, 35:4, pp435–52.

Scanlon, T.M. (2002) 'The diversity of objections to inequality', in Clayton, M. and Williams, A. (eds) *The Ideal of Equality*, Basingstoke: Palgrave Macmillan.

Sevenhuijsen, S. (2003) 'The place of care: the relevance of the feminist ethic of care for social policy', *Feminist Theory*, 4:2, pp179–97.

Sheppard, M. (2002) 'Depressed mothers' experience of partnership in child and family care', *British Journal of Social Work*, 32:1, pp93–112.

Sherman, N. (ed.) (1999) *Aristotle's Ethics: Critical Essays*, Lanham, Md.: Rowman and Littlefield.

Singer, P. (ed.) (1993) *A Companion to Ethics*, Oxford: Blackwell.

Smart, B. (2000) 'Sociology, morality and ethics: on being with others', in Ritzer, G. and Smart, B. (eds) *Handbook of Social Theory*, London: Sage.

Smith, R. (2005) *Values and Practices in Children's Services*, Basingstoke: Palgrave.

Spargo, T. (1999) *Foucault and Queer Theory*, Cambridge: Icon Books.

Squires, J. (1993) 'Introduction', in Squires, J. (ed.) *Principled Positions: Postmodernism and the Rediscovery of Values*, London: Lawrence and Wishart.

Stanley, L. (1990) 'Recovering women in history from feminist deconstruction', *Women's Studies International Forum*, 13:1, pp35–56.

Stanley, L. (1992) *The Auto/Biographical I: The Theory and Practice of Feminist Auto/biography*, Manchester: Manchester University Press.

Stanley, L. and Wise, S. (1983) *Breaking Out: Feminist Consciousness and Feminist Research*, London: Routledge.

Stanley, L. and Wise, S. (1994) *Breaking Out Again: Feminist Ontology and Epistemology*, Manchester: Manchester University Press.

Statman, D. (1997) 'Introduction to virtue ethics', in Statman, D. (ed.) *Virtue Ethics*, Edinburgh: Edinburgh University Press.

Statman, D. (ed.) (1997) *Virtue Ethics*, Edinburgh: Edinburgh University Press.

Stevenson, C.L. (2002) 'The emotive meaning of ethical terms', in Cahn, S.M. and Markie, P. (eds) *Ethics: History, Theory and Contemporary Issues*, Oxford: Oxford University Press.

Summerfield, P. (2000) 'Dis/composing the subject: intersubjectivities in oral history', in Cosslett, T., Lury, C. and Summerfield, P. (eds) *Feminism and Autobiography: Texts, Theories, Methods*, London: Routledge.

Taylor, C. and White, S. (2000) *Practising Reflexivity in Health and Welfare*, Buckingham: Open University Press.

Tew, J. (2006) 'Understanding power and powerlessness', *Journal of Social Work*, 6:1, pp33–51.

Thomson, A. (1999) *Critical Reasoning in Ethics: A Practical Introduction*, London: Routledge.

Thompson, F.E. (2002) 'Moving from codes of ethics to ethical relationships for midwifery practice', *Nursing Ethics*, 9:5, pp522–36.

Thompson, M. (1999) *Ethical Theory*, London: Hodder and Stoughton.

Thompson, N. (1998) *Promoting Equality: Challenging Discrimination and Equality in the Human Services*, London: Macmillan.

Thompson, N. (2007) *Power and Empowerment*, Lyme Regis, Dorset: Russell House Publishing.

Thompson, N. (2008) 'Existentialist ethics: from Nietzsche to Sartre and beyond', *Ethics and Social Welfare*, 2:1, pp10–23.

Tomlinson, D.R. (2001) 'From equal opportunities to anti-oppressive practice: the historical and social context', in Tomlinson, D.R. and Trew, W. (eds) *Equalising Opportunities, Minimising Oppression*, London: Routledge.

Tong, R. (2003) 'Feminist ethics', in Zalta, E.N. (ed.) *The Stanford Encyclopedia of Philosophy* (Winter 2003 edn) <http://plato.stanford.edu/archives/win2003/entries/femuusm-efhics/>.

Training Organisation for Personal Social Services, (2004) *National Occupational Standards*, London: TOPPSS.

Tronto, J.C. (2003) 'Time's place', *Feminist Theory*, 4:2, pp119–38.

Voices in Partnership (2003) 'Comments by service users on the proposed training of social workers in values and ethics on the new B.A.in Social Work', 17 June, Knowsley (unpublished).

Walker, M.U. (1998) *Moral Understandings: A Feminist Study in Ethics*, London: Routledge.

Warnock, M. (1967) *Existentialist Ethics*, London: Macmillan.

Weston, A. (2002) A *Practical Companion to Ethics*, Oxford: Oxford University Press.

Wilks, T. (2005) 'Social work and narrative ethics', *British Journal of Social Work* 35:8, pp1249–64.

Williams, C. (ed.) (2005) *Personal Virtues*, Basingstoke: Palgrave Macmillan.

Williams, J. (2004) 'Social Work, liberty and law', *British Journal of Social Work*, 34:1, pp37–52.

Wilson, A. and Beresford, P. (2000) ' "Anti-oppressive practice" – emancipation or appropriation?' *British Journal of Social Work*, 30:5, pp553–73.

Windheuser, J. (2003) 'An ethical decision-making model', in Banks, S. and Nohr, K. (eds) *Teaching Practical Ethics for the Social Professions* <wwwfeset.dk>: European Social Ethics Project.

Wise, S. (1995) 'Feminist ethics in practice', in Hugman, R. and Smith, D. (eds) *Ethical Issues in Social Work*, London: Routledge, pp104–19.

Wood, A. (2000) 'Marx against morality', in Singer, P. (ed.) A *Companion to Ethics*, Oxford: Blackwell Publishers, pp511–24.

Yip, K.-S. (2004) 'A Chinese cultural critique of the global qualifying standards for social work education', in *Social Work Education*, 23:5, pp597–612.

Young, I.M. (1990) *Justice and the Politics of Difference*, Princeton, NJ: Princeton University Press.

Young, I.M. (1997) *Intersecting Voices: Dilemmas of Gender, Political Philosophy and Policy*, Princeton, NJ: Princeton University Press.

Young, I.M. (2002) 'Displacing the distributive paradigm', in LaFollette, H. (ed.) *Ethics in Practice: An Anthology*, 2nd edn, Oxford: Blackwell Publishers, pp540–50.

Index